1921

EMORY UNIVERSITY 1915-1965

EMORY UNIVERSITY
1915-1965

A Semicentennial History

by

THOMAS H. ENGLISH
Professor Emeritus of English

ATLANTA, GEORGIA
EMORY UNIVERSITY
1966

PRINTED IN THE UNITED STATES OF AMERICA BY
HIGGINS-McARTHUR COMPANY, ATLANTA, GEORGIA

CONTENTS

PREFACE . . . . *ix*

CHRONICLE

   Introduction: Emory College 1836-1915 3
  I Initial Planning, Charter and Bylaws 10
  II The Beginnings of the University, 1915-1926 . . 18
  III Through the Centennial Year, 1927-1936 . . . 33
  IV Through World War II, 1937-1945 47
  V The Postwar Decade, 1946-1955 63
  VI To the Semicentennial of the University, 1956-1965 82

THE DIVISIONS

  Emory College 111
  The School of Business Administration 123
  The Graduate School of Arts and Sciences 129
  The Candler School of Theology 138
  The School of Medicine and the Hospitals 148
  The Lamar School of Law 164
  The Library School—Division of Librarianship . . 170
  The School of Dentistry 172
  The School of Nursing 178
  Oxford and Valdosta Junior Colleges 181
  The Libraries 185

ACTIVITIES

  Student Affairs 197
  Religious Life 210
  Athletics and Physical Education 216
  Public Cultural Activities 224
  The Alumni Association 227

FIFTY YEARS — AND BEYOND 235

APPENDIXES 247

    Buildings

    Fields of Study in Which Degrees Are Offered

    Summary of Enrollment 1964-1965; Degrees Conferred,
        Academic Year 1964-65

    Trustees of Emory University 1915-1965

    Recipients of Honorary Degrees 1915-1965

    Alumni Loyalty Fund

    Bibliography

INDEX 263

LIST OF ILLUSTRATIONS

Facing
Page

End papers: Aerial photographs of University Campus,
   1921 and 1965

Hornbostel Layout of University Campus, 1915 . . . 20

Map of University Campus 1965, with Index 21

Excavating for First Building on Druid Hills Campus . . 36

Bridge between Quadrangle and Dormitory Areas,
   Dobbs Hall in Distance 36

The Log Cabin 36

Commencement in Antoinette Gardens 37

Emory ROTC 37

Freshman-Sophomore Pushball Match 37

Asa Griggs Candler 52

Warren Akin Candler 52

Harvey Warren Cox 53

Goodrich Cook White 53

Sidney Walter Martin 53

Sanford Soverhill Atwood 53

Review of Navy V-12 Unit 68

Trailertown 68

Mudville 68

Glenn Memorial 69

Commemorating Emory Units I and II 69

Executive Committee, Board of Trustees, 1946 . . . 69

The Quadrangle 100

Whitehead Memorial Room 100

Miss Pauline and her Deans 101

Hooding Emory's First Ph.D. 101

Air Force ROTC Holds Retreat 101

Charles Howard Candler 132

Facing
Page

Henry Lumpkin Bowden 132
Bishops at Consecration of Bishops Hall 132
Vice-President Barkley Returns to Oxford 132
Robert W. Woodruff 133
October 1964 Meeting of Board 133
Inauguration of President Atwood 133
Graduation Exercises, June 1963 164
Atlanta Gets her Bottle 164
New and Old on Oxford Campus 164
Page of 14th-Century MS Bible 165
The Woodruff Building 165
Books of Joel Chandler Harris Collection 165
Christmas Carol Concert 165
Dooley and Frolics Queen 196
Lawn Display, Dooley's Frolics 196
The Coke Lounge 196
Coaching Session, Upper Athletic Field 196
Jennie Tourel Sings in Alumni Memorial 197
Secretary of State Dean Rusk at Special Convocation . . 197
Soccer with Vanderbilt 197
Charter Day Dinner 1964 197

Preface

THIS IS THE STORY of the first fifty years of Emory University.

1936 was celebrated as the centennial of Emory College. Among the features of the observance was the publication of a Centennial History, by Henry Morton Bullock, A.B. '24, B.D. '25. The first twelve chapters, pp. 17-280, told the story of Emory College from its founding at Oxford, Georgia, to its removal to Atlanta as the "academic department" of the newly created Emory University. The four concluding chapters, pp. 283-376, besides presenting a continuing account of the College, dealt somewhat more briefly with the already existing institutions brought into the University complex, and the new foundations completing its organization up to the centennial year.

Based on all existing records and personal interviews, with some slight revision it has been accepted as the definitive chronicle of the University and its component schools. It should be stated at the outset that Dr. Bullock's history has been extensively employed in the composition of the present work, although a policy prohibiting footnotes has not permitted calling attention to the Editor's dependence on his predecessor for specific information.

The centennial year may be taken to conclude the first phase of Emory's career as a university. A second phase began immediately, and in spite of the intrusion of the war period, there ensued a rapid fulfillment of promises of development that had been long delayed, but had perhaps gained in definition as in urgency by the delay.

It is this second phase, which brought fruition to the hopes of the planners of the University, that has necessitated the publication of the present volume. Something more than a quarter-century of intense and enlightened effort has gone far to accomplish what had been mapped out in the 'twenties and 'thirties. If Emory has not yet achieved the highest rank among America's institutions of learning, it has at least made fair progress toward the ultimate goal of usefulness and distinction descried by those who have steered its course for the first half-century.

It may be well to outline the procedure adopted for the present work. Following a condensed sketch of old Emory College and an account of the planning for a new university, the career of the latter is chronicled by decades. That is to say, Chapters II-VI present an inclusive narrative of the University from its chartering in 1915 to the close of its semicentennial year, 1965. Then in eleven chapters the divisions of the University are taken up individually in specific detail. A certain amount of repetition will be seen to be inevitable in the method employed, but this is believed not to be excessive. General activities belonging to the institution as a whole are recounted in five chapters. A concluding chapter is addressed to the attempt to state Emory's educational policy, its past achievement, and its plans for the future. Certain statistical materials are included in appendixes.

This history is actually a work of collaboration, in which the Editor has had the constant assistance of his colleagues of the faculty and administrative staff of the University. From the first stages of planning to the completion of the work it has had the oversight of the Editorial Committee: Chancellor Goodrich C. White, Chairman, Vice-President Judson C. Ward, Jr., Mr. Robert F. Whitaker, Professor James G. Lester, Professor Ellis Heber Rece, and Professor James Harvey Young. Besides reading every chapter and making detailed suggestions for revision, they have prepared manuscripts on which sections of the book are directly based. If specific acknowledgment is nowhere given their contributions, it is to be understood that their assistance is pervasive throughout. More than a score of others have given generously of their time and special knowledge; without their help the work could make no claim to authority. The Editor is grateful to all those whose assistance he has sought. Finally special acknowledgment must be made of the constant employment of the volumes of the *Emory Alumnus,* the only full account of the varied activities of the University from 1924 until the present. Nevertheless, in dealing with a theme of such complexity as that presented by fifty years of the life of a university, errors of omission, commission, and emphasis are bound to occur, and for these the Editor must be held solely responsible. He can only hope that his sins have been venial and forgiveable. Yet much of which he has written has come within his own observation in forty years of connection with Emory, and it is his sincere hope that something of the pleasure that he has found in recollections of the past may be conveyed to readers of this volume.

T. H. E.

CHRONICLE

Introduction:

Emory College 1836-1915

EMORY UNIVERSITY in 1965 attained its first half-century, but the division upon which the institution is centered had already registered more than a century and a quarter of service to the South and the nation. Emory College, then being planned at Oxford, Georgia, was granted a charter by the State Legislature on December 10, 1836. And Emory College itself was the outgrowth of the Georgia Conference Manual Labor School, chartered on December 18, 1834.

Emory's history, indeed, begins with a meeting of the Georgia Methodist Conference, held in Washington, Georgia, in 1834, at which the President of Randolph-Macon College in Virginia solicited support for his institution. The Conference was ready to vote its patronage, when to the surprise of the assembly one of the delegates, "Uncle Allen" Turner, rose in opposition, declaring that Georgia Methodists should have their own college. Although the plea was amusedly disregarded at the moment, within the year plans were made to establish a manual labor school at Covington, which was opened in March 1835 with Alexander Means as Superintendent and thirty students.

The school showed no clear signs of prosperity, but already its chief promoter, Ignatius Alphonso Few, was projecting the establishment of a college in the same location. With the consent of the Conference, and after obtaining a charter from the Legislature, a college town was laid out in the woods near Covington and named Oxford for the university of the founder of Methodism. The College was named for Bishop John Emory of Maryland, who had presided at the Washington Conference, and who had been killed in a carriage accident in 1835.

Under President Few classes were organized on September 17, 1838, with fifteen students. The standard classical curriculum was offered, but with Alexander Means on the faculty there was a strong bent toward the natural sciences from the beginnings of the College.

President Few resigning on account of failing health, he was followed in 1840 by Augustus Baldwin Longstreet, the celebrated author of *Georgia Scenes*. Under President Longstreet financial difficulties plagued the young foundation, which was only kept alive by heroic measures. Meanwhile the mounting social and political tensions of the nation were felt even in this remote spot. The concentration of leaders of the Church in the College and village had made Oxford virtually the capital of Southern Methodism. An inheritance of slaves, which the laws of Georgia would not permit him to manumit, brought Bishop James O. Andrew, President of Emory's Trustees, under fire of the Northern members of the Church. At the General Conference of 1844 the controversy, in which Longstreet took an angry part, rose to such heights that the Methodist Church divided on sectional lines.

In 1848 President Longstreet resigned and was succeeded by George Foster Pierce. The College continued to be faced with money problems, but physical facilities were greatly improved and the enrollment was steadily rising. The election of President Pierce as bishop of the Methodist Episcopal Church, South, in 1854, compelled his resignation from the College. He was followed by Alexander Means, who had been a fixture since the organization of the Manual Labor School. Means, however, had accepted the professorship of chemistry in the Atlanta Medical College, and the double appointment was not in Emory's best interest. After one year in the presidency, therefore, he was replaced by James R. Thomas. Although both financial and disciplinary difficulties troubled his administration at the start, after five years it seemed that better times were ahead. For one thing, a spirit of religious fervor swept the campus, in which Young J. Allen '58, later the famous missionary to China, was influential. The "Old Log Prayer-Meeting" of 1858 was marked by a great outpouring of missionary zeal. For another, the enrollment had reached 244, and the College income was meeting current expenses. Then came the Civil War.

In the summer of 1861 the Trustees hopefully proposed keeping the College open, but when it was found that a large part of the students had gone to war and that there were no available funds, on November 30 it was voted to close the College for a year. It was not reopened until January 1866.

In the long hiatus the buildings were used for a time by the Confederate authorities as a hospital center. The little military cemetery on the campus is a memorial of this episode. Later there was occupation by Northern troops, and in between neglect and pillage took their toll of buildings and equipment, so that at the end of the war the little College was a shambles. Moreover, such endowment as had been accumulated was practically wiped out.

Beginning again was a notable act of courage, but some relief was afforded when the Georgia Legislature made provision for the education of poor and disabled veterans, the first "G. I. Bill of Rights." In the academic year 1866-67, 120 students were enrolled of whom ninety-three had been soldiers. President Thomas's last official act was to confer degrees upon members of the Class of 1862 who had left their studies to enter the Confederate armies. In July 1867 he turned over the office to Luther M. Smith '48.

The presidency of Luther M. Smith brought a degree of prosperity to the College, but disagreement with the Trustees on basic policies caused his resignation after three years, and Osborn L. Smith '42 became Emory's seventh President in 1871. The panic of 1873 resulted in a drop in enrollment, and unwise tuition exemptions seriously reduced the income of the College, while the main building, in use for only twenty years, was declared unsafe and was taken down. In this exigency Bishop George F. Pierce came to the rescue. His strenuous exertions brought about the erection of four buildings, including the Prayer Chapel, and as the President reported in 1875, the College had "a better outfit for the work of instruction than she ever had at any time in the past." The most pressing problem, however, was that of providing an endowment, and to this task Atticus Greene Haygood '59, who succeeded Osborn Smith in 1875, bent his energies.

President Haygood's administration marked a turning point in the history of the College. He accomplished much by internal organization, and by an active campaign of publicity he brought Emory's needs to the attention of a large public. But decisive aid came from an unexpected source. Haygood's Thanksgiving sermon, preached on November 25, 1880, in the Oxford Methodist Church, found cause for rejoicing in the improved conditions of the South in the latter days of Reconstruction and her return to the Union. The speaker declared that slavery had been an evil thing, and that with its abolition the South with a clear conscience faced a more prosperous future, if only she would exercise the virtues of industry and economy.

The printed pamphlet of the sermon fell into the hands of the New York banker, George I. Seney, a Northern Methodist who practiced a liberal philanthropy. At a first interview with Haygood in February 1881, Seney gave the College $10,000 to endow a professorship, and before the year was out he had increased his donation to $130,000, an unprecedented gift to Southern education. Of this sum $75,000 was for endowment, $5,000 for debts, and $50,000 for a new building. On its erection, the building, which still occupies the center of the Oxford campus, was named Seney Hall by the Trustees. By the time of his retirement in 1884, President Haygood had raised Emory's endowment to $97,000, and the future of the College was assured.

Atticus Haygood's successor, Isaac Stiles Hopkins '59, is chiefly remembered as Georgia's pioneer in technological education. A hobbyist with a home workshop, he found that students were interested in learning woodworking. From this he developed a Department of Toolcraft and Design, later of Technology, for which a building was provided in 1885. The Department proved to be a drain on the resources of the College, but it drew attention from the state, so that when the Georgia School of Technology was founded in 1889, Hopkins became its first President. On his departure from Emory the Department was discontinued, and soon thereafter the building was refitted as a gymnasium.

With the election of Warren Akin Candler '75 as President in 1888 began what is proudly recalled as the golden age of Old Emory College. In him deep religious conviction was joined with unbounded energy and a dogged determination to accomplish the ends that he conceived vital to the prosperity of the institution of which he was the head. Orthodox in his religious views, he intro-

[6]

duced changes in the curriculum that were regarded as downright heretical by members of his own faculty. The new three-course curriculum that he sponsored, while retaining the classical requirements for the A.B. degree, dispensed with Greek for the B.Ph., and with both learned languages for the B.S.

Business and technological courses were dropped, but it is not often noted that at this time a law course was offered. Although few students were involved, Candler secured from the Legislature the privilege of admission to the bar for its graduates on the same terms as were enjoyed by graduates of the Lumpkin Law School at Athens. A school for preachers never flourished.

Emory's finances engrossed a large part of President Candler's attention. Though the College had a small endowment, and though its enrollment was steadily climbing, so that 1898 found 325 students in attendance, there were debts, and physical facilities remained inadequate. His efforts to secure increased support proved amazingly productive. At his resignation the endowment was valued at $213,955. The most important addition to the campus was a library building that was named in his honor.

During these years a strong alumni loyalty was developed, leading to the incorporation in 1895 of an Alumni Association which began to participate enthusiastically in the affairs of the College.

With Dr. Candler's election as a bishop of the Church in spring 1898 he resigned the presidency, but for the remainder of his life he remained intimately concerned with all matters pertaining to the College and the University with which ultimately it was joined. While his policies were not always approved, his services to the two institutions were of incalculable value, and were known to be so.

In the brief administration of President Charles E. Dowman '73, 1898-1902, no financial campaign was undertaken, although salaries were lowered somewhat, and there was a serious reduction of funds for running expenses. Enrollments fell off also, partly accounted for by the widespread belief that Emory's entrance requirements were higher than those of other Georgia colleges. A good omen for the future, although it may not have been fully recognized at the time, was the election of Asa G. Candler to the

Board of Trustees in 1899.

President Dowman displayed a high order of educational statesmanship. While it failed of appreciation in his own day, it was later to have no inconsiderable effect on the academic standing of the College. He did away with all remaining remnants of professional training. He sought to introduce electives to lessen the rigidity of the required courses of study. Students were assigned to faculty advisers to direct them "in the prosecution of [their] work in any way that may be necessary." The President for the first time attended a session of the Association of Colleges and Preparatory Schools of the Southern States. Most important of all, Emory organized a Joint College Conference with Mercer and the University of Georgia for the purpose of achieving higher and more uniform entrance requirements. These and other forward-looking measures were features of President Dowman's administration. There is reason to believe, however, that the Trustees were unwilling to go along with his more liberal policies, and he left the College in 1902 to become Presiding Elder of the Atlanta District.

In 1902 James Edward Dickey '91 became the twelfth and last President of Old Emory College, to serve until the organization of the University in 1915. A figure of commanding presence, known as "the King" by the students, he proved a notable administrator of the business affairs of the institution. Among his achievements was to raise the endowment to $325,000, and to add four important buildings to the plant. In his time rose Pierce Science Hall, Williams Athletic Hall, Young J. Allen Memorial Church, and Haygood Dormitory. The influence of Bishop Warren A. Candler was powerful in aiding these projects, and the financial assistance of his brother, Asa G. Candler, more than once saved the College from actual embarrassment. Faculty salaries reached new levels, and the student body held to an atendance of above 250, rising in 1910 to 313. At the end of the Dickey era and in the four transition years following, Emory College attained the maturity that fitted it to become the "academic department" of the new University.

The subsequent history of the College at Oxford is related in a later chapter. The memories of the past, however, linger in the oak shades of the old campus. Among modern structures, Seney Hall, the Prayer Chapel, and the halls of the literary societies, Few and Phi Gamma, maintain the dignity of age. The class trees are gathering points for reunions when the alumni come again on pilgrimage to their Alma Mater. Yet the forty miles and fifty years that lie between the two campuses indicate no real separation. The Oxford College of today is as truly a part of Emory University as though they were together in place as they are in function and spirit.

I

Initial Planning, Charter and Bylaws

THE ESTABLISHMENT OF EMORY UNIVERSITY was the direct outgrowth of an extended controversy over the relationship of Vanderbilt University to the Methodist Episcopal Church, South. Vanderbilt University first opened its doors to students in 1875. It had been projected as "Central University" at a meeting in Memphis in January 1872 by representatives of seven annual conferences of the Methodist Episcopal Church, South. Its future was not assured, however, until a gift of $500,000 was received from Commodore Cornelius Vanderbilt in March 1873. On March 26 the Board of Trust voted to change the name to "Vanderbilt." The Commodore's contributions reached a total of $1,000,000 before the University was opened; of this total $600,000 was endowment. Bishop Holland N. McTyiere was the leading figure in the planning and in contacts with Commodore Vanderbilt. As Chairman of the Board of Trust he dominated the scene until his death in 1889. Dr. L. C. Garland had been inaugurated as Chancellor in October 1875; he was succeeded in 1893 by James H. Kirkland, who remained in office until 1937.

From the beginning there had been controversy over the establishment of the University, and it is safe to say that it never had the unreserved support and loyalty of the Church as a whole and of all its leaders. The issues in the controversy were precipitated by disagreements over policy and were complicated by uncertainty as to the legal provisions of the Vanderbilt charter. The legal issues came to focus on two points: (1) the right of the General Conference, the chief governing body of the Church, to *elect* trustees of the University; (2) the "visitorial powers" of the bishops of the Church, *i.e.*, their authority to *veto* actions of the trustees.

For more than a decade the controversy was marked by vigorous debate, at times intensely personal. The leadership of the Church was divided. The "Vanderbilt question" was of major concern to the General Conferences of 1906 and 1910. In 1910 the

General Conference authorized the bishops to carry the issues into the civil courts. The case was filed in the Chancery Court of Davidson County, Tennessee, in 1911; this court's decision was rendered in February 1913. The claims of the Church, as represented by the bishops, were sustained; the right of the General Conference to elect trustees and the veto powers of the bishops were recognized.

The Vanderbilt Board of Trustees promptly appealed the decision.

On March 21, 1914, the Supreme Court of Tennessee rendered a decision reversing the lower court. The visitorial powers of the bishops were denied. The Board of Trustees was held to be self-perpetuating, though elections to the Board were subject to confirmation by the General Conference or its designated agent.

The General Conference of the Church, meeting in May 1914, was largely given over to debate over the Vanderbilt issue. A special committee appointed by the Conference to make recommendations was unable to reach unanimity, and majority and minority reports were submitted. The minority report declared that the court's decision was unjust and did not represent the real equities in the case. Nevertheless the way had been left open for a continuance of the relationship of Vanderbilt to the Church through the authority of the General Conference to confirm trustees. The minority report therefore recommended the continuance of the relationship on this basis.

The majority report of the committee recommended that all relationships with the University be severed. After extended and sometimes bitter debate, the majority report was adopted by a vote of 151 to 140.

Most of the leaders actively engaged in the Vanderbilt controversy are now gone from the scene. The issues so vigorously contested are no longer relevant to Emory's history. It is perhaps worth noting that the bitterness of the controversy did not carry over into the relationships between the administrations and the faculties of Vanderbilt and Emory. Almost from the beginning and increasingly through the years these relationships have been friendly and coöperative.

[11]

The General Conference authorized the naming of an Educational Commission empowered to take positive action looking toward the creation of institutions whose relationship to the Church would be clearly defined. The members of this Commission were to be named by the bishops, the Conference specifying that it should include four bishops, four ministers other than bishops, and eight laymen. The Commission was to "provide at the earliest possible time for the establishment and maintenance of a Biblical School or Department of Theology," making, if necessary, temporary arrangements for such a school or department "either separate from or in conjunction with some institution now under the control and management of" the Church.

More important, however, was the instruction to the Commission "to consider and determine the advisability of establishing an institution or institutions" of university grade, under the auspices of the Church, and to take action toward this end, with the proviso that "the ownership and control of the same in perpetuity" should be vested in the Church.

The General Conference went one step further. Careful not to restrict the Commission in its consideration and action, the Conference expressed the belief that there should be one such institution east of the Mississippi River and one west of the Mississippi River; it recorded its pleasure at the establishment, by the membership of the Church in the State of Texas, of Southern Methodist University; and it "commended" that institution to the Commission for its consideration.

The Educational Commission moved rapidly. There can be little doubt that there had been "a considerable amount of prior planning" well in advance of the action of the General Conference. But the Commission found itself under the necessity of giving at least *pro forma* consideration to a number of different proposals for the location of the institution east of the river.

The Commission met in Birmingham, Alabama, on June 17, 1914, inspected suggested sites, and conferred with representative citizens. Meantime the trustees of Emory College at Oxford, Georgia, on June 8, had resolved that "the authorities of Emory College stand ready to do whatever they can in furtherance of the work" of the Commission.

In mid-July the Commission met in Atlanta. The session held on July 16 was decisive. The Chamber of Commerce of the city had pledged $500,000 if the proposed university were located in the Georgia capital. It had been made clear that an adequate and suitably located tract of land would be made available; that classroom, office, and dormitory space would be ready for the temporary use of the school of theology which, in accordance with the instructions of the General Conference, was to be opened "at the earliest possible time;" and that clinical teaching facilities would be readily available for a contemplated school of medicine.

The climax came with the presentation of the historic and often quoted "million dollar letter."

Addressed to Bishop W. A. Candler, Chairman of the Educational Commission, with the salutation "My dear Brother," the letter is signed "Respectfully, Asa G. Candler."

It is a genuinely moving letter, even as read fifty years later. It offers "to the Educational Commission of the Methodist Episcopal Church, South, charged by the General Conference with the duty of establishing an institution of University grade East of the Mississippi River, the sum of one million dollars ($1,000,000) for the endowment of such an institution, the plans and methods of which are to be definitely directed to the advancement of sound learning and pure religion."

The paragraph in which the offer is explicitly made is preceded and followed by paragraphs explaining the writer's motives, and stating his convictions as to the importance of Christian education under the auspices of the Church. At one point he says, "I do not seek a sectarian end;" again, he records his hope that the type of education in which he believes will "benefit the people of my section and country without regard to denominational lines," and his wish "that the characteristic excellences of our people may be made better and that the things which blemish our lives may be speedily obliterated."

The minutes of the Commission record that "the Presence of God seemed to overshadow the Commission; faith and hope were quickened as by the power and light of inspiration, and the Commission gave thanks to God in prayer, led by Bishop Kilgo."

It is noted that Mr. Candler's letter does not make the location of the university in Atlanta a condition of the offer. Only in the final sentence is there any mention of Atlanta or Georgia. As was clearly to be expected, however, the Commission, voting to accept the offer, also voted to locate the university in Atlanta. Bishop Candler, the chairman of the Commission, was made Chancellor of the University—as yet unnamed. Mr. Asa G. Candler, Bishop Candler, and Mr. William D. Thomson were named as a committee to negotiate with the Trustees of Emory College with a view to making that college the "academic department" of the University.

With basic decisions made, details incident to the actual opening of the University were handled with great expedition. On August 4, 1914, Dr. Plato Durham, a member of the Commission, was elected by its Executive Committee as Dean of the School of Theology, and September 23, 1914, was set as the date for the opening of this division of the University. On August 5, 1914, the "Old Guess Place" was agreed upon as the site of the University. These seventy-five acres, located about six miles northeast of the center of the city of Atlanta, were not formally deeded by "Druid Hills" to the University until June 28, 1915.

It was also on August 5, 1914, that the Trustees of Emory College officially approved the plan for amalgamating with the new university as its "academic department," with the suggestion that "Emory University" be chosen as its name, "so as to preserve and conserve the assets, history and traditions of Emory College and enlarge its usefulness to the M. E. Church, South, and at the same time promote the success of the new University." Other names had been considered, including, of course, "Candler." The Commission authorized a mail ballot among its members and the name *Emory* was approved.

In all these decisions and actions the dominant influence of Bishop Warren A. Candler and his brother, Mr. Asa G. Candler, is clearly evident. It is easy to agree with the conviction expressed by Mr. C. Howard Candler in his biography of his father: "Father and Uncle Warren . . . I believe, had already mapped a possible course of action to repair the loss of Vanderbilt which actually had its fruition in the work of the Commission."

The Bishop was chairman of the Educational Commission and Mr. Asa was treasurer. Both had been intimately related to Emory College for more than two decades. Both had promoted and served as trustees of the Wesley Memorial Enterprises, which included Wesley Memorial Church, the first home of Emory's School of Theology, and Wesley Memorial Hospital, destined to become a teaching hospital of the School of Medicine of Emory University. Closely related to these two dominant figures was Mr. William D. Thomson, an attorney, a member of the Commission, who had major responsibility for the legal procedures incident to setting up the University.

The most important legal step was, of course, the securing of a charter. The petitioning incorporators were the members of the Educational Commission of the Methodist Episcopal Church, South. The charter was granted on January 25, 1915, by Judge C. S. Reid of the Superior Court of DeKalb County. The charter was approved by the Commission on February 20, 1915. The incorporators were to function as an interim board of trustees until the next meeting of the General Conference. The officers of the Board elected were: Asa G. Candler, President; Bishop John C. Kilgo, Vice-President; William D. Thomson, Secretary.

The charter of Emory University explicitly states that "the Methodist Episcopal Church, South, is and shall be always regarded and held to be the founder of the University." It provides for a board of thirty trustees, with the addition, at the Board's discretion, of as many as three trustees named by the alumni. The members of the first Board were to be elected, at its first opportunity, by the General Conference of the Church. Subsequently the Board itself is to fill vacancies, with the proviso that "no person so elected to fill a vacancy on said Board shall become a Trustee, or take any part in the deliberations of said Board, until he shall first have been confirmed by the General Conference of the Methodist Episcopal Church, South, or by some agency designated by it." There is a further provision giving the General Conference the "power to remove for cause, any member of said Board, after

[15]

giving said member opportunity to be heard in his own defense."
A vacancy thus created is to be reported to the Board, which then
itself proceeds to elect a successor, subject again to approval by the
General Conference or its designated agent.

Over the years there has been no instance of rejection of a
trustee elected by the Board nor of any action or suggestion of
action to remove a member already serving.

In still other passages the Emory charter emphasizes the relationship of the University to the Church.

Bylaws were adopted by the interim Board of Trustees on January 12, 1916. The preamble reads:

> Emory University was founded by the Methodist Episcopal
> Church, South, for the promotion of the broadest intellectual
> culture in harmony with the democratic institutions of our
> country and permeated by the principles and influences of the
> Christian religion. It is designed to be a profoundly religious
> institution without being narrowly sectarian. It proposes to
> encourage freedom of thought as liberal as the limitations of
> truth, while maintaining unwavering devotion to the faith
> once for all delivered to the saints.
>
> Emory University belongs to the Methodist Episcopal
> Church, South, and the corporation shall administer the in-
> stitution and all of its properties of every kind for the benefit
> of said Church and under the direction of the General Con-
> ference or other agencies appointed by said Conference for the
> purpose, in accordance with the provisions of the charter of
> the University.

The main body of the bylaws has undergone periodic revision
to meet changing administrative needs. This preamble, however,
has remained unaltered with a single exception incident to the unification of three major Methodist bodies to form The Methodist
Church.*

In this connection it should be noted that the Discipline of the
Methodist Church (its body of laws) requires that not less than
three-fourths of the members of a board of control of any Church-

*In the second paragraph "The Methodist Church" was substituted for "the Meth-
odist Episcopal Church, South," and the "General Conference" was replaced by
"the Southeastern Jurisdictional Conference." The last General Conference of the
Methodist Episcopal Church, South (May 1938), in accordance with the provisions
of the charter, delegated its authority to the Jurisdictional Conference.

sponsored institution must be Methodists. This requirement has been carefully adhered to by the Emory Board of Trustees.

It may be further noted that neither the charter nor the bylaws of the University specify any requirements as to church affiliation or religious faith for students, faculty members, or administrative officers.

II

The Beginnings of the University

1915-1926

AMONG THE INDUCEMENTS to bring the new Methodist university to Atlanta was the availability of Wesley Memorial Church as a home for the school of theology. Although this was only a temporary facility, it certainly had no small influence in deciding the location of the institution. The Church had determined to cut all official connections with Vanderbilt University, including its school of theology. There must, nevertheless, be no interruption in the training of candidates for the Methodist ministry. The Educational Commission, therefore, on June 17, 1914, decreed that a "Biblical and Theological School" be established east of the Mississippi River not later than October 1 of the same year. On receipt of the magnificent gift of Mr. Asa Candler, $500,000 was set aside for that purpose, and on August 4 Dr. Plato Tracy Durham was elected Dean of the School of Theology to be brought into being without delay.

The new school, which in February 1915 was named, over the Bishop's protest, the Candler School of Theology, began operation on September 23, 1914, with an enrollment of sixty-nine, including advanced students transferring from Vanderbilt, and a faculty of seven. It was thus the first division of Emory University to be organized, four months before the granting of the University's charter. It was to continue in its temporary quarters in the heart of the city until the erection of its building on the Druid Hills campus. Dr. Durham held the deanship for four years, until the appointment of Dr. Franklin Nutting Parker in 1919.

At a meeting of the Board of Trustees of Emory College on August 5, 1914, a willingness was expressed for the College to become the "academic department" of the university in planning.

On March 17, 1915, the Newton County Superior Court in Covington amended the charter of the College to permit its inclusion in Emory University, and on April 1 following, a formal transfer of the College to the University was made at a ceremony in Wesley Memorial Church. At the meeting of the Board of Trustees in June, Dr. James E. Dickey, who had been President since 1902, resigned the office, and in December of that year Professor Edgar H. Johnson '91 was named Acting President. This was only a temporary designation, however, for in June 1916 the executive head of the College was given the title of Dean, held by Dr. Johnson until the move to Atlanta was accomplished three years later. In fall 1916 the academic year, that had formerly consisted of two semesters, was divided into four equal quarters, following the plan inaugurated at the University of Chicago. There was, however, no regular summer quarter until the College moved to Atlanta.

Between 1914 and 1919 several men joined the College faculty who were most influential in carrying forward the program of the University. Those years at Oxford, further disorganized by America's entry into World War I, were a period of eager and even restless waiting for members of the faculty. The interval was employed in projecting plans for the operation of the College when the move to Atlanta should be effected. A long series of informal conferences between Professors James Hinton '06 and J. Gordon Stipe '07 were to bear fruit in formal faculty action in the early years on the new campus. The standards then set and the firm commitment of the faculty to ideals of quality brought prompt recognition to the University.

Emory University received a third division in actual being when, on May 24, 1915, the Atlanta Medical College transferred its entire holdings to the University to become its School of Medicine. The Atlanta Medical College, the result of successive mergers of earlier institutions, the first founded in 1854, was an excellent proprietary school which was suffering severely from the increasing costs of equipment and instruction, and the rising standards of medical education enforced by the American Medical Association and the Association of American Medical Colleges. It had become clear that survival depended on a university affiliation. The announcement of Atlanta as the location of the new Emory University caused Dean W. S. Elkin of the Medical College to enter into negotiations with Mr. Asa Candler, which successfully resulted in the addition of a medical division to the already established College and School of Theology. $250,000 was appropriated as endowment for the School of Medicine; classrooms and laboratories on the Druid Hills campus and a new hospital were promised to enlarge its teaching facilities. The School of Medicine continued to occupy its Butler Street premises for the next few years, the freshman and sophomore classes moving to the newly erected buildings on the University campus in the fall of 1917.

On March 31, 1915, the Educational Commission had appointed a building committee, "instructed and empowered to have a plan made for the campus buildings at the earliest moment which the Committee may deem expedient . . . and to proceed with the erection of one or more." The plan of campus development was entrusted to Henry Hornbostel (1867-1961), the distinguished Pittsburgh architect, who had done work for the Coca-Cola Company. Mr. Hornbostel was enamored of northern Italy, and on his visit to Atlanta he was impressed with similarities—"rolling hills, pines, and even marble as native stone"—to his favorite region. The idea of adopting an Italian Renaissance style with a generous employment of marble was proposed to Mr. Asa Candler, who received it favorably.

The campus plan developed in the drafting rooms of Palmer, Hornbostel & Jones was an impressive design, enthusiastically approved by the Building Committee. The central group consisted of a double court of buildings connected by loggias with a high mausoleum-like structure centered near the west end and a lower building with spreading wings closing the east end. To the north across a ravine was placed a large dormitory quadrangle, and beyond it a stadium and field house. Other identifiable features are a circle of fraternity houses, a Greek theater, a group of residences obviously intended for the president and other administrative officers, and a heating plant.

Arthur Tufts, of Baltimore, previously employed by the Coca-

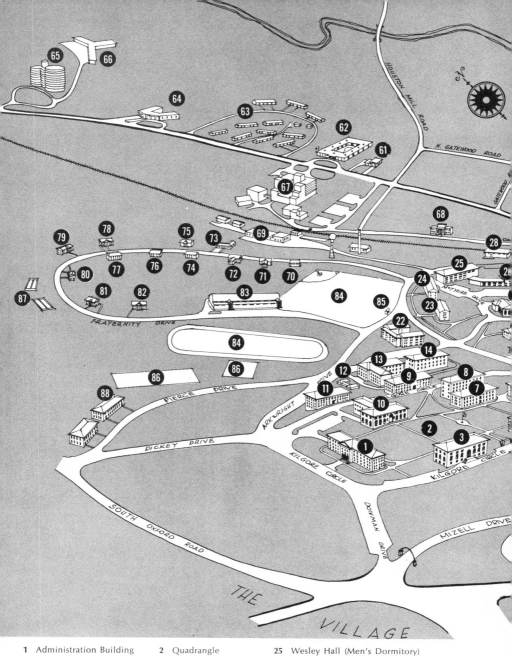

1 Administration Building 2 Quadrangle
3 Lamar School of Law
4 Rich Memorial Building, School of Business
5 History Building 6 Asa Griggs Candler Library
7 Physics Building 8 Chemistry Building
9 Psychology Building 10 Theology Building
11 Bishops Hall, Theology 12 Biology Greenhouse
13 Biology Building 14 Geology Building
15 Cox Hall (Food Services)
16 Emory University Hospital
17 Woodruff Memorial Building (Medical Research)
18 Physiology Building 19 Anatomy Building
20 Alumni Memorial Building (Student Center)
21 Alabama Hall (Women's Dormitory)
22 Dobbs Hall (Men's Dormitory)
23 Winship Hall (Men's Dormitory)
24 McTyeire Hall (Women's Dormitory)

25 Wesley Hall (Men's Dormitory)
26 Longstreet Hall (Men's Dormitory)
27 Means Hall (Men's Dormitory)
28 Seaboard Railroad Station 29 Air Force R.O.T.C
30 Glenn Memorial Auditorium 31 Amphitheater
32 Church School Building
33 Glenn Youth Building 34 Annex C (Music)
35 Fishburne Building 36 Fishburne Annex
37 Nursing School (Annex B)
38 Thomas Hall (Women's Dormitory)
39 Hopkins Hall (Women's Dormitory)
40 Smith Hall (Women's Dormitory)
41 Harris Hall (Women's Dormitory)
42 Baptist Student Union
43 Emory Court Apartments
44 Panhellenic House (Sorority Center)
45 Clifton House (Testing Service)

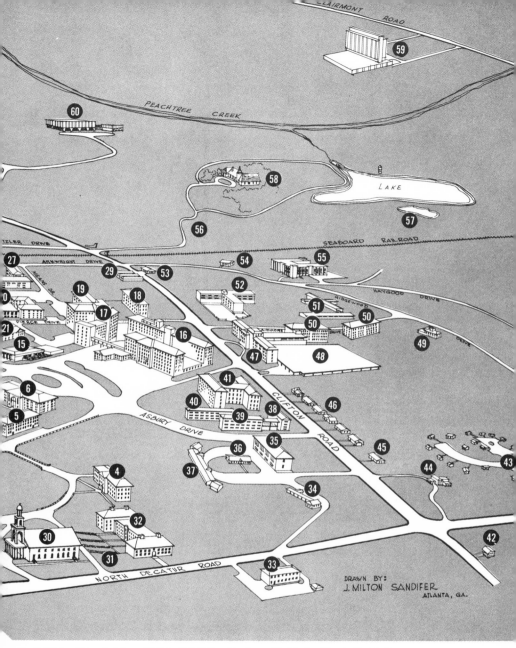

46	Child Psychiatry Buildings (1317 & 1323 Clifton Road)
47	Emory University Clinic
48	Parking Deck for Public
49	Uppergate House 50 Emory Park Apartments
51	Aidmore Children's Hospital
52	Henrietta Egleston Children's Hospital
53	U.S. Post Office
54	Ophthalmic Research Laboratory
55	Graduate Residence Center
56	Lullwater Estate 57 Biology Preserve
58	Lullwater House (President's Home)
59	U.S. Veterans Administration Hospital
60	Yerkes Regional Primate Research Center
61	Fire Station 62 Sheraton Emory Inn
63	Clifton Court Apartments
64	Protestant Radio and Television Center
65	Wesley Woods Residence Center

66	Wesley Woods Health Center
67	U.S.P.H.S. Communicable Disease Center
68	Saunders Hall (Medical Dormitory)
69	Operations Department and Shops
70	Delta Tau Delta House 71 Sigma Chi House
72	Chi Phi House 73 Beta Theta Pi House
74	Sigma Nu House 75 Alpha Epsilon Pi House
76	Alpha Tau Omega House 77 Kappa Alpha House
78	Tau Epsilon Phi House
79	Phi Gamma Delta House
80	Sigma Alpha Epsilon House
81	Phi Delta Theta House 82 Pi Kappa Alpha House
83	Gymnasium and Swimming Pool
84	Athletic Fields 85 Bus Stop Shelter
86	Tennis Courts 87 Tennis Center
88	Thomson Hall
89	Gilbert Hall (Married Students)

Cola Company, was chosen as builder. The site was staked off by the Atlanta architect, W. H. Ivey, who continued as inspector throughout the operations, and the erection of Theology and Law buildings, Dobbs and Winship dormitories was begun immediately. These were completed in 1916; Anatomy, Physiology, and the first two floors of Chemistry, for the accommodation of the School of Medicine, followed in 1917. Two years later Physics and Alabama completed the first major program. All these buildings were constructed with reinforced concrete shells with exterior finish of marble in shades of pink and gray. The idea of varicolored, "quilt pattern," marble veneering for exterior walls is said to have been Mr. Candler's. Col. Sam Tate, the owner of the North Georgia quarries, one of the Methodist leaders involved in establishing the University, encouraged use of the material and contributed marble for the purpose. Although the buildings have been irreverently compared to huge bars of Castile soap, with their red tile roofs they make a pleasingly colorful effect under the bright Southern sky. Of interior detail, the circular staircase of Law Building and the chapel of Theology, with its lighting fixtures of transparent marble, are much admired. Physics, for many years the chief classroom building of the College, however, was badly designed for its purposes, especially in regard to acoustics and traffic.

In later buildings gray marble has largely replaced the pink stone, and off the main quadrangle stucco has replaced marble except for trim, but the original architectural style has been generally adhered to. At a meeting of the Board of Trustees on June 3, 1927, the Committee on Buildings and Grounds stated in their annual report:

In looking over the grounds and buildings we remember that we are working to the completion of a great architectural and landscape gardening design furnished by one of the great architects of America. We are delighted to see this design fulfilling itself in the buildings and in the beautiful driveways through the campus of the University. We believe that the original pattern should always be kept in view in every improvement that is made from year to year and that no detail of the original plan should be lost sight of.

Nevertheless, Mr. Hornbostel's elaborate layout has of necessity been departed from to the extent that the existing campus is only just recognizable in the "bird's-eye view" that his draftsmen prepared fifty years ago.

Occupation of the new campus began with the completion of the first four permanent buildings, which enabled the School of Theology to move from its temporary quarters in downtown Atlanta, and for another division to be added to the University. Thus at the end of September 1916, the Candler School of Theology and the Lamar School of Law faced each other across the yet incomplete main quadrangle. The School of Law was organized under Acting Dean William Danner Thomson '95, with two full-time professors, six Atlanta attorneys on part-time basis, and twenty-seven students. Although the school was not to have a full-time Dean until the appointment of Samuel Cole Williams in 1919, by that time its curriculum and academic procedure was fully established. When in 1917 pre-clinical instruction in the School of Medicine was also transferred to the Druid Hills campus, only the presence of the College was lacking to bring together the traditional four faculties of a university.

Meanwhile World War I seriously hampered the planned development of the University. Enrollments had fallen off, faculty members had gone into the armed services, building operations had been slowed, and finances were made more difficult. An academy had been established, and its growing enrollment came to tax the facilities of the Oxford plant.

Nevertheless, it was found impossible to move the College to Atlanta until after the war. In January 1919 Howard W. Odum '04 was elected Dean of the College, and from his office in Theology Building he perfected plans for the rapid organization of work on the new campus to begin with that summer quarter. In addition to a classroom building near completion and a third dormitory, two temporary frame structures for use as a dining and an assembly hall (they came in the course of time to be referred to as "permanent temporary buildings"), and fourteen houses "suitable for use by the members of the faculty as their homes" were ready by June

1919. The Atlanta housing shortage and the lack of residential development in the neighborhood of the campus had necessitated the construction of "Faculty Row," located along the Seaboard Railway line beyond Clifton Road. Mr. Asa Candler had these houses built on his own land adjoining the eastern line of the campus, and then sold them to the University at a fraction of their value.

The last faculty meeting at Oxford was held on June 4, 1919, after which the professors of the College hastened their exodus to prepare for the summer quarter beginning July 25 on the Atlanta campus. Now a fifth division of the University was established, the School of Business Administration, with Edgar H. Johnson as Dean, and a sixth, the Graduate School, with Theodore H. Jack as Dean. J. Gordon Stipe was appointed to the new office of Registrar. Important additions were made to the faculty. For the summer quarter, classes of the College of Liberal Arts were held in Law and Theology Buildings, occupation of Physics being delayed until the fall quarter.

Dr. Odum served as "organizing dean" for the single year, resigning in 1920 to accept the position of Professor of Sociology at the University of North Carolina; his career at that institution was to make him internationally famous. His departure, however, did not deprive Emory of the secretary whom he had brought with him in 1919. His sister, Miss Pauline Odum, was to continue the mainstay of successive deans for forty-four busy years. On Howard Odum's departure Theodore H. Jack accepted the duties of Dean of the College in addition to those of Dean of the Graduate School.

The primitive conditions encountered on the new campus have long been the subject of amused and rueful reminiscence. Excavation and grading had exposed great areas of red clay, with consequent clouds of dust in dry weather and morasses of mud in wet weather. There were no paved roads until the mid-twenties. The streetcar line stopped at the first intersection of Oxford and North Decatur Roads, though it was later extended to the Log Cabin at the foot of the campus. Any extended rainy spell closed the area to auto traffic and reduced the community to slogging through the mud for all occasions. Community facilities were few, the most important being the Emory station on the Seaboard Railroad. A temporary post office was installed in the basement of Theology; the post office near the bridge on Clifton Road was not occupied until 1923. The nearest market was a small country store on the left side of Clifton Road between the railroad bridge and Gatewood Drive. For several years it was extremely difficult for the newcomers to realize the conveniences of urban life.

The newcomers, however, were not slow to provide the social amenities. The most notable of these was organized by the ladies of the University circle. Since 1919 the Emory Woman's Club has a record of unbroken activity. Its aims have been broadly defined, and besides regular monthly meetings, it has carried on a variety of cultural programs and has served campus and community in many ways. Its offices have proved no sinecures to those who have held them. Appropriately, the Club has taken charge of or assisted at the greater number of the University's major social functions. Its year culminates in a spring luncheon, which brings out a large attendance.

As early as 1919 Bishop Candler asked to be relieved of his duties as Chancellor, a request which the Board of Trustees was unwilling to grant. As a matter of fact, Bishop Candler's great influence in the Church and the community made him almost indispensable in the difficult days of the organization of the University. The variety of services that he had shown himself capable of performing had established him as a key man in many of its undertakings, in spite of the fact that some areas of disagreement with the majority of the Board had developed. Among his enduring benefactions was the successful issue of a twenty-year campaign to release college endowments from taxation. With the exception of investments in real estate, this was finally achieved in 1920. Savings thus afforded have enabled Emory and the other private institutions of Georgia to apply large sums to the improvement of their programs.

For some months of 1920 Dr. Franklin Parker served as Acting Chancellor, then as Acting President when the Bishop reluctantly resumed the chancellorship. In the fall of that year Dr. Harvey

Warren Cox assumed the office of President, Bishop Candler continuing as Chancellor until the final acceptance of his resignation two years later. With the coming of Dr. Cox to the University and his assumption of full administrative responsibility in 1922, the days of beginnings were over.

President Cox, a Nebraska Wesleyan University undergraduate with graduate degrees from Harvard, came to Emory from the University of Florida, where he was Professor of Philosophy and Dean of the Teachers' College. He soon showed himself to be a man of integrity, firmness, and business acumen. Finding at Emory a group of semi-independent schools with little feeling of corporate unity, his first task was to establish among them a sense of the responsible relation of each to the University as a whole. Finances were in bad order, with the University running so heavy a deficit that Mr. Candler had declared that he would no longer contribute to its support. Setting up a firm budget, and holding the divisions and departments within it, the President was able to win back the confidence of Emory's chief benefactor, and within five years the University was again on the move. Dr. Cox was no less determined to maintain the highest academic standards. In 1917 Emory had been admitted to the Southern Association of Colleges and Secondary Schools; in 1924 it was placed on the approved list of the Association of American Universities.

Among pledges made to the Atlanta Medical College on its affiliation with Emory was the provision of a hospital to enlarge its teaching facilities. Wesley Memorial Enterprises, of which Mr. Asa Candler had been a chief patron, in 1905 had established a fifty-bed hospital in the famous old "Calico House" on Auburn Avenue with an associated school of nursing. Within a decade its facilities became inadequate to meet demands made on it, and plans for a new, modern hospital were in the making. Its location was the subject of long controversy, until Mr. Candler took matters in his own hands, announcing that it would be erected on the campus of Emory University. Of its cost of more than $1,750,000 approximately $1,250,000 came out of Mr. Candler's own pocket. New Wesley Memorial Hospital went into operation a fortnight before Christmas 1922. On May 30, 1924, it was transferred to Emory and became Emory University Hospital, although the old name held on for some years.

On June 4, 1920, the Treasurer reported the University's endowment as $2,150,332.15. The School of Medicine was creating a serious financial problem, and the Board of Trustees' Committee on Finance proposed that the General Education Board be applied to for a grant of $500,000, to be made "without other conditions than that it shall be used for medical education." At next year's meeting Emory's Trustees approved the request, over the vigorous protest of Bishop Candler. Two years later the General Education Board made an offer of matching funds considerably below what had been originally sought. The offer was accepted, and with this temporary assistance the School of Medicine operated from 1923 to 1928 without a deficit.

It was clear that there was a pressing need for increased endowment and an expanded plant; otherwise the University was flourishing. Attendance for 1919-20 was 961, and in the quadrennial report to the General Conference it was stated: "The attendance would have been far greater if there had been room for them in the dormitories and lecture rooms."

That conditions of student life in an urban university differed from those in a rural college caused some concern among the Trustees. Atlanta's enthusiasm for intercollegiate athletics, as manifested by the football spirit centered at Georgia Tech and Oglethorpe, raised emulation on the Emory campus. The newly founded student newspaper, the *Emory Wheel,* carried the slogan, "For a Greater Emory and Intercollegiate Athletics," and the Student Council petitioned for a reversal of the policy that had prevailed at Oxford. The Trustees returned a firm refusal, but they were uneasily conscious of the lack of proper facilities for physical education, which was to continue for many years. The medical students were impatient with the traditional discipline to which the College students were subjected. The problem of compulsory church attendance and the expansion of extracurricular activities drew from Bishop Candler the warning: "It is not reassuring to see any slightest tendency to reduce the religious forces of the institution and increase the methods of amusement and diversion." Nevertheless it was found necessary to modify the rules of discipline: the bylaws of the College and the student's matriculation pledge were cautiously liberalized. There were, to be sure, some unpleasant incidents in the student life of these early years. There was an outbreak of hazing which the authorities were forced to put down with a strong hand. The sophomores compelled the freshmen to run a brutal gauntlet on the athletic field, and the dismissal of the ringleaders which was immediately decreed resulted in a tumultuous demonstration at the College assembly. But on the whole it may be stated that the morale of the campus was high. The Class of 1923, the first to spend all four years in Atlanta, is happy in the memory of its undergraduate career and takes a justifiable pride in its record.

Although Emory students, as in duty bound, complained continually about compulsory religious observance, there was a pervasive religious spirit on the campus, perhaps not much stronger in the School of Theology than in the College. There were annual revivals in the 'twenties, of which the most notable was the "Durham Revival" of February 1921. Dr. Plato Durham, an eloquent and fervent preacher, by his sermons created such a furor of religious excitement that by petition of the students the special services continued for a fortnight.

There was great extracurricular activity. The literary societies, Few and Phi Gamma, had accompanied the College in its migration, but they did not flourish in the new environment, although they were not finally disbanded until 1932. The literary magazine, the *Phoenix,* had also been transplanted, to be soon overshadowed by the weekly newspaper, the *Emory Wheel,* the first number of which appeared on December 12, 1919, with Ernest Rogers '20 as Editor. Under Professor Malcolm H. Dewey the Glee Club rapidly became the premier student organization, within a few years reaching an international audience. The Board of Trustees at this time discouraged a dramatic society, but the gap was partially filled by "stunt nights" under the auspices of the Glee Club. An ambitious musical undertaking was Dr. Dewey's Little Symphony, whose concerts attracted audiences from the city as well as from the campus.

A temporary fraternity row was located across the railroad tracks in seven frame cottages. The social life of the fraternities, however, was severely circumscribed, both by the limited accommodations of the chapters and by the University rule forbidding dancing. The ban on dancing was to be a sore point for some years to come, although it came to be pretty openly flouted at the "receptions" and "teas" held in Atlanta clubs, hotels, and the homes of chapter patrons and patronesses, particularly at the March "Little Commencement."

The first summer session on the Atlanta campus in 1919 offered special courses for teachers and school administrators, and teacher education has been a feature of all summer quarters succeeding. Programs have included courses by visiting instructors, workshops, and demonstration schools, and subject matter courses in the College and Graduate School have been available to registrants. Large enrollments from the beginning have shown that the provision of enriched offerings in the field of education at this season have contributed to a real need, and a large and loyal body of Emory alumni is made up of professional educators whose training in whole or in part has been thus obtained.

In the minutes of the Board of Trustees for the first decade of the University a recurring topic of discussion is the establishment of a teachers' college. On June 10, 1916, Chancellor Candler reported that "A contract was made with Rev. F. H. Shuler of the South Carolina Conference, to conduct a campaign in that State to raise $50,000 for the Pedagogical Department of the University, to be called in honor of the late President James H. Carlisle, of Wofford College, The Carlisle Teachers College." A conflict of interest with Conference colleges compelled the campaign to be called off, and without it collections were disappointingly small. But the Chancellor did not dismiss the project, declaring that "no department of the University is more urgently needed than the Teachers College. It is scarcely less important than the School of Theology."

The Chancellor's Report in the minutes for June 3, 1921, returns to the subject:

Looking to the time when the Teachers' College can be opened, an initial course, or a department of a pedagogical character, ought to be provided now, and to this end the building for the Model School should be erected. This would meet the urgent need of the children of members of the faculty, and the children of others living near the University, for a proper school, and would lead naturally to the opening of the "James H. Carlisle Teachers College" in the near future. For this building I believe I can secure the necessary funds.

In the same year Ralph E. Wager was elected Professor of Education, and in 1923 the L. C. Fishburne Building was erected, intended as the first unit of the Teachers' College. Here for several years was located the elementary public school for the Emory neighborhood, in addition to classrooms for the Department of Education, to which in 1925 a second member, Sterling G. Brinkley '07, was added.

At the meeting of the Board on June 5, 1925, Bishop Candler offered the following resolution: "Resolved, That the founding of the Teachers College follow immediately after the completion of the Chemistry Building, as soon thereafter as sufficient funds can be had." Although the resolution was adopted, the plan was eventually abandoned.

In Fall Quarter 1925 the University opened an Extension Department under the direction of Professor Wager, offering afternoon and evening courses for full University credit. A downtown Atlanta branch for evening classes was located in a building at the corner of Spring and Baker Streets, the gift of Mr. Asa G. Candler, and afternoon classes were conducted in Atlanta public schools and neighboring towns, all taught by regular members of the University faculty. Correspondence work was also offered for a few years. All off-campus teaching, however, was discontinued after 1933. Although the extension experiment proved unsatisfactory and the plan for a teachers' college was given up, the Department of Education continued to gather strength and influence, and has been one of Emory's major contributions to the cultural development of Atlanta and Georgia.

Organization and reorganization, involving successive new appointments to key positions, are a constant feature of university administration. In 1923, Goodrich C. White '08 succeeded Theodore H. Jack as Dean of the College. In 1924, George H. Mew, a young accountant with Western Electric, was elected Treasurer of the University, and Comer M. Woodward '00 was appointed Dean of Men. In 1925, Charles J. Hilkey became Dean of the School of Law after an interregnum following the resignation of Judge Samuel Cole Williams, and Russell H. Oppenheimer, Superintendent of Wesley Memorial Hospital, became Dean of the School of Medicine on the retirement of Dr. W. S. Elkin.

The Library School of the Carnegie Library of Atlanta, founded in 1905 by a subsidy from Andrew Carnegie, in 1925, under its Director Miss Tommie Dora Barker, sought affiliation with Emory. Accepted by the Board of Trustees, it nevertheless continued to hold its classes at the Carnegie Library until 1930, when subventions by the Carnegie Corporation and the Rosenwald Fund made possible its reorganization as the Library School of Emory University and its move to quarters in the Asa Griggs Candler Library.

When the College was brought up from Oxford, the library was placed in the basement of Theology Building, where it was to remain with increasing inconvenience for seven years. In 1924 a gift of Mr. Asa G. Candler enabled the Trustees to authorize the erection of a University Library building, to be located at the east end of the Quadrangle. Professor Hinton, after a tour of Northern universities to gather ideas, prepared a report as a basis of planning, a well-known architect in the special field was employed, and in February 1926 the Asa Griggs Candler Library was dedicated by Bishop Candler, his brother the dedicatee too ill to be present at the ceremony. The transfer of books and furniture from Theology was soon effected. But in addition to library uses, the building for nearly thirty years was to double as the administrative center of the University. Offices which had hitherto been mainly crowded into the second floor of Physics, eventually required the whole of the ground and first floors of the Library building. On its transfer to the University campus in 1930, the Library School took over most of the third floor. With the growth of the University Library, collections and services were to suffer severely from restricted space, for which no relief was afforded until the completion of the new Administration Building in 1955.

At the end of the first decade it was clearly seen by President Cox and the Board of Trustees that Emory's progress depended on increased endowment and an enlarged physical plant. In May 1925 the productive endowment amounted to only $2,659,276.70, and every meeting of the Board had heard of the need for new buildings. At the meeting on June 5, 1925, it was determined to launch a campaign for new resources, massive for the time and the region, with the slogan, "Ten Million in Ten Years." $7,000,000 was to be added endowment, and the remainder was for the construction of buildings. Of the total, it may be noted, $1,800,000 was earmarked for the Teachers' College. Great enthusiasm was generated by the successful Atlanta drive for $750,000 in March 1926, of which their quota of $75,000 was oversubscribed by faculty and students in a single day.

An inducement to student participation was a plan to dredge a lake in the low ground along Lullwater Creek, the area of the lower athletic field. Student pledges were to be used for this purpose, and as a start to the project, a holiday was declared on which the University community put in an exciting day's work clearing the ground for the proposed Emory Lake, for which a beautiful drawing had been made by a local landscape architect. Unfortunately, the creek, which carried sewage, was not cleared out, as had been promised by the county commissioners, and a careful study was to prove that if a lake were constructed at the foot of the campus, it would shortly become a huge cesspool. The scheme was therefore given up, long to be the subject of ironic comment.

For 1925-26 the total enrollment of the University was 1,888, almost double the total for the first year that the College had occupied the Atlanta campus. 220 degrees were granted. The College, with a full-time faculty of 49, enrolled 569 students. The Candler School of Theology numbered 99 students, the School of Medicine 199, the Lamar School of Law 65. The Summer Session enrollment of 618 included many teachers in addition to students in attendance during the regular year. There were 380 students, most of them teachers, in the Extension Division. Basic tuition charges were $35 a quarter in the College, $180 for the year in the School of Medicine, and $150 for the year in the School of Law. The faculty of the University, including all divisions, numbered 220, 86 of them full-time, the greater number of the part-time members serving the School of Medicine on a voluntary basis.

By way of summing up, it may be stated that the ten years, in which occurred a major financial depression, did not produce the ten million dollars that had been sought. Emory's resources, however, both in endowment and plant were considerably improved, and a more closely knit academic and financial pattern emerged even from the hard times that lay ahead.

III

Through the Centennial Year

1927-1936

THE SECOND DECADE of the life of the University initiated a new building program. In 1927 a combination dining hall and temporary auditorium was erected in the dormitory area. On the upper floor were held chapel services, concerts, plays, and commencements until all these functions were taken over by Glenn Memorial. The level floor and the uncertain acoustics, however, made the room something less than ideal. The lower floor was occupied by dining hall and kitchens. For the first two years the plan of serving table d'hote meals was continued, but after 1929 a cafeteria line was installed. In 1931 the auditorium was burned out, but was immediately rebuilt. A few years later the cafeteria was moved to the upper floor, and the offices of the Emory Christian Association and student lounges occupied the free space downstairs.

Prior to the construction of the temporary auditorium there had been no fixed place for commencement exercises. The first in Atlanta had been held in Wesley Memorial Church. When they were brought out to the campus, for several years they were conducted in an improvised amphitheater set in Antoinette Gardens. Antoinette Gardens, located in the ravine across the road from the Law Building, had been planted under the supervision of the wife of Bishop Candler and named in her honor. At the commencement held here in June 1925, the president of the ladies' committee of the Stone Mountain Memorial Association presented every member of the graduating class with a memorial half dollar. Commencement of 1926 was held in a tent in front of Fishburne in a blistering hot and humid noonday, an occasion to be recalled with horror.

In 1927 also the Chemistry Building was completed by the addition of two upper floors. The building housed all facilities for both chemistry and biology. A large amphitheater for lecture-demonstrations was installed on the third floor. The Department of Biology was crowded into the ground floor, where it was to remain until the erection of its own building twenty-four years later.

In 1929 the Florence Candler Harris Memorial Nurses' Home on Clifton Road was completed and occupied. Dedicated to the memory of the sister of the three Candler brothers—Asa G., Warren A., and John S.—one of the organizers of the Women's Auxiliary of Wesley Memorial Hospital, nine of her nephews and nieces contributed to the building fund.

Glenn Memorial, at the North Decatur Road entrance to the campus, was completed in 1931 and dedicated on October 4 of that year. The architects were the Atlanta firm of Hentz, Adler, and Schutze, with Hal F. Hentz '04, '36H, the principal designer. This structure, intended both as auditorium and church, is in the general tradition of the work of Sir Christopher Wren, with a commanding tower inspired by that of All Saints' Church, Bristol, England. By an ingenious and beautiful arrangement the east end was originally equipped with both chancel and stage, making it available for public gatherings of the University and community and for formal religious services. Dedicated to the memory of the Reverend Wilbur Fisk Glenn, Class of 1861, a veteran Methodist minister and leader in the Church, among the contributors to its erection were his children, Thomas K. Glenn '43H and Mrs. Charles Howard Candler.

The first house on new Fraternity Row, in the northwestern quarter of the campus, Sigma Alpha Epsilon, was occupied in 1928, to be followed two years later by Sigma Chi, Kappa Alpha, and Chi Phi (Tom Connally Hall). The style adopted was that of the pillared Southern mansion, which has been followed with various adaptions. From the first, these houses, located on University property, and with title vested in the University, have been considered an integral part of the student housing of the institution. In return for exclusive use by their members, the fraternities assume the cost of maintenance and repairs and, over a period of years, reimburse the University for construction cost of the houses. Fraternity affairs otherwise are left in the control of the chapters with a minimum of official regulation.

The chief landmark of the back campus is a spherical water tank, resembling a golf ball perched on a high tee. For this reason the students christened it on sight the Bobby Jones Memorial, the great golfer having attended the School of Law with the Class of 1929. Erected in 1933, it stands 125 feet high and has a capacity of 100,000 gallons, the source of its water being a deep well beneath it. Built to furnish a complete water supply for the campus, it was found inadequate for the purpose, now serving as an auxiliary supply for the steam plant in case of failure of the DeKalb County system, and to maintain pressure in case of fire on Fraternity Row.

The first of Emory's junior colleges off the Atlanta campus was established at Valdosta in 1928. Residents of the South Georgia city conducted a strong campaign for a division of the University to be located there, offering a site, a commodious administration-classroom building, and $200,000 endowment. The offer was accepted by the Trustees, William B. Stubbs '19 was named Associate Dean, and Valdosta Junior College opened under good auspices with fifty students and a staff of seven. In the following year, on petition of a committee from Newton County, a junior college was also established on the old Oxford campus, with Hugh A. Woodward '01 as Associate Dean. Extensive repairs were undertaken, and the plant was restored to its original uses with an enrollment of sixty-three students. Women were admitted as day students. The Academy, which had utilized the facilities from the removal of the College to Atlanta, was discontinued with the inauguration of a four-year Junior College, including the last two years of high school, in fall 1950.

Valdosta and Oxford Junior Colleges conformed to the plan, adopted in 1928, organizing the College into Junior and Senior divisions, the former devoted primarily to required courses, the latter to specialization. The work in the three localities was made uniform, so that a student of any one of the three satisfying the requirements at his junior college, in his third year could be admitted to senior college on the Atlanta campus.

Subvention by the Carnegie Corporation and the Julius Rosenwald Fund, setting up its operations for five years, at length permitted the organization of the Library School on the Emory campus. The upper floor of Asa Griggs Candler Library was transferred to its uses, and the first session began in Fall 1930. Miss Clara E. Howard, formerly Director of the Library School of New Jersey College for Women, was the first Dean, and at her death in December 1935, Miss Lydia M. Gooding served as Acting Dean until the appointment of Miss Tommie Dora Barker '09LS, '30H, to the office in 1936.

In 1926, Perry W. Fattig came to Emory from State Teachers College, Farmville, Virginia, as Curator of the Museum. Located on the first floor of the new Library building, its collections were brought together from various quarters on the Oxford and Atlanta campuses, notable among them the Egyptian-Babylonian collection gathered by Professor William A. Shelton in 1920, the W. H. LaPrade collection of bird skins, the Cobb collection of Indian relics, and several smaller groupings. Mr. Fattig was himself an entomologist, and the collecting and classifying of insects and other biological specimens largely engaged his attention during the twenty-three years that he continued in the position. He was to achieve wide publicity by demonstrating in the court room that various deleterious substances, including ground glass, insects, and snake venom, could be swallowed with a soft drink without harmful after-effects.

The decade brought various changes in the College. In 1927 a Department of Fine Arts was organized under Professor Malcolm H. Dewey, and in 1938 Geology, after many years, was returned to the curriculum as a full-fledged department under Professor James G. Lester. The mineral cabinet that had been the pride of the College at Oxford in the course of time was installed on the ground floor of Physics. From 1932 Latin and Greek were no longer required for the A.B. degree.

In 1930 the Reserve Officers Training Corps was discontinued. On America's entrance into World War I in 1917, compulsory military training, organized the following year as a Student Army Training Corps unit, had been installed at Oxford, to be succeeded in January 1919 by a unit of R.O.T.C. with required participation

Excavating for First Building on Druid Hills Campus, 1915

Bridge between Quadrangle and Dormitory Areas, Dobbs Hall in Distance, ca. 1920

The Log Cabin, End of Car Line, Early 'Twenties

Commencement in Antoinette Gardens, June 1925

Emory R O T C, Late 'Twenties

Freshman-Sophomore Pushball Match, ca. 1928

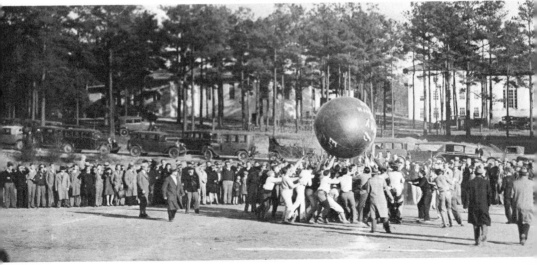

by freshmen and sophomores. Its hours of exercise and drill had made it a useful adjunct to the program of physical education, but by 1930 it was felt that compulsory military training had outlived its usefulness and appropriateness at Emory. The departure of Major Richard T. Taylor, who was popular with the students, and for whom no replacement had been named, suggested the end of an era. At this time the campus was visited by Sherwood Eddy, who delivered a series of pacifist addresses with a violent attack on the R.O.T.C. that aroused considerable excitement. It must be emphasized, however, that this unfortunate incident, deeply resented by the administration of the University, did not determine its action in terminating military training. It was, indeed, to be reintroduced when a national need was again indicated.

In accordance with the pattern set at Oxford the University had chosen to operate on a five-day week, with the holiday on Monday. In 1929 the holiday was changed to the more usual Saturday. Moreover, the Medical, Law, and Library Schools ran on the semester system, while the other divisions were on the quarter plan. In 1931 all divisions alike scheduled their work by quarters. Graduation exercises were held at the close of every quarter through 1927-28; thereafter only the June Commencement and summer graduation exercises were retained. Other minor irregularities were adjusted as convenience permitted.

Coming to Emory in the fall of 1927 as Assistant Professor of History and Government, Cullen B. Gosnell brought with him the idea of community education for political action, and in February 1928 was held the first Southeastern Citizenship Conference, under the direction of Dean Theodore H. Jack, Professor Ross H. McLean, and Professor Gosnell. The four-day program featured a number of distinguished speakers, besides round-tables and a model Assembly of the League of Nations. The success of the conference led to its establishment as an annual affair under Dr. Gosnell's direction. The third session, 1930, was renamed the Institute of Citizenship, and under that title it continued through 1940. Among subjects of discussion were, "The Constitution of the United States," "The Press and Public Opinion," "The New Deal," and

"The Political and Economic Problems of the South." Reactivated in 1954, the Institute functioned until Dr. Gosnell's retirement in 1962, in which year President Kennedy praised it as a forum for the discussion of "national problems and policies which is the life-blood of our democratic process." In 1934 President Roosevelt had written a similar commendation. The participation of public and academic figures speaking with authority on matters of vital concern, the coöperation of organizations dedicated to public affairs, and the attendance of audiences drawn from a wide area, made the Institute of Citizenship an influential medium for the discussion of regional, national, and international problems in the critical years of depression, war, and recovery.

An important milestone was reached by the College in 1929, when a chapter of Phi Beta Kappa, national scholastic fraternity, was installed. Phi Beta Kappa, founded in 1776 at the College of William and Mary, stands for the promotion and recognition of scholarship, of which its key is the universally recognized badge. Emory had presented a petition for membership to the Phi Beta Kappa Senate in December 1927, and after due investigation a charter was granted to Gamma Chapter in the State of Georgia. The charter membership consisted of twenty-one professors who had won their keys at other institutions, and installation ceremonies were held on April 5, 1929, under the direction of national President Clark S. Northrup, of Cornell University. Dr. Theodore H. Jack, Dean of the Graduate School, was elected first President of the Emory chapter; he was to serve as a member of the Senate of Phi Beta Kappa, 1934-52. This was the 108th installation of the fraternity, the third in Georgia, preceded by Alpha Chapter of the University of Georgia in 1914 and Beta Chapter at Agnes Scott College in 1926. Undergraduate members from the junior and senior classes are chosen at meetings of the chapter in fall and spring, alumni members are added on the basis of scholarly attainments after graduation, and occasional honorary membership is granted. Emory has every reason to take pride in its Phi Beta Kappa roll, which holds many individuals who have won high distinction in various fields. It is especially proud of the fact that a foundation member, Goodrich C. White, was elected to the Senate in 1937, and served as President of the United Chapters for the triennium 1952-55.

On the coming of Phi Beta Kappa, the local fraternity recognizing excellence in scholarship, Alpha Epsilon Upsilon, dating back to 1906, became the junior college scholastic honor society, with chapters at Atlanta, Valdosta, and Oxford.

The depression years of the 'thirties did not leave Emory unscathed. The income of the University from all sources took a steep decline, enrollments dropped, plans for expansion were shelved, some permanently, and operating budgets were cut to the bone. Although from 1929 to 1932 the enrollment varied less than five per cent, the loss of attendance was felt severely. One dormitory, Winship, was closed in 1932. All possible economies were put into effect without lowering the quality of instruction and other educational services. At length it was seen that salary cuts were unavoidable. At a called meeting of the faculty President Cox announced that salaries of faculty, administration, and staff would be reduced on a graduated scale from five to eleven per cent. Although there had been previous warning of the probable necessity of this step, the news was unwelcome and depressing. Nevertheless, Professor J. Sam Guy, the "skipper" of the Department of Chemistry, famous for his pugnacious defense of the faculty against possible administrative encroachment, rose to propose a vote of full confidence in the President, which was passed with but a single dissent. The strain had taken its toll of Dr. Cox, and he broke down, the only public show of emotion that he was ever known to exhibit.

The University income, however, continued to fall, and in 1934 another cut was necessitated, this time bringing the reduction of salaries from fifteen to twenty-one per cent. This was a difficult time for all the Emory personnel, but it was borne as hopefully as might be, and the interval was occupied with plans for the development to be anticipated in better days ahead. Nevertheless, it was not until 1935 that a five per cent restoration was found feasible, with full restoration two years later. Prudent management of its resources had enabled Emory to weather the storm, and the

[39]

institution was to emerge from the ordeal, from a sense of hardship honorably shared and overcome, with a greater unified strength than it had possessed before.

In October 1934 Emory found itself unhappily involved in a "red scare." Overzealous officers of DeKalb County raided the home of an alumna of the University where a small meeting discussing the prevention of war was in progress. Six arrests were made on the farcical charge of "inciting insurrection," which under an old Georgia statute carried the death penalty. Among exhibits confiscated were copies of *Liberty* magazine, the *Nation,* the *New Republic,* and a problem in trigonometry, which was interpreted as a code message relating to a Communist plot to overthrow the government of the United States. The prime movers in this ridiculous display of "oppression, suppression, and terrorism," as it was characterized by President Cox, were members of the legal department of Fulton County, who were permitted to prosecute the case in DeKalb.

A graduate assistant in Emory's Department of Chemistry was made the chief defendant. The hostess of the meeting and another guest were alumnae of the University, and these connections encouraged the prosecutor to utter wild and inflammatory charges that Emory was a hotbed of Communism. Professor Guy came vigorously to the defense of his student, and a large deputation of the faculty attended the preliminary hearing, at which, nevertheless, four members of the discussion group were bound over, to remain in the DeKalb County jail for three weeks until the grand jury convened.

Every attempt had been made by those responsible for this misprision of justice to link the University with Communist subversion. Rumors were rife and feeling rose high. It was felt necessary that a public statement be released defining the University's position with regard to Communism and democratic freedom. While in unqualified language opposing "the principles, the objectives, and the methods of the Communist movement," the statement registered "a definite protest against the methods of suppression and terrorism . . . expressing our unwavering faith in the principles of democracy, tolerance, and free discussion." This declaration, signed by sixty-nine members of the faculty, was transmitted to President Cox, who added a strong exposition of Emory's religious, moral, and political convictions, and gave it to the press. The public response was immediate and reassuring. The New York *Times,* the Richmond *Times-Dispatch,* and a number of Georgia weeklies came editorially to the defense, and when the DeKalb grand jury refused to indict, the *Atlanta Journal* spoke out on the unjustifiable employment of "dangerous and undemocratic methods" in combating alleged Communistic activities.

Although one of those active in the prosecution was quoted as declaring that he was determined to put Emory out of business, the long-term effect was to rally the friends of the University to its support in the pursuit of truth and enlightened opinion, and to do much to clear the air of disquieting rumors, of which more than one institution of higher learning at this time was the victim.

When the first two years of medical training were brought out to the Druid Hills campus, the Atlanta Medical College buildings and the J. J. Gray Clinic, erected 1917, were turned over to the City of Atlanta for use as a Negro hospital. Thereafter the Negro Division of Grady Hospital, with approximately 240 beds, became a teaching facility of the Emory School of Medicine. For many years financial conditions permitted only the most limited use of Wesley Memorial Hospital for teaching purposes. On an official visit in 1930, the Secretary of the Association of American Medical Colleges, while complimenting the School on its general progress, insisted that there should be less didactic and more clinical teaching. As a result, formal class instruction for advanced students was largely restricted to the junior year, and the senior program took a chiefly clinical form. In 1931 the white wards of Grady were opened to the Medical School on a limited basis, a move substantially improving the quality of medical care available to patients.

On March 12, 1929, Asa Griggs Candler, Emory's chief patron, President of the Board of Trustees, died at the age of seventy-eight in the hospital that he had founded. The funeral, held in his home on Ponce de Leon Avenue, was attended in a body by the University faculty. Mr. Candler had suffered a protracted illness. The last meeting of the Board of Trustees at which he had presided was that of June 5, 1925; four years earlier he had sought to retire, but his resignation had been declined. Reporting his passing, the newspapers rehearsed at length the story of his financial success, and his multiplied services to the Methodist Episcopal Church, South, the City of Atlanta, the State of Georgia, Emory College, and Emory University. The sum of his benefactions, which had begun long before he achieved dramatic prosperity, would be impossible to calculate with any accuracy. It has been estimated that his gifts to Emory University approximated eight million dollars. His eldest son, Charles Howard Candler '98, '02M, '42H, succeeded his father as President of the Board of Trustees at their meeting on May 21, 1929, an office that he was to hold until his death in 1957.

The office of Vice-President of the University was created in 1929 with Theodore H. Jack the first incumbent. He was replaced as Dean of the Graduate School by Goodrich C. White, who was to hold the appointment for thirteen years. Dr. Jack resigned to accept the presidency of Randolph-Macon Woman's College in 1933, making his farewell to Emory in the baccalaureate address at the June Commencement, when he was awarded the honorary degree of LL.D. In 1934 Raymond R. Paty '21, Associate Professor of Bible and Religious Education, was elected Dean of Men.

This was a great era for student extracurricular activities. In the summer of 1926 the Emory Glee Club sailed to England on its first European concert tour. The invasion of a group of singing American collegians was a novelty at that time, and they were everywhere cordially received. So encouraged, the Club returned to England in summer 1928, extending its tour to the Continent, where they visited Paris and sang in Amsterdam. Veterans of the organization recall their musical journeyings as the high points of their college years.

Emory's first dramatic group, the Emory Players, made their

appearance on "Stunt Night" of 1928, performing Booth Tarkington's one-act *The Trysting Place* in the second half of the program of the evening. From 1928 to 1933 under the direction of Professor Thomas H. English the Players produced a series of one-act and full-length dramas ranging from *Seven Keys to Baldpate* to *She Stoops to Conquer*. In 1934 Professor Garland G. Smith took over the direction, specializing in plays of the contemporary theater, performed with conspicuous success on the stage of Glenn Memorial. The professional finish achieved by Dr. Smith made these notable displays of undergraduate talent.

This was the greatest period in the history of Emory debating on the score of public interest. Coached by Professor Nolan A. Goodyear '04, meets were arranged with leading American universities and with visitors from overseas. In 1929 victories were registered over both Princeton and Harvard. In 1935, Robert Elliott '30, '34L, and Robert Wiggins '36 were chosen by the National Student Federation to make a debate tour of Europe, on which they met fifteen teams in Britain and France. They were accompanied on the tour by Emory benefactor Samuel C. Dobbs '28H, and their arrangements were in the hands of John A. Griffin '35, '38G. In the academic year 1935-36 nineteen Emory debaters competed against thirty different colleges, held the tenth international debate, and engaged in a broadcast event with Catholic University on the question of intercollegiate athletics.

Little Commencement, with its house party week end and round of social functions, for several years served to allay the annual epidemic of spring fever. In 1929, however, it was forbidden for disciplinary reasons, and in the depression year 1932 it was omitted for economy's sake. Certain moribund organizations gave up their charters or simply suspended at this time, but campus affairs were generally thriving. Although a student center and gymnasium were yet far in the future, a swimming pool, adjoining Fraternity Row, was given the students in 1927; at first open to the weather, and therefore not usable throughout the year, it was enclosed in 1932.

Edwin R. Embree, President of the Julius Rosenwald Fund, visited Emory in February 1931. After a detailed inspection of the University, he made the following statement at a called meeting of the faculty:

> My impression of Emory is that you are doing the required work of a university amazingly well, and with astounding modesty, as compared with some other institutions. I believe Emory more nearly approaches Dr. Abraham Flexner's "ideal university" than any other institution in America.

In an address before the Southern Conference on Education in the fall of that year Dr. Embree gave favorable notice to Emory. A few years later he was quoted in a newspaper interview as saying: "If I were putting twenty million dollars into a Southern university, I would put it all into Emory, because I consider it rich in promise."

But on all occasions Dr. Embree pointed out that the South was dissipating its educational energies among a multitude of small, mediocre institutions; that the larger, better-established foundations wastefully duplicated offerings; that it presented few opportunities to advanced students for first-class specialization; and that as a result, promising graduate students and teachers were lured away to Northern and Western universities. He urged that Southern education consolidate its resources, and indicated the possibility of developing at least five university centers, of which Atlanta was one, where graduate work of the highest quality might be pursued. Such a movement he envisaged as a Southern educational renaissance.

In pursuance of this suggestion, President Cox, President J. R. McCain of Agnes Scott, and President M. L. Brittain '86 of Georgia Tech entered into discussions as to the possibility of establishing a university center in Atlanta. The immediate outcome was a petition to the trustees of the Lewis H. Beck Foundation to underwrite a study of the local situation by a committee of educators of national distinction. The petition granted, Dr. George A. Works, of the University of Chicago, who had earlier planned the reorganization of Georgia's state educational system, was named to head the committee. With him were associated five other prominent academic figures, President Robert M. Hutchins, the University of Chicago, President L. D. Coffman, the University of Minnesota, Edmond E. Day, the Rockefeller Foundation, Professor William F. Ogburn, the University of Chicago, and Dr. Embree.

Together they visited Atlanta in January 1934, and from observations made on the scene and from information gathered from various sources they submitted a preliminary report in November of that year, recommending seven major steps toward "the ultimate goal of making Atlanta a regional educational center for graduate and professional work on a high level." Specific recommendations were made for coöperation, consolidation, and development involving the three institutions so far concerned in the plan. Besides noting the need for new buildings, and the enlargement of library and laboratory facilities, however, it was clearly stated that only "an endowment running into millions . . . will make it possible for the proposed university center to attract and hold outstanding scholars in the several fields that are desirable to develop."

In the following years every recommendation of the report and every aspect of coöperation were given the most intensive study by committees of Emory, Agnes Scott, and Georgia Tech, with whom were joined representatives of the University of Georgia, Columbia Theological Seminary, and the High Museum of Art. As will be seen, much was accomplished by the institutions working in concert, although some specific recommendations were found impracticable. But the impetus gained from the movement toward a university center was to carry all the educational institutions of the area to higher levels than they had previously occupied.

One hundred years had elapsed since the chartering of the College at Oxford, years of distinguished service to Georgia, the South, and the Church that gave it birth. In its first century Emory had enrolled 20,251 students and conferred 8,559 degrees. The Centennial of the College, now the central unit of Emory University in Atlanta, was celebrated in an elaborate academic program extending over ten days, Friday, December 4, through Sunday, December 13, 1936. A series of conferences brought to the campus leaders in areas of service to which the University is dedicated, including the physical sciences, the humanities, religion, higher education, medicine, law, government, the press, business. Meetings of the Georgia Section of the American Chemical Society and of the College of Bishops of the Methodist Episcopal Church, South, were held in conjunction with the anniversary, the Emory chapter of Phi Beta Kappa initiated twelve distinguished alumni, and Omicron Delta Kappa welcomed a group of six alumni into its membership. On the day marking the granting of the original charter, Thursday, December 10, the ancient bell in the tower of Seney Hall rang out one hundred strokes, broadcast over Radio Station WSB as highlights in the history of the old College were narrated. On Saturday, December 12, the Centennial Convocation was held in Glenn Memorial, attended by delegates representing more than 200 colleges and learned societies. The main address was delivered by President Daniel L. Marsh of Boston University, and honorary degrees were conferred on seven outstanding Emory alumni. A special program on Sunday, December 6, paid tribute to Emory's grand old man, Bishop Warren A. Candler, and on the following Sunday the morning service was in charge of the College of Bishops, with the sermon preached by Bishop Edwin D. Mouzon. The program bringing the Centennial observance to a close appropriately ushered in the Christmas season with a carol concert by the Glee Club.

The Centennial Committee, under the direction of Robert C. Mizell '11, had worked on the program since Fall 1935, and their efforts were notably successful. Audiences attending the nineteen public sessions were estimated at 15,000, and an indeterminate number of listeners were added by means of eight radio broadcasts. The theme of the celebration, "Emory's century challenges the future," was given permanent form by the publication of *A History of Emory University 1836-1936,* by Henry M. Bullock '24, 25T. During the Centennial Year $200,000 was received in gifts to the University. But at the bell-ringing ceremony President Harvey W. Cox announced a six-million-dollar program of development to build an Emory "sufficient to meet the needs of the present and of the years to come." In 1944, with the payment of the final installment of the grant from the General Education Board in connection with the University Center plan, the program begun at the Centennial observance reached a triumphant conclusion.

IV
Through World War II
1937-1945

THE IDEA OF THE CONSOLIDATION of educational resources in the Atlanta-Athens area was originally conceived by Edwin Embree, but it was taken over by officials of the General Education Board, to whom an application for funds was soon made. Its protagonists were undoubtedly too sanguine in assessing its possibilities, too little impressed by the complications of the local situation, but every attempt was made with sincerity and zeal to explore means of adapting existing resources to the scheme of a university center, and to project future development on the record of past achievement. The university center plan had been successfully adopted by a few institutions in northern United States and Canada, notably the University of Toronto, the University of Rochester, Cornell University, and Syracuse University, and Atlanta groups visited them in May 1938 and October 1939 to take observations.

In 1938 Robert C. Mizell, later Director of Development, set forth the ends and aims of the coöperative project in a pamphlet, *Notes on the Proposed University Center in Atlanta*. Progress in the scheme had not been confined to interminable committee meetings and the drafting of reports. As a beginning, Agnes Scott changed from the semester to the quarter system, so to synchronize its calendar with Emory's, library reciprocity was established between the two institutions, and some exchange of professors was effected.

In January 1939 the General Education Board made grants to Emory and Agnes Scott on a matching basis: $2,000,000 to Emory for $4,000,000 independently raised, $500,000 to Agnes Scott for $1,000,000, these sums not to be entirely available until the completion of the $7,500,000 expansion program. The grants were made for "general endowment, with specific interest in strength-

[47]

ening the library, natural sciences, and departments essential for the proposed graduate program." $200,000 was reserved from the Emory grant for general university center uses. Chancellor S. V. Sanford, of the University System of Georgia, announced that Georgia Tech and the University of Georgia would coöperate fully in the enterprise. Columbia Theological Seminary and the High Museum and School of Art were also involved to a limited extent and participated in all conferences.

Another coöperative activity was early in operation. On November 30, 1939, the General Education Board had made an additional grant of $55,250 for a union catalogue of books in the Atlanta-Athens area. Part of this sum was to be used for cataloguing uncatalogued collections at Athens, part for equipment, and part for the salary of the editor. Although, as will be seen, the project languished for a time, it was effectually revived, and is to be counted one of the most useful achievements of the university center endeavor.

The University Center campaign got off to a strong start when on January 24, 1939, Samuel C. Dobbs announced an unconditional gift of $1,000,000 for Emory's College of Arts and Sciences. On December 1, $250,000 was given to the School of Medicine to endow the Joseph B. Whitehead Chair of Surgery. The clergy of the Southeastern Jurisdiction sponsored a $100,000 Parker Recognition Fund to endow a Chair of Christian Doctrine in the Candler School of Theology. In the Atlanta campaign pledges of $1,300,000 were secured by May 15, 1940, after a twelve-day intensive drive. On Charter Day 1942 President Cox was able to announce final success in the grand effort, pledges and cash having reached a total of $10,027,000, of which approximately $8,500,000 was Emory's share.

The victory was won against great odds, as was pointed out in a statement by President McCain of Agnes Scott:

> On the day the newspapers carried the account of our joint campaign effort, Germany invaded Poland. During the week of intensive solicitation in Atlanta, France fell and the stock market went to pieces. While the appeal was being carried throughout Georgia in the summer of 1941, political interfer-

ence in the state University System greatly discouraged all friends of higher education. When the final efforts were being made in December to bring the campaign to a conclusion, the United States entered the war.

In connection with the drive for endowment a new attempt to secure a student activities-gymnasium building had been set in motion by Alumni President Hal F. Hentz on Charter Day 1939. A student campaign for the same purpose was launched on the following April 7 by Marcus Bartlett, President of the Student Body. The Alumni Council adopted the project on May 15, with a goal of $400,000, but a decade and more was to be required for its realization.

Raymond B. Fosdick, President of the General Education Board 1936-1948, in his review of the university center project in *Adventure in Giving* (1962) gives a rather pessimistic statement of its outcome:

> In retrospect the affiliation of the Atlanta institutions failed to develop in any substantial way into the type of relationship originally envisioned by the General Education Board. Perhaps the concept of regional cooperation was too much of an alien idea, unsuited to the time or the occasion. Perhaps the trend toward sharing libraries, laboratories, and faculties, and away from duplicating specialties, was impeded by too many local difficulties. Whatever the reason, this particular experiment, while not a complete failure, must be written off as one of the less successful ventures of the General Education Board.

It is clear that in the planning there had not been a complete meeting of minds. The statement of the Director of Development, R. C. Mizell, of June 1941, presents the best statement of what had been sought for by those directing the campaign:

> The basic ideas in the University Center plan were: (1) that the several institutions would confer together on the educational problems of the area; (2) each would undertake to strengthen itself in order that it might make a greater contribution to the cause of education; (3) that an effort would be made to reduce the total cost of educational development in the area by avoiding needless duplication.

These aims, more general but not less useful than some that had apparently been intended by the sponsors, were actually achieved, and the benefit to higher education in the area has hardly been less than the hopes originally entertained. The University Center organization has continued, now financially supported by the participating institutions, with a quarterly conference of a Council of Presidents for the discussion of current educational problems. An Advisory Faculty Council allocates grants for research and arranges for visits of distinguished scholars and for interdepartmental meetings. In 1964-65 there were fourteen visiting scholars and twenty-four interdepartmental meetings. Finally, duplication of offerings has probably been brought to an irreducible minimum. The institutions of the Atlanta-Athens area, while not linked in an absolute coöperative relation, are actively allied for the furtherance of scholarship and academic progress.

In the third decade of the University's history there was a succession of high-level appointments. In 1937 Ellis Heber Rece, of the Department of Bible and Religious Education, succeeded Raymond R. Paty as Dean of Men, Paty resigning the office to become Director of Fellowships with the Julius Rosenwald Fund. Henry Burton Trimble, Professor of Homiletics and Pastoral Theology, was elected Dean of the Candler School of Theology on the retirement of Franklin N. Parker. A. Hollis Edens '28 became Dean of Valdosta Junior College, W. B. Stubbs replacing Paty as Associate Professor of Bible on the Atlanta campus. Finally in the same year Robert S. Hudgens '23, '30G, replaced R. H. Oppenheimer as Superintendent of the Emory Hospital, the latter filling the new position of its Medical Director in addition to the deanship of the School of Medicine.

In 1938 Goodrich C. White was appointed Vice-President of the University, continuing as Dean of the Graduate School but relinquishing the deanship of the College to J. Harris Purks, Jr., '23, Professor of Physics. In 1940 Boyce F. Martin, who had taken his college preparatory work at the Oxford Academy, followed Edgar H. Johnson as Dean of the School of Business Administration, a position that he was to fill for only two years.

Harvey W. Cox, first President of Emory University and thirteenth in the succession of the College, announced his retirement to take place in 1942. To his conservative but enlightened leadership must be attributed the laying of strong foundations for a major institution of higher learning in the South. No better summation of his accomplishment can be made than his own statement in a report to the alumni:

> Our most pressing job was to place the entire academic program upon such a sound basis that an Emory diploma would carry prestige wherever sound scholarship is recognized and valued . . . . Its accomplishment means that we have created a *good university*. But with this accomplishment our work had only begun . . . . Our next job was to create a *great university*.

Vice-President White was immediately elevated to the presidency, and Dr. Cox was named Chancellor. To President White was entrusted the task of developing the program of graduate studies that was to be the highest achievement of his administration. But already America was involved in World War II, and for the next years the national emergency was to engross the larger share of Emory's attention and energy. With the cessation of hostilities, however, long hopes became realities. Following a "Report to the President on the Development of the Graduate School," by Dumas Malone '10, '36H, the Board of Trustees on October 16, 1946, authorized the extension of graduate work to the doctoral level and the conferring of the Ph.D. degree. Permission to offer the advanced program was immediately granted to the Departments of Chemistry and Biochemistry.

Alumni Director Robert F. Whitaker '26, '27L, who became Assistant to the President in 1942, was appointed Superintendent of the Emory Hospital on the resignation of Robert S. Hudgens in mid-1944. Illness compelling Dr. Oppenheimer to retire from the deanship of the School of Medicine, Eugene A. Stead '28, '32M, Professor of Medicine, took over that position in 1945. In the same year Virgil Y. C. Eady '36G succeeded George S. Roach as Associate Dean of Emory-at-Oxford.

The increasing complexity of the operations of the University from this time forward necessitated large additions to the staff. In December 1944 Charles W. Hayes was appointed Director of Purchases. Within a year of taking office he was busily engaged in the acquisition of war surplus materials, especially laboratory equipment, as installations were closing. Both the University and Emory-at-Oxford benefited greatly from scientific apparatus thus advantageously secured. Following the resignation of L. Neal Smith '28, for twenty years Superintendent of Buildings and Grounds, Bryan L. Allan was brought to Emory as Director of Operations. It is the efficiency and promptness of the services rendered by his workmen that keep the plant in running order.

On September 25, 1941, Bishop Warren Akin Candler, who may truly be called the father of the University, its first Chancellor, President of Emory College 1888-1898, died at his home near the University campus. He was eighty-four years of age. Funeral services were held in Oxford Old Church, and he was buried in the village cemetery near the other Emory worthies. On December 9, Judge John Slaughter Candler, active in founding the School of Law, first President of the Alumni Association, followed his brother in death.

The year 1944 marked the passing of three Emory builders. Dr. W. S. Elkin, Dean of the Atlanta Medical College under whose leadership it became the Medical School of Emory University, and its first Dean, died on April 24. On July 27, Harvey Warren Cox, first President of the University, died at the age of sixty-nine, two years after his retirement on account of failing health. On September 11, Edgar H. Johnson, first Dean of the School of Business Administration, who had entered Emory College in 1889, and for nearly fifty years had served the College and University in a variety of capacities, died suddenly at his home on Clifton Road. For all these devoted servants the University stands a living monument.

There was a brief flurry of building on the campus before the war made private construction largely impracticable. Five houses were added to Fraternity Row: Delta Tau Delta, Alpha Tau Omega, and Sigma Nu in 1938; Phi Delta Theta in 1940; Pi Kappa Alpha in 1941. The Haygood-Hopkins Memorial Gateway had been erected at the front entrance to the campus in 1937. It was the gift of Linton B. Robeson '86, for fifteen years a member of the College Board of Trustees and for ten years President of its

Asa Griggs Candler, President of Board 1915-29

Warren Akin Candler, Chancellor 1915-21

President Harvey Warren Cox
1920-42

President Goodrich Cook White
1942-57

President Sidney Walter Martin
1957-62

President Sanford Soverhill Atwood
1963-

Alumni Association, and commemorated two presidents of the College, Atticus G. Haygood (1875-1884) and Isaac S. Hopkins (1884-1888). Another dormitory was ready for occupancy in fall 1940, McTyeire Hall, named for Bishop Holland Nimmons McTyeire, a founder of Vanderbilt University. The Glenn Memorial Church School Building was dedicated on September 29; the Little Chapel to the right of the main entrance reproduces in miniature one of the most exquisite of Wren's London churches, St. Stephen Walbrook.

The purchase of 200 acres of land north of the Seaboard Railway in 1938 brought total campus acreage to 550. The W. D. Thomson home, at the corner of North Decatur and Clifton Roads, was bought in 1943 for the President's home. Uppergate House, the Arthur Tufts residence, back from Clifton Road opposite the Hospital, was acquired and remodeled to serve as an additional dormitory for student nurses. In 1937 the business area at the end of the car line was expanded by the erection of six stores. Soon this unattractive but convenient adjunct to the University was to be known as the Village.

The Robert Winship Clinic for the study and treatment of neoplastic diseases was opened in the Emory University Hospital in June 1937. A benefaction of Robert W. Woodruff '12, it was named in honor of his grandfather. Dr. J. Elliott Scarborough was appointed its Director. In the same year, in pursuance of the plan for an expanded medical center, a part of the university center plan, one and a half blocks of land adjoining Grady Hospital were purchased for possible future development of the School of Medicine. Ultimately this land was sold for its original purchase price to Grady Hospital, and on it was erected its magnificent new plant. The proceeds of the sale were used to recondition the buildings in the area belonging to Emory University, the Colored Division of Grady and the J. J. Gray Clinic.

The Crawford W. Long Memorial Hospital in downtown Atlanta was deeded to the University in 1940 by Dr. Luther C. Fischer '99M, its co-founder with Dr. E. C. Davis '30H. The transfer of its management, however, was not to take place until

Dr. Fischer's death, which occurred in 1953.

In September 1944 the Atlanta-Southern Dental College, which had some years before proposed amalgamation, became the Emory University School of Dentistry. It continued to occupy its premises at Forrest Avenue and Courtland Street, and Dr. Ralph R. Byrnes continued as Dean.

In the same year the Emory University Hospital School of Nursing, which granted certificates and produced registered nurses, was elevated to collegiate rank. Miss Julia Miller, Director of Nursing at Emory University Hospital, became Dean of the Emory University School of Nursing, a position that she was to hold until 1950.

In 1943 on two occasions it had been found necessary to make public statements in clarification of Emory's policy of medical education. Oglethorpe University had opened a medical department in 1941. President Thornwell Jacobs, who depended solely on relatively high tuition fees for its operation, sought to bring pressure on the State Board of Medical Examiners to admit its graduates to examination and licensing for practice. This the Board refused to do until accreditation was secured. President Jacobs had proclaimed himself a firm foe of the principle of accreditation. Grady Hospital was applied to for clinical facilities in the white wards. This was denied, the authorities of Emory University contending that the hospital was too small to accommodate two medical schools, and that Emory had earned its right to exclusive use by the expenditure of several hundred thousand dollars for the improvement of facilities and staff. A reorganization of the Oglethorpe school was undertaken, but the Committee on Medical Education and Hospitals of the American Medical Association after a visit of inspection reported such deficiencies as to make accreditation seem hopeless. Nevertheless the dean of the school is said to have maintained that only access to Grady was needed to bring it up to standard. It was charged that only the recalcitrant position of Emory University was standing in the way of an expanded program of medical education in a region that was experiencing a serious shortage of physicians, especially in rural areas. On October 29 a special meeting of the Board of Trustees of Grady was called, at which representatives of Emory presented in clear detail the reasons for its opposition to Oglethorpe's admission to Grady. Leaders of the medical profession in Atlanta, by emphasizing the absolute necessity of the highest standards in medical education and Oglethorpe's inability to provide adequate training, persuaded the Grady Trustees to close the issue by finally denying the petition.

One problem was resolved, but attacks on the School of Medicine continued. These were led by the Secretary-Treasurer of the Medical Association of Georgia, who was also Editor of its *Journal,* and consisted of a series of unsigned articles in the *Journal* that were given wider circulation as reprints without indication of their source. Although they were inspired by personal animus, the attempt was apparently made to have them appear as sanctioned by the Association. The School of Medicine was charged with having embraced a "new philosophy of medical education," leading it to fail an inordinate number of students, and to be guilty of rank favoritism in passing only those who toadied to the professors.

This campaign of vilification was met by the publication of a pamphlet, *Why High Standards in Medical Education?,* setting forth the responsibility of the School to the public that depends on it to supply it with soundly trained practitioners into whose hands the lives of their patients are to be entrusted.

On November 23, 1943, President White addressed a meeting on the campus of the University faculties, Association officers, and local Board members. After reviewing the case in all its aspects, recounting the origins of disaffection with the school and the methods employed in the attack, he replied to the chief charges, making it clear that the development of the School of Medicine had been fully in accord with the program of the profession for raising its educational standards. He cited statistics to prove that the number of student failures ran well with the national average, with the elimination of students largely confined to the first year, and that the percentage of candidates graduated, nearly eighty per cent of those entering as freshmen, also was in line with the national average. The President stated Emory's "philosophy" simply and directly: "Our chief responsibility is to see to it that the doctors Emory graduates shall be good doctors." The University's position so publicly presented, no further notice was taken of the controversy.

The enrollment in Fall Quarter 1938 for the first time rose above 1,500. When Registrar J. G. Stipe was named to the new post of Director of Admissions, the system of accepting candidates for the College freshman class by count of prescribed high-school units of studies was discarded and the more flexible plan of stipulating a generally well-rounded course from an accredited high school was adopted. The Department of Journalism, headed by Professor Raymond B. Nixon '25, began a development that was to bring it accreditation by the American Association of Schools and Departments of Journalism three years later. In 1941 the School of Law opened a fully accredited Evening Division; with the loss of students to the military services, from 1942 only evening sessions were offered until the war's end. Valdosta Junior College also was closed "for the duration," all members of the teaching staff being brought to the Atlanta campus, Hollis Edens becoming Associate Dean in the Undergraduate Divisions and four years later appointed Dean of Administration.

The University did not delay until the cessation of hostilities to plan for progress in the postwar years. In the interval faculty committees actively engaged in a survey of all aspects of the functions and life of the institution, which was given careful study by administrative officers. President White's report to the Board of Trustees on November 10, 1944, separately published and circulated, was "a masterly exposition of Emory's educational philosophy and a program for its development." The University was to reap a rich reward for the thoughtful preparation made at this difficult time for the possibilities and exigencies that the near future was to present. But Emory did not feel compelled to wait to enlarge its scope.

On petition of twenty-eight members of the Society of the Sigma Xi on the faculty and staff of Emory University, September 1943, a charter was granted establishing the Emory Chapter on April 14, 1944. The first President was Osborne R. Quayle, Professor of Chemistry. Sigma Xi, the highest honor society in general science, was founded at Cornell University in 1886 "for the promotion of research in science." Its purpose is to maintain companionship among investigators in the various fields of science. Full membership in the chapter is granted for the publication of research in recognized journals. Associate membership is granted to graduate students on evidence of research potential. An annual citation is made at the fall meeting to a faculty member for the publication of an outstanding research paper. At the spring meeting citations are made to students for outstanding research in fulfillment of requirements for the M.S. and Ph.D. degrees.

The series of brochures, *Emory Sources & Reprints,* was introduced in 1943 with the publication of *Letters of General J. E. B. Stuart to His Wife,* edited by Professor Bingham Duncan. The purpose of the series was to make generally available unique manuscript materials and rare imprints in the collections of the Emory University Library. The project was carried out under the auspices of the University Committee on Research, with Thomas H. English as Editor in Chief. Continuing until 1958, the series finally comprised twenty-eight titles, each edited by a member of the Emory faculty or staff, and produced in a distinguished format in editions of 350 copies. Several of the titles went out of print almost immediately, and they have been frequently cited in footnotes and bibliographies.

The Emory University Quarterly began publication in 1945 as a general magazine with contributions from the Emory faculty, staff, and alumni. The Editor from Volume I through Volume XX, 1964, was Thomas H. English, assisted by an Editorial Board of the University faculty. The contents included essays, verse, editorials, and book reviews. Sources and reprints from unique and rare materials in the Emory University Library, particularly Southern literary and historical documents, were featured, as also a series of frontispieces reproducing portraits in the University collections. Essays ranged through all the fields of learning of the Emory community, presented authoritatively on the basis of sound scholarship, but addressed to non-specialists in a manner to show the wide relevance of academic research. Special issues were occasionally published, as for the 1948 centenary of the birth of Joel Chandler Harris, the twenty-fifth anniversary of the Emory chapter of Phi Beta Kappa, 1954, and the centennial of the School of Medicine, 1954.

The *Quarterly* has been sustained by a University subsidy; its circulation has been approximately 2,000. Files are maintained in the Library of Congress, the British Museum, the Bibliothècque Nationale, Paris, and in more than 200 other institutional libraries at home and abroad. Its handsome format, designed by Richard McArthur, the well-known typographer, has been widely commended.

Very early in the years of World War II the University's slogan became "Get Ready for the Unexpected." That radical change was in store for colleges and universities was keenly realized, and it was undertaken without delay to assess Emory's resources that might contribute to the national effort when and if the United States was drawn into the conflict. In the summer of 1940 a University Council Committee on National Defense was appointed with Dean Purks as Chairman, "to facilitate the cooperation of the University with the government in all matters relating to the defense program." Already so many alumni had entered the armed services that it had become a major task of the office of the Alumni Association to keep in touch with them. A number of students had volunteered, and all of age, which in October 1943 was lowered to eighteen years, were registering for the draft.

On March 11, 1940, the Surgeon General of the Army had requested the reorganization of the Emory Unit, that had served in World War I, as the 43rd General Hospital. Organization was completed by Dr. Ira A. Ferguson '23M, and the Unit was mobilized at Camp Livingston, Louisiana, in September 1942. It was based at Oran, Algeria, in 1944, and at Aix-en-Provence, France, in 1945, and was inactivated in September 1945. The absence of full-time and voluntary clinical faculty on this and other assignments placed a heavy burden on the remaining staff of the School of Medicine, especially when the School adopted an accelerated program adding a summer quarter to the normal schedule.

When the fateful day, December 7, 1941, arrived, the institution went into decisive action. A University Council on the War Emergency was formed with President Cox as Chairman, and its numerous subcommittees sought to anticipate every need of the critical moment. All schools now began to operate around the calendar. In January 1942 a series of short courses on a variety of war-related subjects were offered, whose enrollment totaled 357, including 235 persons from outside the University. In February and March Count Carlo Sforza, former Italian Minister of Foreign Affairs, was Visiting Professor of International Relations under auspices of the Carnegie Foundation for International Peace.

Emory refused to be stampeded, but determined to continue its regular academic program until a call for special services should be made. Provision was made for a class of entering freshmen in the summer quarter. Student morale was good. Early in 1943 Emory was listed for "basic" and pre-medical training in the Navy College Training Program (V-12), and also for medical training in both the Army and Navy. The selection was confirmed late in March, with the announcement that the program would begin on July 1. The following specifications were stated:

It is understood that your institution will make available to the Navy adequate buildings and facilities to house and feed a minimum of 654 trainees (whose status shall be apprentice seamen), and will furnish medical and dental services for such trainees; and that the institution will also make available facilities and teaching staff for instruction in the following curricula:

Basic curriculum	400
Pre-medical curriculum	254

The four campus dormitories were assigned to the Navy, with exclusive use of the cafeteria as its mess. The houses on Fraternity Row were taken over by the University to furnish living quarters for civilian students, who were outnumbered two to one. The Emory Grill, on Clifton Road, was opened as a cafeteria for civilians.

That summer uniforms filled the campus, including those of 200 Marines, who, however, were soon replaced by Navy trainees. The Commanding Officer for Emory, Georgia Tech, and Atlanta-

Southern Dental College was Captain J. V. Babcock, and the Executive Officer for Emory, Commander Thomas L. McCann, whose chief aide was Lieutenant Fred W. Ajax '30. The quota of 654 was maintained to 96% of the total until the quota was lowered on November 1, 1944. When the unit was discontinued on November 1, 1945, more than 2,000 men had received training at Emory. Besides the V-12 unit, there were 159 Army students and 73 Navy students in the School of Medicine, and six pre-chaplain students in the School of Theology. 165 nurses were in training in the Hospital Nursing School, making a very smart appearance in their cadet uniforms.

The V-12 period will be remembered by all participants as a time of hard work on a relentless schedule, but one in which the coöperative effort never faltered. The Navy's prescribed curriculum was basically science, mathematics, English, and history. To staff these courses it was necessary to secure volunteer instructors from other departments. A professor of philosophy took mathematics classes, for example, and a professor of sociology met English sections. Courses not in the regular curriculum had to be supplied: the Department of Mathematics provided a course in navigation, and the Department of Geology, one in meteorology.

The response of the trainees left little to be desired. At first Emory rather puzzled and disappointed some of the newcomers. An institution calling itself a university without intercollegiate football, without even a gymnasium! They were soon too busy to be much concerned about such things, and before long they found themselves caught up in the spirit of the place. Trainees staffed the *Wheel* and tried out for the Glee Club. When extracurricular activities were threatened with extinction because of the loss of student fees, the Navy boys voluntarily assessed themselves to keep them alive. The government did not supply a band; the members of the unit bought instruments, held rehearsals, and soon were performing creditably. Formations became sharper day by day, and retreat began to attract daily groups of spectators around the quadrangle when the band played "The Star-Spangled Banner" and the flag was lowered.

The departure of the Navy unit brought as much regret as relief. The neat appearance of its members, their unfailing courtesy, and their serious application to their studies will long be remembered. Many who left in the fall of 1945 were obviously reluctant to go from a place to which they had become attached in a relatively short time, even though it had not been of their choosing.

A recognition of Emory's rôle in the war effort was the christening of one of the "Victory" ships in its honor. *M. S. Emory Victory,* a 10,700 ton cargo ship, was launched at the Baltimore Bethlehem-Fairchild Shipyards on April 3, 1945. The sponsor was Mrs. Warren H. Cox '35G, President Cox's daughter-in-law. Besides active duty in World War II, it was put back into service in the Korean War. After it was finally decommissioned, its bell was presented to the University in 1964.

More than 3,500 Emory alumni and former students were in the armed services in all theaters of the war; 121 gave their lives in their country's cause. A large number of the faculty and administrative staff were either in the uniformed services or in civilian phases of the war effort. "Four members of the University faculty and seventeen of its graduates participated in the research leading to the development of the atomic bomb." Even before V-J Day servicemen began to return to the University to continue their education under the "G. I. Bill of Rights" (Public Law 346, 78th Congress, Servicemen's Readjustment Act of 1944). To deal with them, the Director of Student Aid and Placement, L. L. Clegg '25, was appointed Coordinator of Veterans Education. Within a few months this office was to become one of the most active and useful on the campus.

Student activities in the prewar years of this decade followed the normal pattern, with one notable exception. The annual pushball battle between freshmen and sophomores continued to be won by the latter except when a tie was declared, but the innocent bystanders, upperclassmen and faculty, became the victims of detrousering by both parties of the belligerents. The ball was twice stolen, but unhappily it was both times recovered.

A tradition that had held for more than a century was shattered on the evening of October 25, 1941, when the first administration-approved on-campus dance was held in the auditorium-dining hall. Long a bone of contention between the student body and the trustees, when the ban against dancing was finally lifted, it attracted hardly any notice.

In early spring 1941 the seasonal tension was eased by the first Dooley's Frolics. Dooley, the Department of Biology's skeleton whose image is now engraved on the University mace, from Oxford days had been the mouthpiece of caustic comment on matters of student interest in the *Phoenix* and *Campus*. Incarnated as the lord of misrule of the undergraduate festivities, he roams the campus for the week end and assumes outrageous privileges on the quadrangle and in the classrooms.

The end of the war ushering in a new era, it was thought advisable to reaffirm the University's policy in regard to intercollegiate athletics. At the meeting of the Board of Trustees on October 16, 1945, in a measured statement the program of athletics for all and sports for physical fitness, including certain intercollegiate contests, was given official approval. But firm opposition was expressed to "participation in those competitive sports which require elaborate and expensive facilities for public entertainment." Specific mention was not made of football, basketball, and baseball, but there could be no question as to the meaning of the pronouncement. Emory was entering upon a new day, but there was no intention of abandoning principles which had given it strength to survive the crises of depression and war through which it had so recently passed.

V

The Postwar Decade 1946-1955

EMORY'S POSTWAR DECADE presents a rich but confused chronicle, of achievement and frustration, of progress and regression, of hope and disappointment. The time is recalled with mixed emotions. But in the long view it is seen that the achievement was permanent and the frustration temporary; the regression was but one step back from many steps forward. The progress made toward the establishment of an institution fulfilling national standards of greatness was decisive. For reasons too various and complex to set forth in detail, the hope of immediate arrival at the goal was premature, and fate intervened with unpredictable checks. Nevertheless, the aims of so much long planning were finally accomplished that 1946-1955 may justly be noted as an era of fruition in the life of the University.

In the first place, the physical plant was greatly expanded with the erection of a score of sorely needed buildings. This brought relief to every division of the University, the congestion of whose facilities had barred the full realization of its potential. New dormitories, new laboratories, new classroom buildings, additions to the Hospital, and an Administration Building greatly reduced overcrowding and permitted extension of all academic activities.

A complete administrative reorganization was carried out with the addition of bureau heads and the redefining of areas of jurisdiction. The increasingly diversified business of the University had outgrown the basic organizational structure, and although the new chart of offices at first raised some questions as to centers of authority, in the end it was found that the transaction of business was expedited by the new order.

Within the divisions there was also extensive reorganization. The Graduate School achieved a new dimension when the first Ph.D. degree, in Chemistry, was conferred at the June 1948 Commencement, and four more departments were authorized to go forward with doctoral programs. The new Institute of the Liberal

Arts offered an advanced curriculum cutting across departmental lines. The Library School became a graduate division. The College, on the other hand, dropped the Departments of Engineering and Journalism, at the same time greatly strengthening both faculty and teaching facilities in other fields. Of the professional schools, the greatest advances were made by the School of Medicine, whose financial status was at length largely freed from the uncertainty that had plagued it from its beginning, and for which opportunity was now afforded to enter into varied fields of research. The School of Business Administration, by the provision of its own building and a separate operating fund through the generosity of the Rich Foundation, ceased to be little more than an appendage of the College. The School of Law was making a more modest recovery from the setback it had suffered in the war years, but a prosperous future now seemed to be assured. The Schools of Nursing and Dentistry both profited from the organization of a Division of Basic Sciences in the Health Services. Increased enrollments, however, had so taxed all its facilities that the School of Theology found itself in a more disadvantageous position than any other division. It was clear that only with an added building would it be able effectively to perform its functions in the future.

Both faculty and students were made happy by tangible and substantial evidences of the administration's concern for their welfare. For the faculty a salary raise of $500 across the board in most divisions in 1951 did something to meet increased costs of living, and there was a promise of further relief not long to be delayed. Although many students single and married continued for a time to be housed in rather primitive conditions, the erection of more suitable quarters was carried on with all possible speed. Meanwhile the long-desired Field House and a student center became realities. By the end of the period most comforts and conveniences of university community life had been fairly provided.

So much and more was accomplished, not without great expense of energy in meeting and overcoming almost daily recurring problems presented by the changing times. The impressive sum total was achieved in the face of unforeseeable circumstances of difficulty and discouragement, not the least of which was the outbreak of war in Korea. The crisis, however, was soon past, and in the period of comparative calm that succeeded, the University was able to survey its record of progress and make plans for a new advance.

Veterans of World War II, eager to take advantage of the educational opportunity offered by the "G. I. Bill of Rights," in Winter Quarter 1946 brought Emory's enrollment to 2,045, with 550 of the number servicemen. In Fall Quarter there were 3,583 students on the campus, about half of whom were veterans. In 1947, the peak year, servicemen in residence numbered 2,200. Facilities of the University, particularly housing, were unequal to accommodation of the influx, but the authorities were not caught unprepared. University Treasurer George Mew had already visited the atom bomb project at Oak Ridge, Tennessee, and put in a bid for war surplus trailers. The first of the more than one hundred that were to be lined up between Winship Hall and Clifton Road made their appearance on the morning of February 1, 1946. "Trailertown" was to remain a picturesque feature of the University scene until September 1952.

More living space was needed, however, and three Federal Public Housing dormitories were brought in and set up beyond the railroad, in which 384 men shivered in winter and baked in summer. By a happy inspiration this development was immediately christened "Lower Slobbovia." It was not until 1955 that the last of these eyesores was dismantled. Other plywood and tar paper barracks were erected for married couples farther out Clifton Road, long to be remembered without affection as "Mudville." And still housing was unequal to the demand, so that arrangements were made with the Naval Air Station at Chamblee for the use of two former officers' quarters, able to accommodate 288 single men. Commuter busses were provided to carry their residents to and from the campus.

With all the makeshift arrangements of a pioneer settlement, this will be recalled by most of the inhabitants of trailers and barracks as a happy time. A limited number of married theologues had occupied the outskirts of the campus for several years, but now domesticity was brought right into the Quadrangle. Wives doing their marketing and babies taking their sunning were as much a part of the daily scene as students going to and from classes. The new aspect of student life was soon accepted as a matter of course. Trailertown at all times presented a neat and cheerful appearance, and the young people who began family life in its straitened bounds gave every appearance of savoring the experience. It is gratifying to note that the unions so initiated have proved extraordinarily durable.

On the other side of the picture, no professor who taught classes of veterans will ever forget their earnestness, their eager receptiveness, their intensity of application. Their war service had brought them to a rapid maturity without, it should be emphasized, dampening the enthusiasm of youth. Their spirit was even communicated to their classmates who had not been in uniform, and for a time the mere tolerance of instruction that is the teacher's bane virtually disappeared from lecture room and laboratory. When three and four years later servicemen were largely replaced by high school graduates, and the more familiar lackadaisical attitude was again encountered in otherwise attractive and intelligent youngsters, there were those who sighed for the strenuous and challenging times that were past.

Large additions to the faculty were required to cope with swollen enrollment, and for these also a housing problem had to be solved. By the purchase of the Emory Court Apartments, 2080 (now 1766) North Decatur Road, and the erection of numerous small houses, ninety-eight residence units were made available in 1946. In 1947 three temporary classroom buildings were erected, Annexes A, B, and C, whose meager facilities it has not yet been found possible to dispense with. But as a foretaste of better things, in this year the Rich Memorial Building was occupied by the School of Business Administration, and Gilbert and Thomson Halls, on Pierce Drive at South Oxford Road, provided efficiency apartments for married students, Gilbert given over to the School of Theology. The new Field House was opened in fall 1948, and with the completion of the swimming pool in the following year the Department of Physical Education went into full operation. The photograph on the cover of the *Alumnus* for October 1947 of President White ferociously attacking the dilapidated old basketball shell with an ax vividly portrays the prevailing mood of those who at last saw the end of deplored halfway measures.

The project with which the fortunes of the gymnasium had been twinned, the Alumni Memorial student center, was put in use in 1950, and a great chorus of rejoicing went up for the realization of the long-awaited event. The greater part of the ground floor was given over to the Alumni Association, that at last secured adequate space for its multifarious activities. A feature of the main floor is the Goodrich C. White, Jr., Memorial Music Room, beautifully furnished by friends of Lt. White '40, Army Air Corps, who died in combat over the Baltic Sea on September 12, 1944. At its dedication on October 27, 1950, was inaugurated the Emory Chamber Music Series, with the performance of some of Lt. White's own compositions. Off the mezzanine is a tiny Meditation Chapel, the gift of alumni and friends of the Oxford District. Above the altar is a stained glass window of Christ teaching His disciples the Lord's Prayer, designed and executed by Henry Lee Willet of Philadelphia. The ground floor of the adjoining cafeteria building was equipped as a snack bar and recreation room, named Dooley's Den after the patron of the spring frolics.

Between 1949 and 1951 four new fraternity houses were added to the Row: Sigma Pi (replaced in 1962 by Phi Gamma Delta), Alpha Epsilon Pi, Beta Theta Pi, and Tau Epsilon Phi. Thirteen houses now make up the complement of homes of the social fraternities. While there has been much reconstruction and enlargement, the number has for fifteen years remained constant.

An impressive building project of 1944-46 was the construction of the Conkey Pate Whitehead Surgical Pavilion with related additions to the Emory University Hospital. By the generosity of Mrs. Letitia Pate Evans, the only woman member of Emory's Board of Trustees, the front elevation was extended to almost twice its width by a seven-story addition, a six-story front wing was placed at the entrance, and a smaller service wing was added in the rear. The final result was a modernization of the plant and an expansion of its services, with beauty as well as efficiency achieved throughout. A Memorial Room is situated at the north end of the second floor. Designed by Philip Shutze, this contains what is probably the finest wood carving in America, carried out over four years by H. J. Millard in the style of the seventeenth-century craftsman, Grinling Gibbons. The cornice, the door frame, the doors, and especially the elaborate garlands of fruits and flowers of the four seasons surrounding portraits of the Whitehead family, are unsurpassed examples of the woodcarver's art. Not inferior in beauty is the molded plaster ceiling. The room is lavishly furnished with period pieces.

The completion and occupation of ten new buildings in 1951 made this a banner year in University construction. The Geology Building was the first classroom-laboratory building erected on the campus since Fishburne. Built on Pierce Drive with funds secured from an Atlanta foundation, according to plans and specifications by Professor James G. Lester, here and at the Geology Camp established at Ringgold in North Georgia a year earlier, the Department of Geology has conducted a greatly enlarged program of study. By the transfer of a grant originally secured for a nurses' home at Grady and no longer needed for that purpose, the adjoining Biology Building was constructed in the same year. Two years later a small greenhouse augmented its facilities, and in 1962 a wing including a large lecture room was added to the main building. The removal of these departments to some degree relieved the strain on the Departments of Chemistry and Physics, whose buildings they had previously shared. A Basic Science Building on Kilgo Circle centered preclinical instruction for the Schools of Dentistry and Nursing. With later developments of the Division of Basic Health Sciences the Department of Psychology succeeded in occupation. A classroom building on the Quadrangle was dedicated to history, but other departments of the humanities and the social sciences were also allotted space in it. Wesley Hall, across Arkwright Drive from the railroad station, was erected as a dormitory for unmarried theology students, and Emory Park Apartments 1 and 2, on Uppergate Drive, provided living room for married students and University personnel. A new dormitory was also built

Review of Navy V-12 Unit

Trailertown

Mudville

Glenn Memorial

Commemorating Emory Units I and II (Trustee James C. Malone, Dr. Ira A. Ferguson, Emory Unit II, Dr. C. W. Strickler, Emory Unit I, President White)

Executive Committee, Board of Trustees, 1946 (Preston S. Arkwright, Charles Howard Candler, Robert W. Woodruff, F. Phinizy Calhoun, W. D. Thomson, James C. Malone, H. Y. McCord)

on the campus of Valdosta Junior College.

The Woodruff Memorial Building for medical research, adjoining Emory University Hospital, began to be occupied in 1952. Dedicated to the memory of Ernest Woodruff, father of Robert W. and George W. Woodruff, it was erected in large part by a gift of the Emily and Ernest Woodruff Foundation. The main section has eight floors and the south wing seven. The upper floors remained unfinished until 1958. The addition of this facility permitted an enormous expansion of research activities of the School of Medicine, besides centralizing its functions and freeing needed space in the Hospital and elsewhere. The third floor was devoted entirely to the Calhoun Medical Library. The building was enlarged by the addition of a north wing in 1965.

In 1954 a wing was added to Harris Hall for women students, and Alabama Hall, for men, was thoroughly renovated. In the following year, two modern dormitories, Longstreet and Means, named for early presidents of the College, located at the farther side of Alumni Memorial, made room for more than 300 men.

The erection in 1955 of an Administration Building at the west end of the Quadrangle at long last fulfilled a cherished anticipation. The gift of Charles Howard Candler, Chairman of the Board of Trustees, on its four ample floors were brought together offices that for forty years had rivalled the wanderings of the Children of Israel. Among its dispositions, a Trustees' Room on the top floor provided a spacious and dignified setting for University councils. Following the removal of administrative offices from the Asa Griggs Candler Library, an intensive task of reconditioning was entered upon immediately to relieve overcrowded conditions of library space and services that had come near to paralyzing its functions. The relief was admittedly temporary, but with use of the entire building began a new era of library development.

A large number of administrative changes occurred in this period. In 1946 Dr. R. Hugh Wood replaced Dr. Eugene A. Stead as Dean of the School of Medicine. Leroy E. Loemker, Professor of Philosophy, took over the deanship of the Graduate School from J. Harris Purks, to be succeeded in 1952 by Howard M. Phillips,

Professor of Biology. George S. Craft '30, on his release from active duty in the Navy, came in as Dean of the School of Business Administration, and was followed in that office two years later by Gordon Siefkin, a fellow Rhodes Scholar at Oxford University. In 1947 L. L. Clegg relieved J. Gordon Stipe of the duties of Registrar. In 1948 Dean Purks assumed the directorship of the University Center, and Judson C. Ward, Jr. '33, '34G, became Dean of the College. Dean Byrnes having retired the previous year, Dr. John E. Buhler was brought from Temple University to head the School of Dentistry.

In 1947 A. Hollis Edens accepted the office of Vice-Chancellor of the University System of Georgia, and the following year Boisfeuillet Jones '34, '37L, became Dean of Administration. Charles O. Emmerich came in as Business Manager, and George H. Mew took the title of Treasurer and Controller. A much-needed new bureau was added with the appointment of Orie E. Myers, Jr. '41, '57G, as Director of Personnel. J. Gordon Stipe was elected to the newly established position of Dean of the Faculties. An important development of 1948 was the constitution of a Central Administration, of five officers of the University: President White, Vice-President and Dean of the Faculties Stipe, Dean of Administration Jones, Director of Development and Finance Mizell, and Treasurer and Controller Mew. A sixth member was added in 1951 when Ernest C. Colwell '23, '27T, '44H, formerly President of the University of Chicago, became Dean of the Faculties. The death of Mr. Stipe in June 1953 vacated the office of Vice-President, but by an amendment of the bylaws of the University later in the year, provision was made for the election of "one or more vice-presidents," and in 1954 Colwell and Jones were elevated to that rank. In 1953 a division was made of the functions of Treasurer and Controller, Mr. Mew retaining the former office, with the administration of capital funds, and Ewell E. Bessent '34B appointed to the latter for the accounting and reporting of current funds.

A new Health Services Board of five members of the Board of Trustees, under the chairmanship of James D. Robinson, Jr. '25, was established in 1953 to direct the affairs of the Schools of Medicine, Dentistry, and Nursing, the hospitals, and related activities. By them Boisfeuillet Jones was named Acting Administrator. In the fall the Departments of Anatomy, Bacteriology, Biochemistry, Pharmacology, and Physiology were grouped in a unified division of Basic Sciences in the Health Services under the supervision of the Deans of Medicine, Dentistry, Nursing, and the Graduate School. Dr. Arthur P. Richardson, Associate Dean of Medicine, Chairman of the Department of Pharmacology, was named Director of the new division.

In 1948 L. L. Clegg had relieved J. Gordon Stipe as Director of Admissions, and I. W. Brock '27, '30G, took over as Registrar. Henry L. Bowden '32, '34L, '59H, succeeded W. D. Thomson as legal counsel of the University following the death of the latter on April 30, 1952. Mr. Thomson, a member of the Educational Commission of the Methodist Episcopal Church, South, that had been responsible for Emory's creation, had served the University for thirty-eight years; at the time of his death he was Executive Vice-Chairman of the Board of Trustees. Burwell W. Humphrey '37, '48L, took over the superintendency of the Hospital from R. F. Whitaker, who became Associate Director of Development.

Charles J. Hilkey retired as Dean of the School of Law in September 1948, and for the ensuing year the School was operated on an interim basis. William M. Hepburn, Dean of the University of Alabama School of Law, accepted the appointment to Emory in the spring of 1949, taking over the deanship on January 1, 1950. In 1950 Miss Ada Fort became Dean of the School of Nursing. In 1953 William Ragsdale Cannon succeeded H. B. Trimble as Dean of the School of Theology, the latter remaining active as Field Representative for Development and Public Relations, seeking to inspire the leadership of the Church to provide adequate training for its ministry. Miss Evalene Jackson in 1954 followed Miss Barker as head of the Division of Librarianship. Miss Margaret Jemison, the organizer of the Emory University Library, retired after thirty-three years of effective service, and Guy R. Lyle was brought from Louisiana State University as Director of Libraries.

The question whether or not to admit women to Emory University was debated from the start. In the Chancellor's Report to the annual meeting of the Board of Trustees on June 7, 1919, at Oxford, Bishop Candler declared his position in no uncertain terms:

> *The Issue of Co-Education.* At this session of the Board of Trustees the policy of the University with reference to co-education should be finally settled. In my judgment co-education is a mistaken policy. It is proper doubtless to open the Teachers College and the Summer Course for Teachers to female students, but in all other departments the University should be for male students only. The departments of law and medicine especially should not be open to women. Young men and young women working together in a dissecting room, or hearing together lectures on physiology and anatomy, would in my judgment create a most indelicate and injurious situation. And women lawyers would not promote justice in the courts.

When coeducation came to the College in 1953, nevertheless, it was no stranger to the campus. Actually the University had been coeducational from the start; that is to say, every division had at one time and another enrolled women students and granted them degrees. From another point of view, however, one division had not operated on a coeducational plan, since the School of Nursing up until this time had received no application from a male candidate. The Library School had not enrolled men until 1930. Theology had graduated its first woman in 1938, and Medicine in 1946. The Law, Graduate, and Dental Schools had never made difficulties for the enrollment of women. Nominally the College and School of Business Administration were for men only, but under various arrangements a limited number of women had been constantly in attendance. The policy for admitting women to the College had never been clearly set forth. Every case was treated as an exceptional one, but it might also be stated that women were let in because under a wide variety of circumstances they could not justifiably be kept out.

It should be noted that a large number of upper division courses in the College were acceptable offerings for the master's degree in the coeducational Graduate School. When the School of Nursing was raised to collegiate level in 1944, its enrollees were admitted to courses in the junior college. Reciprocity with Agnes Scott brought a limited number of its students to the Emory campus. And these were only a few of the ways by which women found entry into what was defined as a preserve for male students. Finally, summer quarters had always been coeducational, with women in attendance frequently outnumbering men, although undergraduate women attendants were considered as transients, whose course credits would be transferred to other institutions.

But the ultimate letting down of bars was no mere recognition of a *status quo*. An agreement concerning the enrollment of women in the College had been entered into with Agnes Scott in connection with the University Center plan, and it was strongly felt that Emory, the Methodist university, should not compete with Wesleyan, the Methodist woman's college. Even when these sister institutions had indicated that they did not oppose the change, there was continued opposition within Emory's Board of Trustees to so definite an alteration of policy. The final action was by a divided vote.

For a time no social change was to be noted. Until dormitory room was provided, women in the College remained only day students in restricted numbers. Nevertheless in 1951-52, of the total enrollment of the University, 4,282, more than twenty-five per cent, 1,095, were women. The proportion began to climb with the opening of residence halls for their accommodation on the campus: the addition to Harris Hall in 1954; Alabama in 1955; Thomas, Hopkins, and Smith in 1958. Minimum requirements for the admission of women to the College are somewhat higher than those for men, and the ratio of women to men admitted to a freshman class of 600 is fixed at 225 to 375.

One reason why the coeducational plan was adopted for the College was that it might redress the balance between the liberal arts and preprofessional education. The greater number of male students were candidates for the professions of dentistry, law, medicine, and the ministry. It was assumed that women would for the most part take straight courses in the liberal arts and sciences. And so it turned out, with the women putting the men to shame with their grade records. This had been prefigured when at the initiation of the first class of undergraduates by Phi Beta Kappa in 1930 three of the five were women. A Women's Honor Organization (WHO), recognizing leadership, was formed in 1954.

Meanwhile social groups began to coalesce, so that in 1954 there were six active women's clubs, two more the next year, all with unofficial connections with national sororities. While the 508 coeds of 1954 were in a proportion of only one to five with the men, Dean of Students Rece was acquiring experience at an accelerated speed. The influence of the coeds was indeed pervasive both socially and academically, but few serious problems were raised, and what in some quarters had been viewed as a doubtful venture proved highly successful.

On June 25, 1950, North Korean troops crossed the 38th parallel and the brief and uneasy peace crashed to a close. The first question raised on the Emory campus was that of the status of veterans of World War II on active and inactive reserve. Close behind came the question of liability for selective service of students who had reached or were about to reach draft age. A general state of uncertainty greatly affecting campus morale might have been more disruptive had it not been for the ready assistance in solving the problems of individual students given by Charles N. Watson, who had previously had charge of veterans' affairs. The call to service was not long delayed; by spring 1951 eleven faculty and staff members had left for various assignments, and more were to follow. June Commencement was again a war commencement, with Millard F. Caldwell, Jr., Federal Civil Defense Administrator, the speaker.

In fall 1950 enrollments in the College, School of Business Administration, and Law School, whose students enjoyed no special exemption, sharply declined. In the College the drop was from 1,539 in fall 1949, to 1,168 in fall 1950, to 907 in 1951, 837 in 1952. In Business Administration the score was from 152 in 1949, to 127 in 1950, to 89 in 1951, rising to 101 in 1952, and declining to 88 in 1953. In Law there was a steady decrease from 332 to 227, to 193, to 146, to 128. Total enrollments on the Atlanta campus ran as follows: fall 1949, 3,544; 1950, 3,142; 1951, 2,839; 1952, 2,653. Paradoxically, in this same period

Theology registered consistent gains. From 1946 to 1950 there had been a 262 per cent increase, from 113 to 296; in fall 1951 attendance rose to 382, and in 1953 to 391. From Fall Quarter 1953, following the armistice on July 27, enrollments of most divisions picked up again. Meanwhile the falling ratio of tuition fees to the total educational budget had made it necessary somewhat to raise the former; with a continuing disproportion a further increase of the tuition charge was reluctantly resorted to in 1955.

Enrollment had been stabilized to some extent by bringing a military training unit to the campus. At the invitation of the U. S. Air Force, in February 1951 Emory applied for one of the sixty-two Reserve Officers Training Corps units that it planned to establish in colleges across the country. Notification was received on April 20 that the application was approved, and instruction in air science and tactics for students of the College and School of Business Administration began in Fall Quarter. The unit was located in Annex A, across Clifton Road from the post office, with Lt. Col. Robert M. Lawson the officer in charge of the program. Enrollment, on a voluntary basis, in fall 1951 was 285 on the Atlanta campus, and with the addition of the subsidiary wings at Oxford and Valdosta, 461. In 1952 the staff included six officers and seven non-commissioned officers. Within a few months formations had shaped up so that review on the drill field and retreat on the Quadrangle, accompanied by the music of the band, made a fine martial display. After the armistice the A.F.R.O.T.C. had fewer elections, but it had earned and has retained permanent status.

The student activities building was planned by the alumni as a memorial to the University's war dead. When the Alumni Memorial Building was dedicated on April 14, 1956, a bronze plaque within the entrance bore 145 gold star names: eight for World War I, 121 for World War II, sixteen for the Korean War. Their sacrifice is a challenge to Emory men who continue to serve their country throughout the world.

It is an inescapable fact that the closest relations exist between university finances and university development. In this decade the former showed marked improvement, encouraging large hopes for the latter. Emory's general endowment was increased by something in the neighborhood of $5,000,000 when in August 1947 Mr. Charles Howard Candler presented the University with one-half of the stock of Asa G. Candler, Inc., Atlanta's great real-estate corporation. The remainder of the stock was secured by purchase, so that Emory came into possession of large holdings of properties in Atlanta and other cities. This virtually doubled the University's endowment, as it had been doubled in the previous decade.

Recurring annual deficits had made it extremely difficult to activate divisional programs long in planning, since current operations more than exhausted available funds. The establishment of an Emory Loyalty Fund in 1949, a plan of annual giving, was a step forward, but the augmentation of resources by large capital additions was indispensable if Emory was to fulfill its promise of regional leadership and national prestige.

At the meeting of the Board of Trustees on October 30, 1951, President White presented a special report, "A Review of Fifteen Years of Progress and a New Program of Development." A comprehensive survey of the achievements of the last years with a clearly thought-out plan for growth in academic stature, it was received with enthusiasm. After calling attention to the fact that the University's assets had been doubled twice within a period of fifteen years, its basic recommendation was stated as follows: "I now propose that, as we look ahead and plan for the next ten years, we should purpose again to double the University's assets, and that, again, at least three-fourths of the added resources should be for endowment." In 1951, it should be noted, the total assets of the University were $41,922,382, this figure not including a trust fund established by Samuel Candler Dobbs. The new development program contemplated the addition of $40,000,000, $32,000,-000 to be devoted to support of the graduate program.

A request for a grant was made to the General Education Board, that had already shown interest, and in December 1951 it was announced that it had set aside $7,000,000 for the purpose, to be claimed in installments as matching sums were obtained. The news of this unprecedented grant was electrifying, but the conditions annexed were difficult and complicated. Administrative officers at once embarked on a program of planning and solicitation beyond anything in their past experience, mapping strategy in a week-long conference held early in 1953 at the Cumberland Island estate of the Chairman of the Board of Trustees. Deaths of two key figures in the campaign, however, of Mr. Stipe on June 8, 1953, of Mr. Mizell on December 13, 1955, were blows from which it was found impossible to recover.

Nevertheless, matching funds in excess of $6,000,000 were reported in April 1954, by which a first $2,000,000 was claimed from the General Education Board. A major portion of these were received from the Emily and Ernest Woodruff Foundation designated for the School of Medicine, finally permitting it to operate without an annual deficit. The largest matching gift in direct support of graduate education so far received was $600,000, which came at the end of November 1955 from the Commonwealth Fund of New York. And soon after, the Ford Foundation made the dramatic announcement that it would distribute $500,000,000 among privately supported colleges, hospitals, and medical schools in 1956 and 1957. However the campaign might eventuate, in its course Emory was sure to benefit largely.

So much was happening in the ten years under present survey that little more than a listing is possible here; for some of the items further details will be added in later chapters.

With Eugene D. Whisonant as Associate Dean, Valdosta Junior College reopened in September 1946. Good enrollments brought a brief flourishing period, until Georgia State Woman's College, located in the same city, becoming coeducational, attendance fell off sharply and it was deemed necessary that Emory's Valdosta division be discontinued. In 1953 the plant was offered to and accepted by the University System of Georgia. At Oxford a four-year junior college program for students who had completed only two years of high school entered the planning stage in fall 1949. The new curriculum went into operation three years later.

On the Atlanta campus, in 1951 a University Senate was organized, "subject to the powers vested in the President of the University and the Board of Trustees, [to] consider and act upon all educational matters which concern the University as a whole or which affect more than one school or college of the University," to which was added, consideration of and "recommendations on any other matter affecting the interests of the University." Its composition at first included twenty-six administrative officers *ex-officio,* with twenty-seven members representing the several faculties. Although for some years the Senate failed to realize its potential, with later reorganization as a smaller body it began to play an important part in the general administration.

The inauguration of a program of adult education in 1951, presenting non-credit evening courses in a wide range of subjects, has been the most popular of Emory's contributions to community service. Originally planned by John A. Griffin, after his resignation in 1959 Miss Dora Byron '50G took over the direction of short courses. With more than 1,000 courses offered, with 300 teachers and 20,000 participants in its fifteen years, this is the largest project of its kind in the Southeast. The enthusiasm with which it has been received is attested by its current registration of 800 per quarter.

Of the many visitors to the campus two deserve special mention. The Commencement of June 4, 1949, will be remembered as the Barkley Commencement. Alben William Barkley, Vice-President of the United States 1949-53, a member of the Class of 1900, was on that day a guest of the College at Oxford and of the University in Atlanta. At the former he joined a group of his classmates at a barbecue under the oaks of the old campus, and at the latter he delivered the graduation address. As souvenirs of the occasion he carried away with him a Phi Beta Kappa key from the Emory chapter and the hood of an honorary LL.D. bestowed by the University. This was the first Emory event ever to be televised. In the year following, the very active Emory Debate Forum renamed itself the Barkley Forum.

In Winter Quarter 1951, Sir Richard Livingstone, the distinguished British educator, President of Corpus Christi College, Oxford, 1933-50, and sometime Vice-Chancellor of the University, was in residence at Emory. Offering a course, Greek Plays in

Translation, in the general humanities program of the College, he also took part in conferences and lectured extensively. Before his return to England he had crossed the continent, visiting a large number of educational institutions in the United States and Canada.

To the generosity of Walter Turner Candler '07 the University owes two endowed lectureships. The Candler Lectureship, established in 1951, since 1952 has been filled by a succession of outstanding figures in humanistic scholarship. The John Gordon Stipe Memorial Lectureship in Spanish Culture was founded on the death of his classmate in 1953. The first series, delivered in May 1954, began appropriately with a lecture on Cervantes, Mr. Stipe's favorite author.

On the death of Dr. Luther C. Fischer on April 29, 1953, the University took over the operation of Crawford W. Long Memorial Hospital, which had been deeded to Emory in 1940. With 480 beds and 120 bassinets Crawford Long was the largest all-private hospital in the Southeast.

In the same year the Emory University Clinic was organized in the Emory University Hospital. The Clinic is a partnership of physicians engaged in private practice while giving a large part of their time to teaching and research. The original group of seventeen members of the medical faculty was greatly augmented in numbers after the new Clinic building was ready for occupancy in 1956.

In 1954 the School of Medicine observed the centennial of the unbroken line of foundations that had culminated in that division of Emory University. On October 4-5 a large gathering of alumni, together with representatives of medical schools and societies, took part in a series of convocations, luncheons, and a reception and banquet. At the convocation of the second day honorary degrees were conferred on six distinguished physicians.

Gamma Chapter of Georgia, Phi Beta Kappa, celebrated its silver anniversary in a series of meetings, including an all-day program on April 9, 1954. Five alumni of the chapter were invited to speak on aspects of "The American Mind, 1929-1954" in two daytime sessions. At the evening banquet Guy Stanton Ford, who had immediately preceded Dr. White as President of the United

Chapters, delivered an address on the subject, "Teacher and Taught." At the June initiation meeting the speaker was William T. Hastings, Professor of English, Brown University, President of the United Chapters succeeding Dr. White.

The School of Theology, whose needs were acute, was soon to receive help. In order to strengthen the ties between the University and the Church that was its founder, the Board of Trustees in 1954 created the Committee of One Hundred. This is an advisory group including representative laymen from the nine-state Southeastern Jurisdiction. Close contact is maintained between Emory and the Committee, with one meeting of the full membership held on the campus each year. A primary concern has been the stimulation of interest in and the financial support of ministerial education. In 1955 the Methodist Fund for Ministerial Education was established. The 1% Plan, by which congregations of the Southeastern Jurisdiction make annual contributions of approximately one per cent of their budgets for minister training, in which the Candler School participates largely, has gone far toward maintaining the position and service of the Methodist Church in this region.

The International Greek New Testament Project was transferred from the University of Chicago to Emory in 1955. The task assigned is by the collation of all extant manuscripts to produce a more authoritative text of the Greek New Testament than has been hitherto available. To this end have been gathered more than one thousand photographic facsimiles of ancient manuscripts, some of them recently discovered. The meticulous and unhurried work of a large corps of scholars here and abroad under the direction of Dr. Merrill M. Parvis, assessing the evidence of the versions, should at length establish a definitive text of Christianity's basic documents.

Among student activities, the Glee Club continued to flourish, making its third European tour in the summer of 1953, when it visited ten countries, including Army and Air Force installations in West Germany. On the other hand, pushball contests, that had been annual events since 1923 with only one year's omission, came to an end in 1955. The mass encounter of freshmen and sophomores had ceased to be a sport, and injuries resulting from the melee finally brought about its abolition. It went without protest.

Emory was keeping up with the times. By 1946 the campus had traffic and parking problems. New marked parking spaces afforded temporary relief, but the situation continued to worsen. A three-man police force secured by arrangement with DeKalb County in 1948 began the regulation of traffic, besides taking over the guardianship of University property formerly assigned to part-time student watchmen. In 1955 there was compulsory registration of campus cars and assigned parking. Still administrative officers, faculty, students, employees, and visitors milled about in an apparently inextricable confusion. A few cars in a clump of pines opposite Physics Building fifty years ago was the whole motor population; in four decades that particular population explosion had become a problem whose solution continues to elude campus planners.

VI

To the Semicentennial of the University 1956-1965

THE ANNOUNCEMENT BY DR. GOODRICH C. WHITE in spring of 1956 that he purposed to retire from the presidency at the close of the next academic year began a pattern of top-level reorganization that was to continue for much of this period.

Since his entrance at Oxford in 1905, for all but the six years following his graduation, Goodrich White had been connected with Emory College and University; in 1957 he completed his fifteenth year as President. Through all the years of the University his contribution has been notable, and his was the leadership in the difficult decade and a half following 1942. Dr. White became a national academic figure, and his personal reputation aided in raising the status of the institution to which he has given his full devotion. His continuance in the office of Chancellor has ensured the University the benefit of his experienced wisdom.

With timely notice the Board of Trustees immediately launched a search for a new president. On April 18, 1957, they were able to report that he had been found in the person of Sidney Walter Martin, Dean of the Franklin College of Arts and Sciences at the University of Georgia. On the day of his election, when he emerged from the meeting of the Trustees in the Administration Building, the tower of Glenn Memorial gave out with "Glory, Glory to Old Georgia." A Southern historian, an outstanding lay leader of the Methodist Church, Dr. Martin was highly regarded in Athens, and from his arrival on the Emory campus his fine spirit was at once recognized. His announcement as a major policy of his administration the undertaking to raise professors' salaries won the immediate favor of the faculty. The very considerable achievements of this transitional period will be set forth in later detail. After five years, however, Walter Martin resigned in April 1962 to rejoin the University System of Georgia as Vice-Chancellor, and the search for a president was on again.

In the meantime, in the second month of Dr. Martin's presidency, Emory lost the Chairman of its Board of Trustees and a great benefactor of the University, Charles Howard Candler, who died on October 1, 1957. Henry L. Bowden was named to succeed him; it was he who presided at the inauguration of President Martin on November 15, and upon him in 1962 fell the chief burden of finding a replacement for the office.

For the interim an administrative committee of three—Chairman of the Board Bowden, Vice-President Ward, Chancellor White—was set up, which was soon popularly known as the "Troika," as the Administration Building had earlier been christened the "Kremlin." The day-to-day routine of running the University fell to the lot of the Vice-President. The active and wide-ranging search for an administrative head, carried on by a nine-man committee, quite early turned up the name of the Provost of Cornell University, but at the time it appeared that he was not available. Nevertheless, when in late spring of 1963 a settled conviction had developed that he was a most desirable choice, he was visited at Ithaca, brought to Atlanta to view the ground, and on July 8 his election was announced with immense satisfaction.

Dr. Sanford Soverhill Atwood, a native of Wisconsin, holder of three earned degrees from the University of Wisconsin, a specialist in the field of plant cytology, went to Cornell in 1944, where he was successively professor, department chairman, Dean of the Graduate School, and Provost, administrative second-in-command under President Malott. After conferences with the committee of selection, an inspection of Emory's plant, and a study of its resources and past progress, he responded promptly to the challenge of a University that appeared to him to be on the threshold of a bright future. At his inauguration on November 15 a party of his Cornell friends were present to wish him well, to whom if the words of the Emory *Alma Mater* were strange, the tune was familiar.

A rapid review of appointments, resignations, and general reorganization in the higher brackets will indicate something of the increasing complexity of university administration. Yet in spite of a constantly shifting bureaucracy, of which only a condensed view is here presented, it must be emphasized that the business of education, which has become big business, has been carried on with less confusion and delay at Emory than would be taken for granted in the industrial world.

In 1956, Bradford D. Ansley '39, was named Director of Development and Public Relations. During his tenure the promotional literature prepared to acquaint the public with the varied activities of the University won national recognition and the flow of financial aid from many sources increased materially. Following Ansley's resignation to enter private business, Dyar Massey, Director of Development at Furman University, was appointed to fill his place. In preparation for a substantial enlargement of the University's program of service and support, Norman C. Smith was brought from Vassar College in July 1964 as Vice-President for Development and Planning. The large function of his office is the oversight and coördination of public relations, alumni affairs, and development.

On the resignation in 1956 of Dr. R. Hugh Wood for reasons of health, Dr. Arthur P. Richardson took over as Dean of the School of Medicine, with Dr. Evangeline Papageorge '29G, of the Department of Biochemistry, as Assistant Dean. Dr. J. Elliott Scarborough became Director of the University Clinic, including the Robert Winship Clinic for Neoplastic Diseases. Dr. Carl C. Pfeiffer, Chairman of Pharmacology, was chosen as acting head of the Division of Basic Health Sciences, assuming full directorship the next year. In 1960, on Dr. Pfeiffer's resignation, Dr. James A. Bain, also of the Department of Pharmacology, succeeded as Director of the Division.

In 1957, Ernest C. Colwell, Vice-President and Dean of the Faculties, left Emory to accept the presidency of Southern California School of Theology, Claremont, and his place was taken by Judson C. Ward, Jr., Dean of the College. William A. Beardslee, Director of the Graduate Institute in 1958 served as Acting Dean of the College until the arrival on July 1 of William C. Archie, brought from Wake Forest College, Winston-Salem, North

Carolina, where he was Dean and Professor of Romance Languages. When Dean Archie resigned three years later to become Director of the North Carolina Board of Higher Education, John C. Stephens, Jr., '37, '38G, Chairman of the Department of English, moved up to the deanship of the College of Arts and Sciences.

1957 brought two other high administrative resignations. The election of Howard M. Phillips as President of Alabama College, Montevallo, vacated the office of Dean of the Graduate School, filled by Charles T. Lester '32, '34G, Chairman of the Department of Chemistry. George H. Mew, after thirty-four years of invaluable service as Treasurer of the University, retired from the position, although continuing to serve as part-time financial consultant. Ewell E. Bessent, was elected to succeed him, reuniting the functions of Treasurer and Controller.

A new appointment in 1958 was that of Director of the Summer School, for which William H. Jones '24, Professor of Chemistry, was chosen to direct the activities of the quarter, recently greatly expanded by specialized institutes in addition to the regular curriculum. Ill health forcing Gordon Siefkin to resign as Dean of Business Administration, Professor John H. Goff served in an acting capacity until the post was filled in September 1959 by Guy W. Trump, Dean of the U. S. Merchant Marine Academy, Kings Point, New York.

On the recommendation of Dean of Students E. H. Rece '25G, and after careful study of the problem, the University created the office of Dean of Student Affairs, to coördinate all phases of student life outside the classroom. To fill the position David W. Robinson was brought from Baldwin-Wallace College, Berea, Ohio, where he was Dean of Students, entering upon his new duties in June 1959. Mr. Rece resumed his former title of Dean of Men, and Miss Nina Rusk '35N, '51G, Assistant Dean of Students, since 1954 in charge of women's activities, became Emory's first Dean of Women. At his own request Dean Rece relinquished the title that he had held since 1937 to return as full-time Professor of Bible and Religion, and John J. Pershing, Associate Dean of Students at Georgia Institute of Technology, moved into his place. Dean Pershing resigning in Spring 1965, E. Jerome Zeller '50,

'53T, '62G, was appointed to take over the office on September first. On the resignation of Miss Rusk, Dr. Bonnie Ruth Strickland, of the Department of Psychology, in August 1964 was named Dean of Women.

In 1959 Robert F. Whitaker resumed his former position as Assistant to the President. John Rozier '40, '47G, of the editorial staff of the *Atlanta Constitution,* was appointed Director of the Emory News Bureau. The office is set up to perform the double duty of keeping the divisions of the University fully informed of one another's activities and of reporting all matters of interest to the public news media.

On the election of Charles O. Emmerich to the chairmanship of the DeKalb County Commission in 1960, Orie E. Myers, Jr., Director of Personnel, became Business Manager, John M. Outler III '51 succeeding as Director of Personnel. In the following year Mr. Myers's authority was enlarged as Dean of Administration and Director of Health Services, supervising the office of business management and coördinating programs in the health areas, in the latter replacing Vice-President Boisfeuillet Jones, on leave in Washington as Special Assistant for Health in the Department of Health, Education and Welfare. In May 1964 the Trustees elected Mr. Myers Vice-President for Business and Director of Health Services. In February John T. McTier '54, '57L, had been promoted from Assistant Business Manager to Business Manager.

The death of Dean of Law William M. Hepburn in 1960 placed the School in charge of Professor G. Stanley Joslin, until the appointment of Ben F. Johnson '39L in the year following. A new position, Dean of Alumni, was created in 1960 for the purpose of providing a closer personal communication between the University and the alumni and of securing larger financial support from them. The place was filled by H. Prentice Miller '27, '28G, Dean of the Lower Division in the College, who had for some time been serving these functions in a part-time capacity.

Dr. John E. Buhler resigning in 1961, Dr. George H. Moulton, Chairman of the Department of Crown and Bridge Dentistry and Director of Clinics, received the appointment of Dean of the School of Dentistry.

The two best-known members of the University's clerical staff retired together in 1963. Miss Pauline Odum, Secretary of the College since 1919, yielded to no one in length of service, and although Miss Maude Hilley had taken up the duties of Recorder seven years later, she was scarcely less taken for granted.

In April 1958 the Trustees chartered the Board of Visitors, an advisory and assisting group, for liaison between the University and the community that it seeks to serve. Its members have been chosen from the area through which Emory's influence chiefly extends, to support and interpret its activities, and to assist it in reaching important decisions and in initiating action in the public interest.

Building operations, including large-scale renovation, and additions to the campus and its various facilities have proceeded steadily throughout the past decade. Even more extensive building, now in the blueprint stage, waits only on the provision of necessary funds.

But before construction in this latest era had even begun, the University suffered its most disastrous fire, when on September 21, 1956, the upper floor and roof of the Administration Building burned, causing considerable damage to other parts of the structure. A tar paper covering was immediately spread, but when four days later Hurricane Flossie brought a torrential downpour to Atlanta, the temporary protection proved inadequate, and water damage succeeded that of the fire. Repair was begun without delay, and within a few months all traces of the destruction had been erased.

The University Clinic building, facing the Hospital on Clifton Road, was completed and occupied in 1956, the south wing, however, only "shelled in" until 1959. With another wing added in 1963, the Clinic now accommodates one hundred doctors representing most specializations. In the latter year was completed the thorough remodeling of Asa Griggs Candler Library for the effective utilization of all its available space. Plans have been drawn for a new Library of Advanced Studies, to be erected across Kilgo Circle as soon as financial arrangements can be made. On the Oxford campus a men's domitory was built, named Dickey Hall in honor of the last President of the College.

With the erection in 1957 of Bishops Hall, conveniently situated across Arkwright Drive, the School of Theology at last secured relief from the overcrowding that had severely restricted its activities. The lower floor was assigned the University Museum; for the first time its collections were brought together in an effective display, and a program of further acquisition was begun under the direction of Professor W. B. Baker.

A monumental addition was the Mizell Memorial Stairway, leading up to the Quadrangle from Kilgo Circle. Constructed of Georgia marble, it was dedicated to the memory of the former Director of Development who had died two years earlier.

Following the death of her husband, Mrs. Charles Howard Candler announced her intention to present her beautiful estate, "Callanwolde," 980 Briarcliff Road, to the University. The property consists of twenty-seven acres, finely wooded and landscaped, with a magnificent residence in the Tudor style of architecture at its center. Various plans were proposed for its utilization, but eventually in conferences between Mrs. Candler and administrative officials of the University it was determined that "Callanwolde" could be employed for more effective use than was practicable to Emory, and the estate was otherwise bestowed by its generous owner. In lieu of the property, Mrs. Candler made a capital gift equivalent to its value, which with her permission was applied to increase the Charles Howard Candler Memorial Professorship endowment established a few years earlier.

In 1958 Emory purchased the 185 acre estate of Walter T. Candler, adjoining the campus on the east beyond the line of the Seaboard Railway. "Lullwater House," a great mansion in the Elizabethan style, was occupied in August 1963 by Dr. and Mrs. Atwood as the official residence of the President of the University. The former president's home at the corner of Clifton and North Decatur Roads was assigned to the sororities for a Panhellenic House.

Housing for 332 women students was provided when Thomas, Hopkins, and Smith Halls, just south of Harris Hall on Clifton

Road, were occupied in Fall Quarter 1958. In the course of the next year, Clifton Court Apartments replaced the former "Mudville," with 100 units in thirteen buildings. At Oxford two new dormitories, Bonnell and Stone Halls, furnished beds for sixty-four students each, with Dickey Hall making quarters for 180 men. On the Atlanta campus, Dobbs and Winship Halls were modernized in 1962, and Dobbs was enlarged by a full-width addition at its rear. The Graduate and Professional Housing Center, on Haygood Drive, was a major project of 1964. Its three wings contain private bedroom-studies for 200 occupants, besides lounge and recreation rooms. Saunders Hall, a dormitory for medical students, on Dantzler Drive across the tracks from the railroad station, was occupied early in 1965. University owned and operated, members of the Phi Chi fraternity are given preference in housing assignments.

In 1959 the Trustees gave special consideration to the campus area, which in past years had grown rather haphazardly. It was concluded that a northern boundary should be set at Peachtree Creek, with west-south-east lines roughly following Lullwater Creek, Oxford Road, North Decatur Road, Clifton Road, the Seaboard Railroad tracks, and Clairmont Road. Within these limits are about 620 acres, the greater part already in the possession of the University. With the eventual acquisition of parcels still in private ownership, Emory will have a compact and unified campus suitable for all foreseeable needs.

Crawford Long Hospital in 1958 completed a remodeling program, and Emory University Hospital began one. The latter operation, which was only concluded in 1964, renovated or replaced outmoded facilities and virtually made a new hospital out of an old one at a cost of $4,750,000. In 1965, the former J. J. Gray Clinic, in the Grady Hospital area, renovated and rebuilt as the Woodruff Memorial Building—Henry Woodruff Extension, provided enlarged space needed by clinical specialists working at New Grady.

Campus food services were centered in a new building across the bridge on Asbury Drive in 1960, named Cox Hall in memory of the University's first President. Dooley's Den was brought from

[89]

the old cafeteria and located on the ground floor of Cox. With the removal of the cafeteria and the snack bar, the former dining area once more became an auditorium, the kitchens were taken for offices of student activities, and the ground floor made room for the University Book Store and the post office.

Old Pierce Science Hall at Oxford after many years had outlived its usefulness. It was therefore razed, and new Pierce Hall built on its site was put in service in 1961. On the Atlanta campus Glenn Memorial interior was remodeled, with the substitution of a deep chancel for the stage and the installation of a new organ. While it is still available as an auditorium for convocations, lectures, concerts, and recitals, its arrangements are now primarily churchly.

The independent institutions of the medical center that has grown up about the University campus have close affiliations with Emory, and furnish extensive clinical and research facilities in addition to those afforded by its own laboratories and the older hospitals which Emory supervises. Elks' Aidmore Convalescent Hospital for crippled children was opened just off Ridgewood Drive in November 1954, to which a $600,000 addition was made in 1961. Henrietta Egleston Hospital for Children, with 100 beds, was brought in 1959 to a location adjacent to the University Clinic on the north. These hospitals have made possible a great expansion of pediatric training. The Communicable Disease Center of the United States Public Health Service, an immense research and training facility, was erected in 1960 on Clifton Road beyond the railway line. In 1964 a $12,000,000 addition was begun, increasing immeasurably the scope of its operations. The members of the School of Medicine are also directly involved in medical services and the residency training program at the new Veterans Administration Hospital on Clairmont Road put in service in 1966.

The most exciting news of 1955 was that the Ford Foundation would distribute $550,000,000 among the nation's privately supported colleges, universities, and hospitals. Emory was to benefit largely from this unprecedented philanthropy, in 1956-57 receiving $3,961,100 for the University and its hospitals. This was allocated as follows: $2,000,000 for the School of Medicine; $158,100 for the University Hospital; $243,500 for Crawford Long; $1,559,500 for faculty salaries in the University. $597,000 of the latter sum was described as an Accomplishment Grant, awarded to 126 institutions "in recognition of the fact that these institutions have taken the lead in their regions in improving the status and compensation of American college teachers."

The Ford money was a timely windfall, enabling Emory in December 1957 to claim a third million of the General Education Board's grant of December 1951. In order to secure the entire $7,000,000 earmarked for Emory by the G. E. B., however, it was necessary to secure $33,000,000 from other sources, $25,000,000 to be in support of the program of graduate education. After five years it was manifest that these conditions could not be met. Negotiations by the officers of the University resulted in the payment of a fourth million, with the final three millions of the original grant reverting to the General Education Board.

From 1951 to 1958, nevertheless, more than $20,000,000 had been added to the assets of the University, although only a little more than $6,000,000 was in support of the Graduate School, which had been the chief concern of the General Education Board. In *Adventure in Giving* Raymond B. Fosdick summed up with an attempt at impartiality: "It was a somewhat unsatisfactory end to an ambitious plan, and the Board cannot escape its share of the responsibility in attempting too eagerly to strengthen graduate facilities in a location where perhaps the conditions for such a development were not sufficiently matured." The statement is not altogether unfair; it may be questioned, however, whether the extraordinary conditions annexed to the grant might not have been found insuperably difficult by almost every American institution, not only in the South, at that time.

Among numerous grants in aid of Emory's programs may be mentioned $96,000 for the support, over three years, of the Graduate Institute of the Liberal Arts, secured in 1958 from the Carnegie Corporation. In 1961 the Ford Foundation for the Advancement of Teaching made $740,000 available for teacher training, $525,000 for teachers in elementary and secondary schools, $215,-000 for college teachers. The latter grant supports Emory's Career

Scholars program under the direction of Professor William H. Jones, whose participants are selected from high-ranking sophomores to undertake three-year studies leading to the master's degree in preparation for college teaching.

DeKalb County's attempt in 1960 to levy taxes on the houses in Fraternity Row as private rather than institutional properties caused some concern. Taken to the Georgia Supreme Court, the ruling was made that the fraternity houses, owned by the University and on the campus, are an integral part of its system of student housing, and that threat to Emory's finances was averted. In 1962 welcome relief came with the exemption of independent educational institutions from the Georgia Sales tax in the purchase of equipment and supplies for educational purposes. This added to the exemption from federal excise taxes granted in 1961, has resulted in large savings, difficult to calculate but probably not less than $75,000 a year.

The expense to the University of providing an education for its students has risen greatly in past years and continues to rise. Costs of building, equipment, supplies, and compensation to its personnel, including equitable and attractive professors' salaries, have mounted to heights scarcely dreamed of fifty years ago. Education under private auspices could not be maintained were it not for the provision of large endowments and a constant flow of gifts and grants. The individual student is not required to pay more than a part of what his schooling costs the institution, estimated as somewhere in the neighborhood of fifty percent. Tuition fees cannot be held to a constant figure, but must rise in some proportion with the overall financial situation of the institution. This may be illustrated by the pattern of tuition charges in the College at Emory. From 1915 to 1956 they rose from $225 (plus incidental fees) to $525 (fees included). Then they began to spiral: 1956-57, $600; 1957-58, $705; 1959-60, $795; 1961-62, $900; 1963-64, $1,095; 1964-65, $1,245; 1965-66, $1,395.

It is recognized that as the cost increases, it becomes increasingly more difficult for many young people to make financial arrangements to carry them through the four years of college, and quite impossible to provide for postgraduate study. Emory, therefore, has undertaken to furnish assistance grants for students who give evidence of doing well in higher studies, and this undertaking has been generously supported by the alumni and other individual donors and by the foundations. From its own resources in 1963-64 the College extended financial aid to 713 students in the sum of $335,162; the University for all students made 1,897 grants, totalling $912,085. Besides those whom it supports directly, many Emory students are maintained in whole or in part by scholarships and fellowships from outside sources not in the gift of the University.

A great institution must have great resources. With the constantly expanding needs of a university committed to the ideal of a first-class education comparatively great resources are not equivalent to wealth. On August 31, 1964, the total market value of Emory's endowments and trust funds was $87,360,447. This figure includes a trust fund established for the School of Medicine in 1953 by the Woodruff Foundation transferred to the University in this year. The value of the plants—cost value not replacement value—was $47,781,172. It is worth noting that the 1951 proposal to double the University's assets had been met and considerably exceeded. These are large figures, but they do not mean that Emory is rich. On the contrary, if Emory is to live up to its possibilities of service to the South and the nation, if even it is to maintain the standards that it has rigorously imposed on itself, they must be largely increased.

For its first thirty years Emory University devoted almost the whole of its energies and physical resources to teaching, to which research was only incidental. Individual professors, particularly in medicine and law, engaged in private research projects, and a slender stream of journal contributions, mostly from the departments of the sciences, bore witness to the University's latent capability. Even though the work of the Graduate School proceeded only to the master's degree, a large number of Emory M.A.'s going forward to the doctorate at other universities conclusively demonstrated their grounding in the principles and practice of research, frequently in the productive scholarship of their maturity bringing to conclusion studies begun in their first graduate year.

Even though the record of faculty research for the years preceding World War II is not impressive, there had been throughout the period a growing concern for its expansion. Heavy teaching loads and committee assignments allowed little opportunity for a relatively small faculty to carry on concurrent investigations, even when laboratory and library facilities were sufficient. The first breakthrough occurred when university center planning emphasized the development of Emory's Graduate School. A University Research Committee was set up as early as 1938, and with the accession of funds from the campaign, grants were made for research and publication. A University Center Research Fund for five years or a little longer gave encouragement to members of the Center institutions while the latter were making their own financial arrangements. From these combined resources Emory was able in 1945-46 to make grants of $6,739 to thirteen faculty members, at the same time increasing allowances for laboratory equipment and library books. In this year, moreover, grants from outside sources for specific scientific objectives totalled $60,000. So promoted, faculty research has burgeoned, and as productive investigations have multiplied, University funds have been released in greater volume. But while research and publication in the humanities and the non-quantitative social sciences continue to be largely supported by the University's unrestricted account, from the war years to the present, subsidies have been obtained from government and other sources for the biological (including medical and dental), physical, and behavioral sciences in sums greatly in excess of those allocated by the University Research Committee. Funds from government sources expended for research and training in all areas during 1963-64 amounted to $5,225,506, in 1964-65 to $6,097,733.

Long-range programs have been initiated in all divisions of the University, of which a partial list will reveal the scope and importance of current activities.

The School of Business Administration in 1949 established a Business Executives Research Committee to begin a study of the South's opportunities and problems. From this have evolved conferences and publications that have established Emory's leadership in the economics of the Southern region. The International Greek New Testament Project of the School of Theology has already been described.

In 1956 Yale University made Emory the gift of its Yerkes Laboratories of Primate Biology located at Orange Park, Florida, inconveniently placed for the Connecticut institution to make the fullest use of the facility. Originally a colony of fifty-eight chimpanzees, it now consists of more than 200 apes and monkeys of nearly a score of species. Renamed the Yerkes Regional Primate Research Center of Emory University, it was moved in 1965 into new buildings on the north edge of the campus financed by a grant from the National Heart Institute. Here a permanent staff, Emory faculty and graduate students, and research workers from around the world are engaged in social, psychological, and medical investigations in which the animals nearest to man in the scale of nature will aid in solving problems vitally important to human life. From its establishment the Center has been supported by funds from government and foundation sources.

Among the achievements of the School of Law's Bureau of Legal Research and Service was the publication in 1957 of *Georgia Procedure and Practice,* a reference volume of 1,000 pages three years in the making. Besides various charts and pamphlets, the School since 1952 has published the semiannual *Journal of Public Law.*

Reference has already been made to the Geology Camp for field studies in the mountains of North Georgia, erected on a thirty-acre tract given by Jeff McCord '16. The Department of Biology has two experiment stations on the campus. The Radiation Research Field was established to study the effects of atomic radiation on experimental plants and animals. The program initiated in 1956 was expanded in 1958 at the request of the Atomic Energy Commission and the Air Force, using the Lockheed Aircraft Corporation's reactor field at Dawsonville in North Georgia. The Lullwater Biology Field Laboratory, set apart in 1961, is a twenty-acre enclosure on the Walter Candler estate in the northeastern section of the campus, where widely varying fresh-water and terrestrial habitats are available for teaching and research. The

Department maintains active summer programs at Woods Hole Biological Laboratories on the Massachusetts coast and at the Sapelo Island Marine Laboratory on the Georgia coast. It is also a member of the Highlands Biological Station in North Carolina.

The connection with the Oak Ridge National Laboratory for nuclear research, begun during World War II, has been maintained by members of the Departments of Chemistry and Physics. Members of the Emory faculty have been summer research participants, short-term employees, and consultants, and specific research programs have involved both Oak Ridge and Emory.

An Ophthalmological Research Center was established in 1963. The Emory Biomedical Data Processing and Analysis Center of the Department of Biometrics was financed by a federal grant from the National Institutes of Health for use in all health-related areas for the rapid processing of research data. Other computers assist research in the Department of Chemistry and the School of Business Administration.

In recent years members of the School of Theology have joined archaeological expeditions in Jordan and Israel. In the summer months of 1963, 1964, and 1965 Dr. Immanuel Ben-Dor, Professor of Biblical Archaeology, has conducted courses for the Institute for Mediterranean Studies in the Negev Desert.

In connection with the development of the Graduate School the University has instituted a generous policy permitting leaves of absence by faculty members for study at home and abroad, for research and teaching fellowships, of which there have been many recipients of prestigious awards. Emory scholars have been academic sojourners in Great Britain, France, Germany, Norway, and other parts of Europe, in Turkey, Jordan, and Israel, in Japan, Taiwan, and India, in Mexico and Argentina, and in Australia. Visiting scholars brought to the campus from other universities have enriched the experience of faculty and students in almost every area of learning.

Only a sampling can here be presented of the research activities of the University. Particularly in the areas of the health sciences there has been an immense expansion over many fields. An impression of its growth can be gained by comparing government grants of 1955-56, $614,000, with those of 1963-64, $6,602,343. The grants of government agencies, industry, and the foundations for research and training now form a large part of the annual budget.

It is not, however, to be inferred that the new emphasis on research has been at the expense of the teaching function of the University. On the contrary, research activity has the usual effect of imparting life and relevancy to teaching. At Emory those who carry on the research programs with few exceptions are also the teachers of undergraduate, graduate, and professional students. In an elaborate self-study completed in 1961, designed to bring out the resources and the deficiencies of the institution as seen by its own members, almost equal attention is given to both functions, with detailed recommendations for their improvement. Emory's ideal is to achieve the most complete intellectual life for both teacher and taught, to make each of them an active participant in the progress of region and nation.

Enrollment figures tell only a part of the story of Emory's progressive development as an institution of higher education. Without interpretation all along the way they can be quite misleading. They show clearly enough that what began as a small foundation became increasingly larger, numbering 452 students in 1918, more than doubling the attendance in 1920 to 958, and doubling again in 1925 to 1,905. For twenty years enrollments held at around 2,000, except for wartime. Then returning servicemen taking advantage of the "G. I. Bill of Rights" brought them to new highs. The condensed record of full-time students for the last fifteen years, including Oxford College but excluding registrants for the A. A. T. E. S. program, is as follows: 1950, 4,928; 1955, 3,667; 1960, 4,691; 1965, 5,649.

It is taken for granted by the University planners that in the next ten years it will be necessary to admit substantially larger numbers to all divisions, probably to a total of 7,500. Expansion of the admissions policy will depend on two factors, the academic qualifications of candidates, and the extent of available educational facilities. Some schools are already operating at capacity, and the enlargement of their resources will not easily be achieved, but in all divisions it will be necessary to add faculty members, classrooms and laboratories and their equipment, and library collections to accommodate an appreciable rise in enrollments.

Emory College has set a high level for the qualification of entering freshmen. It seeks all possible assurance that the candidate, in addition to good moral character, has shown high-grade performance in his secondary schooling and possesses the ability and the will to go on to higher studies. This does not amount to a policy of exclusion, but it is definitely a policy of conservation of energy and resources to ensure a favorable environment for teaching and learning of a truly advanced nature. Since 1957 applicants for admission have been required to take the Scholastic Aptitude Test given by the College Entrance Examination Board, and scores made on its two parts, verbal and mathematics, are among the data determining acceptance or rejection. Current results are most gratifying. The Dean of the Faculties reported in October 1964: "In the College, the number of freshman applicants grew in number and quality. A class of 630 was chosen from 2,800 applicants. The class admitted in the fall of 1964 is better prepared than any of its predecessors."

Requirements for admission to other divisions of the University are correspondingly high, with the greatest selectivity necessarily employed by the School of Medicine, which can accept an entering class of no more than seventy-two. In 1964 there were more than 800 applications for these places. Law, Business, and Nursing have experienced considerable fluctuations in enrollment, but Law and Nursing report a healthy upward trend. Undergraduate enrollments in the School of Business have been on the decline, since its "highly theoretical and basic orientation has not appealed to students seeking a vocational education." It is anticipated that the School in the near future will devote itself entirely to graduate education.

From its beginning Emory University has operated on an academic calendar of four quarters, anticipating the trend of the open campus that in these latter years is becoming nation-wide. The Schools of Medicine and Dentistry, however, do not offer work in the summer. For the first decades the summer quarter was devoted to a course schedule similar to that of the other three quarters and allowing equal credit toward graduation. To this was added an augmented program of teacher education. In the regular summer session enrollment appears to have reached a plateau, but the development of special programs has greatly increased the activity of the season and has extended its educational usefulness. Ten workshops and institutes, half of them supported by grants from national foundations, brought selected teachers, specially talented high school students, ministers and other religious workers to the campus in the summer of 1965.

A grant from the federal government subsidized in 1960-61 a year-long institute for high school teachers of French at Emory. In the summers of 1962 and 1963 French Institutes were conducted by Emory professors at Besançon, France.

While subject matter and, to some degree, teaching method, undergo constant revision in the College, especially in the departments of science and mathematics, the chief trend has been away from the elementary nature of freshman courses, due in the past to deficient preparation for advanced study revealed by high school graduates. A notable improvement of secondary education in recent years has permitted upgrading of all beginning college work. While there has been a general enrichment of the offering of all departments, perhaps the most important addition to the curriculum has been the addition of courses in Russian language and literature begun in 1959.

The extension of the curriculum of the School of Medicine will be given special attention in a later chapter. Among departments added or notably developed in the decade are anesthesiology, biometrics, ophthalmology, pediatrics, preventive medicine and community health, and psychiatry. But in all areas of teaching as in research the division presents an outstanding record of progress.

1958-1961 were critical years for Georgia's educational system, with Emory deeply involved in the outcome of the segregation-integration controversy. While the U. S. Supreme Court was ruling against segregated public schools, the Governor and Legislature of Georgia were holding the line against integration. In view of

[99]

the strong probability that the Court would order the desegregation of an Atlanta school, the authorities were prepared at once to close the entire Atlanta system rather than allow any degree of racial integration. It would logically follow that Atlanta, not permitted to use its tax money for the support of its own schools, would institute court proceedings to prevent its being used elsewhere. And so in consequence there might be a closing of schools throughout the state.

The threat was serious, and Emory soon began to feel its effect. In the first place, College and University encountered increasing difficulty in interesting teachers from out of the state to consider appointments in Atlanta. In the second place, Emory professors with children to educate were becoming restive, and the possibility of the loss of key faculty members was a real menace. Finally to be taken into account was the possible disruption of public education, which would very soon shut off or largely diminish supplies of college entrants.

These were the practical aspects of the situation. But in the broader view the social results of closing the public schools would be nothing less than disastrous. This moved the University body to release a statement to the press on Sunday, November 30, 1958, signed by 250 full-time members of the Emory faculties, which began: "We the undersigned . . . are opposed to the closing of the public schools in any section of the United States. We wish to point out the irreparable damage that will result from the closing of public schools, not only to the people of any particular community, but also to the state and the nation at large."

The brief but closely argued and moderately worded declaration of principle was soon followed by manifestos of other educational and professional groups. While some voices were raised in angry reply, the public response was increasingly favorable. This does not mean that the general sentiment was for integration, but that a realization grew that Georgia could not afford to close its schools, a judgment concurred in by a number of outspoken segregationists. The matter was not resolved before the occurrence of an unhappy incident on the campus of a state institution that gave the Georgia situation unwelcome nation-wide publicity. But in

The Quadrangle

Whitehead Memorial Room, University Hospital

Miss Pauline and her Deans, 1948 (J. Harris Purks, Jr., Theodore H. Jack, Judson C. Ward, Jr., J. Gordon Stipe, Goodrich C. White, Miss Pauline Odum)

Hooding Emory's First Ph.D., 1948

Air Force R O T C Holds Retreat

January 1961 the Governor and General Assembly finally made the decision to remove from the statute books laws requiring total racial segregation of educational facilities, and a great sigh of relief went up that the stalemate was broken.

The decision, however, related strictly to public education. Private institutions were compelled to continue to operate on a segregated basis, because exemption from taxation by the state depended on that proviso in the constitution and statutes. While the University of Georgia and the Georgia Institute of Technology had already accepted Negro students, Emory, whose "charter and bylaws have never required admission or rejection of students on the basis of race," was held to an all-white constituency, since loss of exemption from taxation would be simply ruinous.

Emory finding itself in an ambiguous situation, in which it was denied the right to make its own admissions policy, and held to one counter to the policy adopted by members of the Georgia state system, determined to seek clarification in the courts. At the November 1961 meeting of the University Board of Trustees a resolution was passed that Emory would consider applications from candidates for admission "without regard to race, color, or creed" as soon as tax laws made this possible. On March 21, 1962, following the application of a Negro to the School of Dentistry, the University filed a "Petition for Declaratory Judgment and Injunction" in the Fulton County Superior Court, from which it was transferred to the Superior Court of DeKalb County. Emory's case was prepared and presented by Henry L. Bowden, Chairman of the Board and University Counsel, and Dean Ben F. Johnson of the School of Law. After unfavorable action in the lower courts, the case was carried to the Georgia Supreme Court, which on September 15 handed down a ruling for the University. When the decision was challenged, the Court denied a rehearing, and Emory's tax exempt status was confirmed. What was determined at law was simply that the University and all other of Georgia's private educational institutions were free to admit any applicant on merit alone.

The first Negro student was registered by the Atlanta Area Teacher Education Service in fall 1962. The first full-time students were two women enrolled in the School of Nursing, graduated in

June 1964. In fall 1964 the Rockefeller Foundation made Emory a grant of $250,000 for financial aid to needy students, particularly Negroes, by which nine qualified Negro students were admitted to the College. In Fall Quarter 1964 eighteen full-time Negro students were enrolled in four divisions of the University.

The dialogue by which Emory University assumed a position of leadership in Georgia educational action had been stimulated by John A. Griffin in forum discussions and by Randolph Fort in *Alumnus* articles. The part played by the Board of Trustees in obtaining a final decision on a problem vitally concerning academic freedom was given national recognition when in April 1963 the Alexander Meiklejohn Award was presented to Henry L. Bowden by the American Association of University Professors. A matter of particular pride to Mr. Bowden and to Emory men generally is that a highly controversial issue was brought to a settlement by Georgians in their own courts.

For those unfamiliar with the local geography, the United States post office address, "Emory University, Georgia," has only caused confusion. Identification of the University with the city in whose suburbs it is situated has long been realized as most advantageous, but attempts to make its post office a station of the Atlanta system met with no success until the spring of 1958. On May 1 of that year, however, the changeover was at length achieved, and the address became Atlanta 22, since the adoption of the zip code, Atlanta, Georgia 30322. Most recently a student post office has been installed on the ground floor of Alumni Memorial.

On May 30, 1960, the names of the first Charles Howard Candler Professors were announced at a dinner in their honor. A memorial tribute to a great benefactor of the University, an endowment had been set up to provide recognition and augmented stipends for a group of distinguished faculty members, able teachers and contributors to the store of knowledge. The twelve first so designated were: Jacob H. Goldstein, chemistry; Chauncey G. Goodchild, biology; Charles Hartshorne and Leroy E. Loemker, philosophy; G. Ray Jordan, theology; G. Stanley Joslin, law; James G. Lester, geology; Joseph J. Mathews and Bell I. Wiley, history;

H. Stephen Weens, radiology; W. Tate Whitman, economics; Alfred E. Wilhelmi, biochemistry.

The Thomas Jefferson Award, made possible by a grant from the Robert Earl McConnell Foundation of New York, honors members of faculty or staff who exhibit qualities that "Mr. Jefferson would have considered essential to the intellectual, social, and political advancement of society." The first recipient, in 1962, was Woolford B. Baker '20G, Professor of Biology. In 1963 the Award was made to William A. Strozier '19, Professor of Romance Languages, in 1964 to Edwin T. Martin '28, '29G, Professor of English, in 1965 to Ellis Heber Rece '25G, Professor of Bible and Religion.

The Candler School of Theology celebrated its semicentenary at its thirtieth Ministers' Week on January 20-23, 1964. A large attendance of churchmen heard addresses by such distinguished visitors as Ernest Gordon, Dean of the Chapel at Princeton University, Glenn T. Seaborg, Chairman of the Atomic Energy Commission, and Robert F. Goheen, President of Princeton. At the opening session Dean Cannon presented citations to ten laymen for their service to ministerial education and support of the Candler School. At the closing convocation five honorary degrees were conferred. The convocation speaker was F. Gerald Ensley, Bishop of the Methodist Church, Iowa Area, who emphasized the need of the times for an educated ministry.

A full campus, an active and varied student life have characterized the past decade. In general the morale has been high, though on occasion the serenity has been clouded by misunderstanding of the attitudes of administrative officials and faculty members. No violent controversy nor long-standing grievance is to be recorded. This has been so characteristic of the spirit of the place that there have been charges of student apathy. The allegation is not to be taken too seriously. Our young people are normal in all respects, and if they have found less destructive ways to blow off steam than some academic communities, this should be set down to their credit.

The continuous rise of undergraduate scholarship has received official recognition by the creation of a new student honor. In 1957 the first group of John Gordon Stipe Scholars was chosen from among entering freshmen. Between sixty-five and seventy students are now selected each year, twenty from incoming freshmen who show academic promise, and fifteen from each of the other classes on the basis of distinguished records of performance. The Stipe Scholarships do not themselves carry financial compensation, but if one of their holders requires assistance, he is eligible for a grant up to $1,000 a year.

A short-lived campaign for intercollegiate athletics was conducted in 1957-58 by the *Wheel* and some student groups. This time the cry was for intercollegiate basketball. The Department of Physical Education showed no enthusiasm, there was no likelihood of the Trustees reconsidering their ruling, and after a time the movement lost whatever impetus it had begun with.

On the other hand, in 1958 compulsory chapel was discontinued. The student community has shown an extraordinary religious commitment, but agitation against institutional religious services with absenteeism penalized is one of the oldest traditions of college life. Practical difficulties in finding hours for weekday chapel have beset the University with the growing complexity of class schedules, and with the rise of enrollments the largest available auditorium will accommodate only a fraction of the student body. Voluntary worship services for denominational groups are well-attended, and a general Sunday service has recently been established. Times and circumstances have changed, but the ideal of education as a Christian heritage still prevails on the Emory campus.

When Emory College became officially coeducational, the women students began at once to organize social clubs, looking toward their establishment as chapters of national sororities. After a period of probation they were allowed to petition for national status, and on May 8, 1959, charters were delivered for chapters of Alpha Chi Omega, Alpha Delta Pi, Alpha Epsilon Phi, Chi Omega, Delta Delta Delta, Delta Gamma, Kappa Alpha Theta, Kappa Delta, Kappa Kappa Gamma, and Phi Mu, with 473 charter members. At the same time, the Panhellenic Council was chartered as a coördinating agency for the sororities. The convocation address was delivered by Dean of Students Rece, for which he received a standing ovation. Emory has no sorority houses, and until the Council can build its own center it is quartered in the former President's House at the corner of Clifton and North Decatur Roads, where ceremonials and social affairs are held.

A few days after the chartering ceremony, at the spring Honors Day convocation, the Interclub Council President, Nancy King '59, Fleur-de-Lis club and Kappa Kappa Gamma sorority, received the Brittain award by unanimous consent of the committee of selection. "The Brittain Award, named for Marion Luther Brittain ['86, '28H, long-time President of Georgia Tech], is made each year to a student who has rendered notable service to the University." Twelfth recipient, Miss King was the first woman to win this highest honor. But not the last, for in 1963 senior Melinda Whitman, and in 1964 senior Hoda Levine were given the award, the latter from the hands of Mrs. Lady Bird Johnson, who had delivered the Honors Day address.

These have been good years for the male-dominated student newspaper and the debating organization. "The South's most independent collegiate newspaper" sometimes appears to go out of its way to raise controversial issues to vindicate its independence, but since its first appearance it has been a force on the campus. The Associated Collegiate Press has repeatedly given it Honor Ratings for makeup, coverage, style, and features, the twenty-sixth for the issues of Fall Quarter 1964.

Intercollegiate debates no longer draw the large audiences that they did thirty years ago, but the activity is still flourishing. Teams of the Barkley Forum have competed widely and successfully, winning scores of trophies. Each year it sponsors a High School Debate Tournament on the Emory campus. In the spring of 1965 the Emory debaters obtained the regional championship in nine undefeated rounds, winning the right to represent the South at the West Point Tournament, recognized as the national championship contest for college debating. At West Point the Forum won first and second place in six rounds, besides two other awards for individual performance.

Plans for the observance of Emory's fiftieth anniversary were held in abeyance until after the inauguration of President Atwood. It was not until March 1964 that it was possible to give consideration to an appropriate way of signalizing the arrival at this important milestone in the history of the University.

After thoughtful discussion it was determined that the celebration should be limited to a few major features, with the semicentennial theme carried through all the normal activities of the academic year. The observance began with a convocation on the afternoon of Charter Day, January 25. At the convocation, after an impressive academic procession, the University was formally presented with a gold and silver mace, the gift of D.V.S., the College Senior Honor Society. Honorary degrees were conferred on Atlanta business leaders Harllee W. Branch, Jr., '31L, and Richard H. Rich, Congressman Carl Vinson, and Chancellor Goodrich C. White. The address was delivered by Eugene Patterson, Editor of the *Atlanta Constitution*. At the Anniversary Dinner that evening Harllee Branch, President of The Southern Company and Emory Trustee, delivered the address. During the month of January special exhibits in the windows of Atlanta department stores brought the Emory semicentennial to the attention of the general public.

Various publications were arranged for, with a Semicentennial History and a special number of the *Atlanta Journal and Constitution Magazine* heading the list. The latter, appearing Sunday, October 24, carried illustrated feature stories setting forth Emory's contributions to the region and the nation. The leading article was written by Eugene Patterson, and other articles were by Emory administrators and faculty members. The *Emory Wheel* printed a series of historical supplements written by sophomore Robert Rohrer, in which epochal events in Emory's past were presented as current news stories. At Honors Day 1965 the young journalist received the Raymond B. Nixon Award for this outstanding contribution.

While the program of the year was not greatly expanded, particular care was taken to make its events noteworthy. The traditional pageantry of academic ceremonies received increased emphasis which added color and interest to them. Distinctive costumes have been created for the President and marshals, and a University mace, an historic emblem of authority, executed after an original design by the Worshipful Company of Goldsmiths in London, is borne in procession before the President of the University by the President of the Student Senate. The dignity of age and reputation achieved by Emory University in its first half-century is thus visually displayed.

THE DIVISIONS

Emory College

THE SMALL COLLEGE AT OXFORD until its migration to Atlanta furnished an education that was largely an end in itself. At the close of its era, however, a change in its function was beginning to develop. In the years just preceding World War I the professions were prescribing formal college training as a requirement for entry into professional schools, which in turn had supplanted the older system of apprenticeship. In law, medicine, dentistry, the ministry—in the higher professions generally—there was a demand for academic training based on a foundation of preparatory work in a college of the liberal arts and sciences. The college, as a result, was becoming the portal through which candidates entered the specialized disciplines. When Emory College became a part of a university complex, its function was revolutionized. No longer could it be mainly concerned with the education of a gentleman, as in the preceding century; now it must be occupied with fitting a large proportion of its students with the prerequisites for vocational training in the professional schools of which it was the center. If the College, however, had lost its former independent status, it had discovered an opportunity for higher usefulness to the community than it had known in the past. All over America colleges were rising to meet the challenge, and Emory College, keenly realizing the claims of a new day, put forth all its energies to their fulfillment.

The curriculum, the course of supervised studies, is the college's basic offering to students. The classical curriculum of the past was mainly disciplinary in purpose. While the contemporary curriculum has not lost its disciplinary intention, since World War I there has been a notable movement toward more inclusive aims. That is to say, the college still seeks to cultivate the minds of its students, to teach them to think, but the materials that it employs are more and more those that possess a special relevance to contemporary life, both in its vocational and avocational aspects. Since, moreover, this is an age of rapid change in the realms both of action and of thought, the past half-century has been marked by constantly shifting directions and emphases in college curricula.

In constructing the college curriculum certain guide-lines have been followed. The range of studies is broadly classified under three heads: the humanities, social studies, mathematics and the physical sciences. It is taken for granted that a man must have a general acquaintance with these three areas if he is to enjoy both a useful and a rich life. "Reading maketh a full man" wrote Francis Bacon; no further justification should be required for the book-learning represented by a large part of the offerings in humanities and social studies. If in most literary and historical courses attention is largely focused on the past, only with such preparation can the modern world be understood in its outward forms and inward mind. In an age of headlong scientific advancement, some acquaintance with scientific principles and processes is requisite. And so the college attempts to give the student both an intellectual grasp of the time in which he lives, and resources by which he may to a degree maintain mental and spiritual freedom in a world of change. The college of liberal arts and sciences still cherishes the ideal of liberation as its distinctive feature.

When Emory College became a part of Emory University, there had already occurred a movement away from the curriculum centered on study of the Greek and Latin classics. For some years after the migration, however, candidates for the Bachelor of Arts degree were required to present at least thirty quarter hours in the classics; a Bachelor of Philosophy degree was provided for students majoring in non-scientific subjects without classics, and the Bachelor of Science degree was offered for science majors. The decline of the classics following World War I was accompanied by the rise of English and modern foreign languages, and they in turn in the era of World War II by the rise of social studies. These successive changes are faithfully reflected in curricular requirements and offerings of the College. The dominant position of the School of Medicine from the 'twenties placed more and more stress on premedical studies—chemistry, biology, physics—and a strong vocational tinge was imparted to the curriculum pursued by large numbers of students of the College.

In order to redress the balance of heavily weighted science programs, as well as other specializations that showed a tendency to get out of hand, in 1928 there was a basic reorganization of the curriculum, between Junior College (later, Lower Division), including freshman and sophomore years, and Senior College (Upper Division), junior and senior years. In Junior College, courses were largely prescribed and distributed among a wide and varied number of subjects to form as broad a cultural background as possible. Specialization was reserved for Senior College, in which the student satisfied the requirements of his major, with supporting and tool subjects, together with some freedom of election. At the beginning, a general or comprehensive examination was required for graduation; this requirement was found impracticable and after a time was dropped. In conformity with a standardization of the curriculum, it was determined to bestow the degree of Bachelor of Arts on all graduates. The last Bachelor of Philosophy degrees were conferred in 1943, the last Bachelor of Science in 1945. There was, however, a return to the Bachelor of Science in 1962.

In 1962 also the classification Lower Division-Upper Division was eliminated in favor of a regular four-year plan of progression. Basic course requirements of the former system, a "core curriculum" of elementary subjects and concentration in a major, were largely retained, but there was less prescription and considerably more flexibility in the scheme.

From the organization of the College on the quarter system in 1916 the basic course pattern was one of five class meetings each week, and the student load was normally three courses each quarter. Occasional deviations from the pattern occurred, but they were generally discouraged because of difficulties of fitting them into the schedule.

It must be emphasized that throughout the more recent history of the College there has been constant modification of the curricular plan, so that even the annual catalogues furnish no entirely dependable record. This process has been greatly hastened in the past decade by the realization that even a relative fixation of undergraduate offerings and requirements cannot stand against the ever-rising tides of change. The emergence of new subjects, and of new approaches to the traditional ones, is no new phenomenon, but the present era is marked by a regrouping and realignment of subject matters that have transcended the old classifications.

For several years now an intensive study of the Emory College curriculum has sought to construct a program of superior breadth and flexibility, aimed at providing means of keeping pace with contemporary cultural trends and the scientific advance. This has been made possible in part by the general improvement of high school work, enabling levels of courses in the lower classes of the College to be raised above the elementary. In part also the more rigorous selection of candidates for college entrance has permitted upgrading courses in freshman and sophomore years. In the spring of 1964 such a curriculum was approved in its main outlines. Among its features may be noted an over-all cultural enrichment, a redistribution of weights among subjects with a new pattern of the undergraduate's quarter course program and new combinations of major and minor subjects. Provision has also been made for honors programs on a scale hitherto unattempted. Since the new plan involves a number of administrative details still to be worked out, it has not yet gone into effect. Its spirit, however, has already had an influence on the work of the College, and some of its specific proposals have already been adopted.

Emory's insistent emphasis has been upon the ideal of a liberal, general education as against vocationalism and narrow specialization. Repeatedly there has been rephrasing of the objectives of the College, but with this emphasis always uppermost. Its practice has in large measure made reality of the profession of loyalty to the liberal ideal. On occasion this has dictated radical changes in the curriculum.

In the early years of the University there was frequent reference to the need for a teachers' college. The idea was abandoned, and the Department of Education assumed parity with the other departments of the College of Arts and Sciences. Since the mid-twenties there has been consistent adherence to the policy of keeping teacher education under the auspices of the faculty of arts and sciences, both on the undergraduate and graduate level. The responsibility for the education of teachers has been shared with the subject-matter departments. The Division of Teacher Education has welcomed and has enlisted their coöperation, and faculty members of the Department of Education have been fully recognized as colleagues in the work of College and Graduate School.

The program in engineering was discontinued in 1950. The program had developed at Oxford, growing out of the teaching of "applied mathematics," first by Professor Harry Stone '80 and subsequently by Professor J. B. Peebles, a professional engineer. On a restricted scale it was highly successful, enrolling each year a small group of students who on graduation were readily placed with engineering firms. In the early years on the Atlanta campus there was suggestion that the program should be expanded; it came to be realized, however, that it would be unwise even to continue it. Little justification could be found for duplicating specialized courses of the Georgia School of Technology. With the development of the University Center idea it was inevitable that engineering should be phased out, and this was accomplished with complete acceptance on the part of all those involved.

Journalism was discontinued in June 1953. Raymond B. Nixon '25, Director of the Division of Journalism, had resigned the previous year to accept a professorship at the University of Minnesota. The program in journalism had been developed by Professor Nixon, who had practical newspaper experience before coming to Emory. The program was a good one, with maximum emphasis upon background in history, economics, and political science, and with minimal, though adequate, training in techniques. It was nevertheless realized that to continue the program would be expensive, diverting funds needed elsewhere, with the inevitability of pressure for expansion. Moreover, at the University of Georgia was the Henry Grady School of Journalism, with large enrollment and a measure of national recognition. The decision to abandon journalism evoked vigorous protest both on and off campus, but the considered judgment of the administration stood.

Careful distinction must be made between vocational and pre-professional training. While it is true that for many years the specializations of Emory students tended to be concerned largely with prerequisites for admission to the professional schools, this tendency has been to a considerable degree modified, as it has been realized that generalization as well as specialization in his undergraduate studies makes for the rounded professional man. By this realization a better balance has been attained in student programs, as the admission of women to the College has resulted in a better balance between the areas of study.

When the move was made from Oxford, ten members of President Dickey's faculty transferred to the new campus: Clarence Eugene Boyd (Greek), Nolan A. Goodyear '04 (French), Edgar H. Johnson '91 (History and Political Economy), Wightman F. Melton (English), John B. Peebles (Applied Mathematics), Mansfield Theodore Peed (Pure Mathematics), Douglas Rumble '04 (Mathematics), John Gordon Stipe '07 (Spanish), Edward Kimbrough Turner (Latin), Goodrich C. White '08 (Mental and Moral Science). Five new appointments were made while the College lingered at Oxford: J. Samuel Guy (Chemistry), Christian Hamff (German), James Hinton '06 (English), Theodore H. Jack (History), Robert C. Rhodes (Biology). On the removal there were six additions: Malcolm H. Dewey (Romance Languages), James G. Lester '18 (Engineering), Ross H. McLean (History), J. Fred Messick (Mathematics), William S. Nelms (Physics), J. M. Steadman, Jr. (English).

These were the men who made the new curriculum, set the standards, and ensured the progressive policy of the College. They were good scholars, but throughout their academic careers they were to employ their talents in teaching almost to the exclusion of research and publication. That they were notable teachers will be borne witness to by their students, many of them high in the scholarly professions. And this was fortunate for Emory, for upon the base of sound personal teaching was built the future development of the University. In the early years a closer association between teacher and student was possible than in later times of swollen enrollments, but the tradition holds, and personal relationships remain a valuable feature of the educative experience at Emory.

Departments have been continuously strengthened and additions have been made to the offerings of the College as its focus has widened. In 1921 Ralph E. Wager came to organize the Department of Education, in which he was joined four years later by Sterling G. Brinkley '07. The projected School of Education never came into existence, but the Division of Teacher Education remains one of the most influential parts of the University. With the appointment in 1924 of Osborne R. Quayle to join Professor Guy, the Department of Chemistry began a development that was to bring it to early academic leadership. Professor Malcolm H. Dewey in 1927 left the Department of Romance Languages to found the Department of Fine Arts. In the same year Cullen B. Gosnell was brought to establish a Department of Political Science. The Department of Philosophy was reinvigorated in 1929 with the coming of Leroy E. Loemker. In 1938 the Department of Geology was installed under James G. Lester, who transferred from the Department of Engineering soon to be discontinued.

These data, obviously incomplete, will serve to illustrate the growth and diversification of the faculty of the College up to the turning point of the Centennial year. The growth has continued with acceleration. In 1945 four departments — biology, chemistry, English, history—were noted as far enough advanced in their organization to be permitted to make preparation for initiating programs of doctoral studies. But the undergraduate curriculum has not been overshadowed by the graduate curriculum. There has been a constant enrichment in all areas. The Department of English, for example, has augmented its courses in American literature. The Department of History has increased its offerings both in the American and modern European fields. Courses in anthropology have been added by the Department of Sociology. The divisional program in the humanities cuts across departmental lines.

It has not been a simple matter to build a staff of specialists who are not narrowly confined to their specialties and who are also stimulating classroom teachers. Yet it may confidently be stated that in 1965 the faculty is one of scholar-teachers unsurpassed in Emory's history. The roll is too long to be entered here, but it contains the names of several who have achieved national and international reputations in their fields and whose students are making reputations for themselves. Emory professors have been the recipients of Rosenwald, Guggenheim, Ford, Fulbright, and Dan-forth fellowships, with grants from numerous other foundations for travel and research at home and abroad.

As has been true of Southern institutions generally, the salary scale in the past has been well below the national norm. Heroic efforts have been made to improve the situation, and a much hap-pier state of affairs prevails now than in the 'thirties. Meanwhile there has been a liberal provision of fringe benefits. The faculty came under the protection of group life insurance in 1928. In 1937 retirement annuities were provided, at which time compulsory re-tirement was fixed at age sixty-eight. A number of programs against illness and accident are participated in by the faculty under the aegis of the University, the first of these, the Blue Cross hospitali-zation plan, installed in 1939. Members of the University have also been covered by Social Security since 1951. That the situation as regards compensation has been substantially improved is indi-cated by the fact that in these last years salaries for most ranks have moved up one place on the national rating scale of the Ameri-can Association of University Professors. It will be understood that these benefits are University-wide, and need not be specified in chapters dealing with other divisions.

For more than half of the life of the University, College class-rooms and offices centered in the Physics Building. At least a dozen departments have at one time and another shared its facilities, con-testing every inch of space with the Department of Physics. Tight schedules, however, have forced constant migration of classes in the Divisions of the Humanities and the Social Sciences, so that their departments have taught in half-a-dozen buildings on and off the Quadrangle. Office space has always been at a premium, and conference rooms have only lately been meagerly provided. The provision of large lecture rooms on the campus remains inadequate. This has seldom critically affected instruction, since Emory has sought to keep its sections small enough that the lecture-discussion plan of teaching was feasible. A service of audio-visual teaching aids has been developed under the direction of Albert F. Cox '39. Films and recordings are much in requisition by many departments, but unfortunately many classrooms are ill-adapted for their use.

Of the sciences, biology and geology for many years worked under the strictest space limitations. Securing their own buildings in 1951, they have since operated without the handicap that virtually forbade development. Chemistry has outgrown its quarters, and physics is in a really desperate situation in an era when that science holds a definite supremacy. The projected Science Center aims to accommodate the Departments of Chemistry, Physics, and Mathematics, together with the science library. With this facility all members of the division will be able to carry on both teaching and research under the most favorable conditions. Much has been accomplished in the past, but frequently with a wasteful expense of energy in adapting methods to available means. With the eventual occupation of both Physics and Chemistry Buildings by departments of the humanities and the social sciences the chief problems of space for these divisions will also be solved.

The Department of Fine Arts, now divided into the separate Department of the History of Art and the Department of Music, has been a nomad of the campus. Its courses have been popular with the students and its cultural influence has been highly regarded by faculty and administration, but it has not yet been given quarters specially adapted to its needs. The various extemporizations to which it has been subjected have not allowed the Department to make the impact that is felt generally desirable. The ultimate provision of a Fine Arts Center will add a new dimension to Emory's program of the liberal arts.

It has been repeatedly observed that Emory's entering freshmen are better prepared for advanced studies than in the past. This is indicated by higher scores on College Entrance Board tests, now required of all candidates for admission. As has been noted, the quality of work in secondary schools has greatly improved in recent years, and Emory has been able to make up its quotas for entrance from the highest ranking high school students. In the fall of 1964 a freshman class of 630 was selected from 2,800 applicants.

As a consequence of the improvement of preparation for college, it has been found possible to abandon many of the elementary courses formerly offered in freshman year. Particularly in English, mathematics, and the natural sciences first-year students now begin college study on higher levels than before. Higher levels of performance have validated this upgrading. In 1963-64 for the entire College student body only twenty-four were excluded permanently for academic failure. Approximately fifteen per cent of the College students made the Dean's List, which requires a minimum grade record of A, B, B. The "gentleman's C" of former times is no longer considered a desirable mark.

The record of student honors is a generally impressive one. The number of juniors and seniors eligible for Phi Beta Kappa has steadily risen. There is no difficulty in filling the quotas for Stipe Scholars, whose eligibility is based on academic promise for freshmen and continued performance for sophomores, juniors, and seniors. The Career Scholars program, begun in 1962, whose long-range objective is the promotion of careers in college teaching, selects about thirty-five students each year for individually planned honors-type studies. From 1945-46 to 1963-64 Emory students have secured thirty-seven Woodrow Wilson Fellowships, the highest number thus far allotted in the region. On the other hand, from 1918 to 1955 only eight Rhodes Scholars have been chosen from Emory.

A matter of special pride has been the effective working of the honor system, whose strength lies in the fact that it is self-imposed by the student body. Examinations are not monitored, and there is no need for extraordinary vigilance on the part of the instructor to prevent cheating. Violations of the code, of course, do occur, and instructors from time to time will discover cases of flagrant dishonesty. When evidence against a student is taken to the undergraduate Honor Council, it is weighed with judicious objectivity, and there is no hesitation in imposing penalties for established guilt. The basic policy, however, is one of prevention rather than of punishment. In Freshman Week, the indoctrination period for entering students, upperclassmen carefully explain the meaning of the honor system, and instructors are urged to inform their classes how it may specifically apply to their courses. The result has been a general relief of tensions and the promotion of mutual respect.

For many years rules prescribing unbroken class attendance were rigidly enforced, with lowered grades the penalty for unexcused absences. Gradually the rules were liberalized: first a limited number of free cuts were allowed; then, more recently, absences of juniors and seniors were not taken official cognizance of. Finally in 1962, rules of class attendance for all four years were abolished. There is not quite unanimity of opinion as to the wisdom of allowing this perfect freedom. It is argued with some justice that young people will not achieve maturity unless they are freed from the leading strings on which immaturity depends. On the other hand, it is observed that in the heedlessness and overconfidence of youth it is easy to underestimate the values of system and routine, frequently with unhappy results.

Students who have sought advice on academic or personal problems have seldom been disappointed in the attention they have received from members of the Emory faculty and administration. An open door for the puzzled and the troubled is one of the oldest and finest of their traditions. Personal counselling has, however, until quite recent years been on a purely informal basis. In 1959 with the aid of a foundation grant a formal system was set up by which freshmen were assigned to special advisers, who received extra remuneration for maintaining helpful relations with their charges. There are conflicting reports on the success of the venture.

Since World War II those "traditions," some of them having an antiquity of more than ten years, that were largely designed to keep freshmen in their place, have disappeared from the Quadrangle, though a few persist on Fraternity Row. It is hard to remember when the last "rat cap" was seen. Dooley's Frolics, a useful safety valve for pent-up energies, seem to have come to stay. Every spring the members of Kappa Alpha fraternity in the martial panoply of whiskers and Confederate uniforms proclaim that "the South will rise again." Sadie Hawkins Day presents a lively scramble between the sexes not unworthy of Dogpatch. Twice a year the campus is disfigured with election posters and banners whose tattered fragments may linger for weeks. If these things may be taken as evidence, then "college spirit" is certainly not dead at Emory, as is frequently charged.

[121]

But the Emory undergraduate does not conform to the Hollywood stereotype. In this day when courses do not depend solely on prescribed textbooks, students throng the library reading rooms, whose capacity is a constant anxiety of the Director of Libraries. They occupy every chair in the periodical alcove, and the Candler Library does not subscribe to *Playboy*. Musical interest has always been high on the campus, even if rock and roll and "folk singing" divide the students' allegiance. A score of extracurricular activities seriously pursued further the process of education, so that the Emory product is as well-rounded as any American institution can boast.

The School of
Business Administration

At the February 18, 1919, meeting of the Executive Committee of the Board of Trustees Dean Odum presented the following recommendation:

Public service to city, county, state and national governments; training for business methods in the operation of community industry, both private and public; training for social efficiency alongside financial development—these constitute one of the obligations of the University to its constituency. This is especially true at this time when the world of capital and labor need new and stabilizing relationships; and the public utilities need careful study and control. Emory ought to be specially fitted to render such a service by giving courses in economics, finance, business administration, corporations, railway problems, accounting, and other that may be necessary.

I recommend, therefore, that the Board authorize the beginning of a School of Business Administration and that Dr. E. H. Johnson be instructed to undertake further plans and organization. Dr. Johnson has already made plans to study the similar schools at both Harvard and Chicago this summer and will plan to spend all his vacation in this pursuit. I know, too, that Dr. Johnson is enthusiastic concerning this work, and that he has been wanted by other universities for similar work.

The School of Economics and Business Administration (the title was soon shortened) was organized in fall 1919 with Dr. Johnson as Dean. Its work was closely associated with that of the College, courses in economics, accounting, and business law, the three heads of its special curriculum, being added to the requirements of the first two years. The headquarters of the School were located in the Law Building, from which they were transferred in 1938 to Fishburne. At the beginning Dean Johnson had a single full-time assistant. In 1925-26 business courses were taught by a staff of five, there was an enrollment of 145 students, and the degree of Bachelor of Business Administration was conferred upon eight candidates. In 1939-40, after which Dr. Johnson retired from the deanship, the staff consisted of seven members, the enrollment stood at 133, and twenty-one students received the B.B.A.

From 1940 to 1942 Boyce F. Martin, former Assistant Dean of the Harvard Graduate School of Business Administration, served as Dean of Emory's division. On his resignation to become defense expediter for a private company, Robert C. Mizell stepped in as Acting Dean. The war years dealt hardly with the School of Business Administration, so that in 1943 its program was merged with that of the College, and Professor Albert Griffin was the only faculty member on the campus. It was obvious that its reorganization was called for in the postwar development of the University. A committee was appointed to survey the situation, and in 1945 George S. Craft '30, who had studied at the Harvard School of Business, was chosen to lay out a new program.

On his release from the Navy in 1946 Mr. Craft moved into the deanship and began at once the task of reorganization. It was his conviction that the work of the School should be broad in scope and liberal in philosophy, concerned with basic principles rather than with special techniques. This was in agreement with recommendations presented by President White in 1944 to the Board of Trustees and unanimously approved by them. Atlanta businessmen had also been asked to make suggestions, many of which were included in the final plans.

Through the generosity of Walter H. Rich, President of Atlanta's Rich Foundation, Emory in 1945 had received $250,000 for the erection of a building for the School of Business Administration, as a memorial to the three brothers, Morris, Daniel, and Emanuel Rich, who in 1867 had founded what was to become a great modern department store. The Foundation also pledged continuing support of an expanded program, to consist of $10,000 a year for ten years. The Rich Memorial Building, situated on Mizell Drive, was occupied in October 1947, and was formally dedicated "to the development of Southern leadership in the field of business" on November 10, 1949.

Dean Craft reëstablished the school with a two-year upper division curriculum, completion of work in the lower division of the College or its equivalent being required for admission. He recruited a strong staff, and when the new program was fully operational, resigned in January 1948 to accept a senior vice-presidency with the Trust Company of Georgia, with which he had a previous connection.

He was succeeded by Gordon Siefkin, Chairman of the Department of Economics. At the suggestion of the National Committee for Economic Development and aided by a grant from the C. E. D., a Business Executives Research Committee of young business leaders of the Atlanta area was formed in March 1948 to begin a long-range survey of the South's business problems and opportunities. An intensive study was projected of the relations between business, industry, and agriculture. Professor John H. Goff was appointed full-time research adviser. *Studies in Business and Economics* was inaugurated in 1949 with the publication of *Problems in Forest Development and Conservation,* prepared by the Committee. Nine titles appeared in the series. The final report, *A Look at Georgia Manufacturing Industries,* was written by Professor Alan L. Ritter, who was named Research Adviser when the Committee was reactivated in 1956. As a result of the success of the project in Atlanta, the Committee for Economic Development constituted other such committees in major cities throughout the nation, with educational institutions as sponsors.

Research activity at Emory was spurred by numerous requests from business firms, associations, and agencies to conduct special investigations, and a Division of Research was set up to administer the grants by which they were carried on.

Reorganization was rewarded with national recognition. Emory's School of Business Administration was admitted to the American Association of Collegiate Schools of Business in 1949, the only one of fourteen petitioning schools awarded full membership in that year. In January 1950 a chapter of Beta Gamma Sigma, national scholastic honor society in business and commerce, was installed. In 1952 the School was elected an institutional member of the American Management Association. It was already on the approved list of the New York State Board of C. P. A. Examiners. The student body was alert to its opportunities. In 1950 it formed a chapter of the Society for the Advancement of Management, and a Student Marketing Club, which planned and carried out a clinic on market research. Liaison established with Atlanta executives brought the students into direct contact with the current organization and conduct of business in the area. The Business School Alumni Association of Greater Atlanta was organized in 1952 under the presidency of S. Russell Bridges, Jr. '33B.

In 1947-48 enrollment rose to 276, falling off to 117 in 1951-52, partly as a result of the Korean War but largely because the theoretical and non-vocational aim of the curriculum was failing to attract undergraduates, and never since reaching the higher figure. Meanwhile plans had matured for adding a graduate program leading to the degree of Master of Arts in Business Administration. This was initiated in fall 1954 with nineteen students registered. "Its aim is to acquaint the student with the theory, the principles and the technique of analysis, organization, planning and control common to all business. It does not pretend to be a complete substitute for training in specific routine tasks which can best be acquired in business itself." When the American Association of Collegiate Schools of Business began accrediting master's programs in 1961, Emory's M.B.A. was in the first group approved. Its success in attracting increased numbers of students and in placing graduates in key business positions across the nation has encouraged the School to move toward a fuller development of its graduate curriculum. The Emory Board of Trustees in November 1964 authorized a change of name to the Graduate School of Business Administration.

The W. K. Kellogg Foundation in 1955 made a grant of $130,000 to set up a program for training hospital administrators, to continue for four years from 1956. An M. B. A. course in hospital administration was offered until the expiration of the grant in 1960.

In September 1958 Gordon Siefkin resigned the deanship because of failing health, and Professor John H. Goff was appointed Acting Dean. Choice of a successor fell on Guy W. Trump, Dean of the U. S. Merchant Marine Academy, Kings Point, New York, who took office in Fall Quarter 1959. On his resignation after six years Professor James M. Hund was named Dean.

On invitation of the Associated Industries of Georgia, the School in 1959 conducted its first A. I. G. Advanced Management Program for executives in the upper brackets. Held annually at Sea Island, Georgia, and continuing for six weeks, it has achieved the reputation of being one of the best of its kind in the nation. In addition, Emory has more lately offered semi-annual two-weeks Middle Management Conferences, concentrated on developing more specialized business skills. In the area of community service the School of Business Administration has been host to various conferences and professional meetings, such as World Trade Clinics, the Georgia Bankers Study Conference, the Credit Union Institute, and numerous others. In the spring of 1962 an Advisory Committee on Business Community Relations was organized, with Marcus Bartlett '39, General Manager of WSB-TV, as Chairman.

In 1959 two reports were published describing the state of business education in the United States. In an effort to improve the quality of the nation's business schools, the Ford Foundation sponsored a survey by Robert Aaron Gordon and James Edwin Howell. After visits to many institutions, including Emory, they wrote *Higher Education for Business* (Columbia University Press), setting forth their findings. The Carnegie Corporation of New York sponsored Frank C. Pierson, who made an intensive study of university and college programs in business administration, resulting in a critical analysis entitled *The Education of American Businessmen* (McGraw-Hill Book Company). This report revealed great weaknesses in many programs, but gave due credit to those schools that were high in quality. Emory came out well, being specifically cited as a good example in several places in the book. What Pierson most commended in Emory's School of Business was its policy of requiring a broad liberal arts basis for its degree candidates, and for "giving more explicit attention to the contributions which humanists, scientists, and social scientists can make to the solution of business problems."

Besides a busy routine of teaching, conferring, and counseling, the staff of the School of Business Administration has carried on an active program of research. The range of its interests may be indicated by a random selection of book titles with their authors:

Joseph Airov '49B, '53G, *The Location of the Synthetic-Fiber Industry* (Technology Press of the Massachusetts Institute of Technology, 1959); Frank J. Charvat, *Supermarketing* (Macmillan, 1961); Charles Sidney Cottle and W. Tate Whitman, *Investment Timing, the Formula Plan Approach* (McGraw-Hill, 1953); Arthur T. Dietz, *An Introduction to the Antitrust Laws* (Bookman Associates, 1951); Harold L. Johnson, *The Christian as a Businessman* (Association Press, 1964).

The Graduate School of Arts and Sciences

CHANCELLOR GOODRICH C. WHITE, who during his presidency took the leading rôle in the development of the Graduate School, has described the changes wrought in the pattern of Emory life and spirit:

Until the mid-forties and later the general atmosphere of the campus was that of a good undergraduate college for men, as distinguished from that of a "real university." The professional schools conducted their programs with little if any tie-in with the faculty of the College and its work, except as students entered the professional schools after finishing in the College requirements for admission. It was not until the beginning of advanced graduate work leading to the Ph.D. degree that a university atmosphere began to pervade the campus. This involved, of course, an increasing interest in and emphasis upon research. The most significant aspect of the University's development from 1950 on has, therefore, been the development of the Graduate School. This has affected and involved all the professional school faculties, so that throughout the University there is an emphasis upon research activity as well as upon teaching, the emphasis that distinguishes the university from the independent undergraduate college.

At times concern has been expressed that this emphasis on research would minimize the importance of good teaching, that the college especially would suffer. Testimony to the contrary can, however, be mustered. If undergraduate teaching and undergraduate life do not quite dominate the scene as they did in earlier years of the University, this would in part be accounted for by growth in size, by new pressures for academic excellence, and by deëmphasis of college antics—a new seriousness in undergraduate student bodies—as well as by the emphasis upon research incident to the graduate school development.

There can be no doubt, however, that the pattern of Emory life, both for faculty and students, has greatly changed since the late 'forties. Once the veterans' rush was over, Emory advanced steadily toward the attainment of its goal of becoming a "real university." It cannot be denied that this has involved the loss of some values that inhere in the intimacy of the independent liberal arts college and the concentration upon teaching undergraduates. The faculty has grown in size so that not everybody knows everybody else. Counseling of students has to be organized and systematized; spontaneous friendly contact between students and instructors is no longer the rule. Faculty people are more apt to be career men, with devotion to ideals of specialized scholarship rivalling the devotion to Emory which was so characteristic of the faculty of earlier years.

All this means that Emory has attained in large measure the university status that has been deliberately set as a goal, and that it has had to sacrifice some of the values that have been a part of the heritage from earlier and simpler days.

When the Graduate School was organized in 1919 under Dean Theodore H. Jack, the only degrees to be conferred were the Master of Arts and the Master of Science. Requirements were rigorous: three quarters of residence, eight courses, a written thesis, oral and written examinations. A reading knowledge of one or more foreign languages was at first strongly recommended and later prescribed. In time the course requirement was somewhat relaxed, but it was not intended that the degree should be a sinecure, and there were few who earned it in the minimum period. Students who went on for the Doctor of Philosophy degree at other universities found that their Emory training had placed them in a position of advantage.

In 1941-42 the Master of Arts in Teaching degree was offered for the benefit of graduate students who were teachers in secondary schools or who contemplated entering that field of service. The candidate's program was under the joint direction of a subject-matter department and the Department of Education, with work shared equally with both. No thesis was required, but minimum residence was extended to four quarters rather than three. The purpose of the course was to prepare teachers who were both well-grounded in a subject matter and equipped with the techniques of teaching. An M.A.T. internship program was instituted in 1963 with a Ford Foundation grant of $525,000. To enroll in the program it is necessary for the student to contract for one semester's salaried employment as an intern in one of the coöperating public school systems.

In the deanship of Goodrich C. White, 1929-42, the goal of Graduate School development was constantly in view. This was to be Emory's specific contribution to the University Center, projected in 1938. A start was made with a vigorous effort to strengthen library collections, primarily achieved by grants from the Lewis H. Beck Foundation, beginning in 1937 and continuing to the present. The Union Catalogue of Books in the Atlanta-Athens area was established in 1939 as a tool for research by a General Education Board subvention. When Dr. White was elevated to the presidency of the University, his work was carried on by J. Harris Purks, Acting Dean 1942-46, though in the midst of the war years there could be little decisive planning.

Nevertheless, in the *Report of the President to the Board of Trustees,* December 1, 1944, Dr. White wrote:

There has been talk for a dozen years of offering the Ph.D. degree. I am glad that we have up to the present refused to do so. Our answer has uniformly been: "We hope that we can—someday. We shall not do it except under conditions that will insure its quality and its recognition." I believe the time is near when those conditions can be met and we can offer the advanced degree in a limited number of fields: biology, chemistry, English, history, to begin with.

Early in 1945 Dr. Dumas Malone '10, '36H, Professor of History, Columbia University, was called in as a special adviser on the plans and programs of the Graduate School. After several visits and extensive rounds of conferences he submitted a report on July 31, in which he commended progress already made and encouraged extension of the program:

I am convinced that a vital graduate school can be developed at Emory in the near future and that in the course of time it can become strong. This is not to say that at the present moment either the facilities or the personnel are sufficient for the performance of a greatly increased function . . . .

On the other hand, it seems to me unquestionable that Emory now possesses the nucleus and the prime essentials for the development of a first-class graduate school.

Dr. Malone specifically recommended that the beginning of doctor's work should be in chemistry and biology, on a strictly limited and selective basis. On October 16 the Board of Trustees authorized the offering of a program leading to the degree of Doctor of Philosophy by those departments which might be found adequately staffed and equipped.

The Atlanta Area Teacher Education Service has been an extraordinarily successful project of the University Center plan. Organized in 1945 as a coöperative arrangement between Emory University, the University of Georgia, and the public school systems of Atlanta, Decatur, Fulton County, and Marietta, it has enabled thousands of teachers to take postgraduate courses on an in-service schedule. The AATES program is administered by an Executive Committee and the Office of the Coördinator, the latter maintained on the Emory campus, in 1965 under the direction of Professor Lynn F. Shufelt. Although it is a division of the Graduate School, it is not possible for its enrollees to satisfy all the requirements for a degree by taking courses in the program. Its work, however, is recognized by the State Department of Education as a major service for the improvement of teaching.

In 1946 Leroy E. Loemker, Professor of Philosophy, was appointed Dean of the Graduate School, and in monthly meetings a committee of his appointment sought solutions for problems arising in connection with the expansion of graduate studies. The Department of Chemistry was first given permission to extend its program, followed by the Department of Biochemistry. The first blue and gold doctor's hood was placed around the shoulders of Thomas P. Johnston '40, '41G, at the June Commencement of 1948. In 1949 anatomy, biology, English, and history were permitted to begin doctoral work, and psychology was included in 1951. On the resignation of Dean Loemker and after a brief interregnum, in 1952 Howard M. Phillips, Professor of Biology, became Dean.

The new program of development launched in October 1951 was particularly aimed at undergirding the Graduate School. Following a conditional grant of $7,000,000 by the General Education Board a five-year campaign was waged to secure matching gifts. While the disappointing discovery was made that it was impossible at that time to create much enthusiasm for the promotion of

Charles Howard Candler
Chairman Board of Trustees
1929-57

Henry Lumpkin Bowden
Chairman Board of Trustees
1957-

Methodist Bishops at Consecration of Bishops Hall, 1957

Vice-President Barkley Returns to Oxford, 1949

Robert W. Woodruff
Benefactor

October 1964 Meeting of Board of Trustees

Inauguration of President Atwood, November 15, 1963

higher studies in the fields of the liberal arts and sciences, nevertheless something more than $6,000,000 was added to the endowment in support of graduate education.

The Graduate Institute of the Liberal Arts was established in fall 1952 by Dean of the Faculties Ernest C. Colwell, who served as Director until 1957. Dr. George P. Cuttino, Department of History, was appointed Secretary of the Institute. Its program combined the disciplines of liberal learning by pooling the scholarly resources of the University, chiefly in the humanities and social sciences, in a broad examination of the issues in which all specializations are concerned. Its basic staff is complemented with members drawn from several departments, who take part in seminar discussions dealing with general topics of wide importance in Western civilization. When the student's special interests are determined, by formal courses and tutorial conferences he carries on individual studies leading to the presentation of a doctor's dissertation and the passing of an oral examination defending his thesis. Since 1960 the Institute has offered a program in comparative literature for both the doctor's and master's degree, and since 1962 a program of American studies in both, but the M. A. is not intended to be terminal. The interdisciplinary nature of the programs is fully maintained.

On Dr. Colwell's resignation from Emory, Professor William A. Beardslee, Department of Bible and Religion, assumed the directorship from 1957 to 1961, succeeded in turn by Professor James M. Smith, Department of Romance Languages. In 1958 a grant of $96,000 was received from the Carnegie Corporation, to be paid in three equal installments for the maintenance of the Institute. In 1962 a series of seminar presentations by members of the staff was published by Prentice-Hall under the title of *Truth, Myth and Symbol*.

The Ph.D. program has continued to expand. In 1953 it was extended to the Division of Basic Sciences in the Health Services, subsuming the earlier included Departments of Anatomy and Biochemistry. For the Division two years later the J. M. Tull Foundation of Atlanta provided a fellowship fund of $100,000. The Departments of Philosophy and Political Science in 1956, the Departments of Sociology-Anthropology and Religion in 1958 moved into the field of doctoral studies. In 1963 a biometry program was instituted, operating on a training grant from the National Institutes of Health. The latest addition, 1964, was the Department of Mathematics. The Doctor of Philosophy degree is now offered to majors in seventeen disciplines.

In 1957 Charles T. Lester '32, '34G, Professor of Chemistry, became Dean of the Graduate School. At the June 1959 Commencement the one-hundredth Ph.D. was conferred. The two-hundredth Ph.D. was conferred only four years later. Beginning in 1959, fellowship grants were awarded under the National Defense Education Act, Title 4. The intent of the Act was to increase the nation's supply of college teachers, and funds were made available to maintain candidates through a three-years course of study and to assist institutions to support the programs in which they were enrolled. The programs for which Emory received grants were Old Testament, philosophy, chemistry, English (American and Victorian literature), history, comparative literature, sociology, political science, and mathematics, in every field the offerings to extend beyond those already provided.

At the organization in 1960 of the Council of Graduate Schools in the United States Emory became a charter member. The Council, with a membership of approximately 250 institutions, works for the establishment of high standards in graduate education and serves as a consultative body for agencies of the United States government.

In 1965 the Graduate School offered the following degrees: Master of Arts, with majors in twenty-three subjects; Master of Science, with majors in eleven subjects; Master of Arts in Teaching, with majors in eight subjects; Master of Education; Master of Librarianship; Doctor of Philosophy, in seventeen fields of specialization.

A fundamental problem of today's graduate school is to provide adequate fellowships, scholarships, and other grants-in-aid. It is realized that it is greatly disadvantageous for a teacher to enter upon his professional career with a burden of debt. As a matter of fact, this has in the past discouraged many well-qualified individuals from pursuing formal scholarship. This has more recently been compensated for to some extent by the demand for holders of the higher degrees, not only in teaching, but in business and industry, which offer more attractive remuneration and more rapid promotion. Nevertheless, with constantly rising costs of education, there are large numbers of young people who must have financial assistance if they are to proceed with graduate studies.

Competition is keen among American universities for the most talented college graduates, and every effort has been made to secure endowments and special subventions to attract those whose undergraduate records promise scholarly fulfillment. The cost of graduate teaching is high, and if it is not expended on good human material, the outlay is wasted. Emory, therefore, from the inception of its Ph.D. program has sought by all means to provide scholarship funds that would enable it to stand on even ground with its academic competitors. It has not yet achieved complete success, but the quality of its candidates has risen steadily, and among the holders of its advanced degrees are many who are making their mark in the intellectual world.

The faculty of the Graduate School is composed of those instructors who regularly teach graduate courses, but there are no instructors whose teaching is solely in the graduate curriculum. Instruction in the College and professional schools and the Graduate School is therefore kept closely related, since there is no body of faculty scholars who do not teach either undergraduate or professional school courses. No member of the faculty devotes his full time to research. Research and classroom teaching are functions shared by all.

The Emory University faculty does not live under the threat of "Publish or perish," but with the development of the Graduate School individual research and publication of its results have been immensely stimulated. A faculty of the highest calibre not only works with books but makes them too. It may be admitted that a candidate for an Emory appointment who has publication to his credit, other things being equal, is more likely to be accepted than one who has not published or who does not show promise of publishing. Furthermore, the University makes provision for allowing its members free time in which to carry on study and research, including leaves of absence. This frequently entails shifting of course schedules and even bringing in a visiting instructor to fill the place of the absentee. Limited funds are budgeted for the support of research and to subsidize publication, and Emory scholars are encouraged to apply to the national foundations for grants-in-aid.

This enlightened policy has yielded rather imposing results, especially when it is noted that the Emory faculty is probably younger than most. In the past twenty years something in the neighborhood of 150 titles in a wide range of subjects have been authored and edited by members of the faculty. It would be difficult to ascertain the very much greater numbers of journal contributions that have appeared in the same period. A considerable amount of the research of graduate students also has taken form in books and articles. While a large part of this writing has been severely technical, a good portion has been directed to a larger public than that of specialists in the fields of academic learning. Contributions to the *Emory University Quarterly* demonstrate the ability of our scholars to present their knowledge in an attractive dress.

Besides textbooks in almost every subject of the curricula of the University which have secured wide adoption, Emory authors have written both for the specialist and the general reader. An almost random selection of a dozen titles will give some idea of the range of subject matter represented in a constantly growing bibliography: *Thomas Jefferson: Scientist,* by Edwin T. Martin; *Poland 1914-1962,* by Richard F. Staar; *The Road to Appomattox,* by Bell Irvin Wiley; *The Toadstool Millionaires,* by James Harvey Young; *Comintern and World Revolution,* by Kermit E. McKenzie; *Leibniz's Philosophical Papers and Letters,* translated by Leroy E. Loemker; *Estates General in Renaissance France,* by J. Russell Major; *The Spiritual Gospel,* by Wyatt Aiken Smart; *Confederate Music,* by Richard Barksdale Harwell; *The Administration of the College Library,* by Guy R. Lyle; *Journeys after St. Paul,* by William Ragsdale Cannon; *Thomas Wolfe's Characters,* by Floyd C. Watkins.

The function of a graduate school is to propagate sound learning in the public service. To this end Emory University has bent its energies. Teaching and conferring, study and writing have been given equal place in the academic routine. There is good evidence that Professor Dumas Malone's prediction that "a vital graduate school can be developed at Emory" is being fulfilled.

The Candler School of Theology

THE IMMEDIATE NEED of an official seminary to educate ministers for the Methodist Episcopal Church, South, brought about the paradoxical situation that the School of Theology was actually in operation before a charter had been granted the new university. The Educational Commission created in Oklahoma City in May 1914 had been instructed by the General Conference "to provide at the earliest possible time for a Biblical School or Department of Theology." How the project developed in subsequent meetings of the Commission in Birmingham in June and in Atlanta in July of the same year has already been related.

At the Birmingham meeting a committee consisting of Bishop Warren A. Candler, Bishop W. B. Murrah, and Dr. Plato T. Durham was given the responsibility of getting a theological seminary in operation by October 1, three months distant. The task was somewhat simplified by the possibility of using the large plant of Wesley Memorial Church in midtown Atlanta, which had space for classrooms, offices, and dormitories for unmarried students, and was already provided with a dining room and kitchen, even a small gymnasium. Two houses adjoining the church furnished additional living quarters for married students. Hugh H. Harris, who since 1912 had directed the community activities of Wesley Memorial, was called back from his summer vacation to ready the plant for the reception of the new school of theology. The availability of Wesley Memorial was one factor, a lesser factor to be sure, in the choice of Atlanta for the seat of the new university.

Bishop Candler was naturally the leader in the exigent task of recruiting a seminary faculty. Dr. Durham was named Dean, and he was soon joined by six other outstanding figures of the Church. The first faculty with their original assignments was as follows: Plato T. Durham, Dean and Professor of Church History; Hugh H. Harris, Professor of Religious Education and Acting Professor of Sociology; Harry C. Howard, Professor of Systematic Theology; William A. Shelton, Professor of Hebrew and Old Testament; Andrew Sledd, Professor of Greek and New Testament;

Wyatt Aiken Smart, Professor of Biblical Theology; Walter J. Young, Professor of Homiletics and Pastoral Theology. In the second year of operation Professor Howard was transferred to homiletics, Professor Young was given the newly established Department of Missions, and an eighth member, Franklin Nutting Parker '51H, was named to the chair of systematic theology.

This was a strong faculty, in spite of the fact that only three of them—Durham, Shelton, and Sledd—could be considered academics, and only Sledd was a regular scholar. In a reminiscential essay in the *Emory Alumnus* for October 1957 Dr. Smart states a more general qualification:

> The others were well-educated men but not specialists, and they were chosen largely for their professional attainments as ministers. In the main they were successful preachers, chosen to teach young men how to become successful preachers. . . . It was, on the whole, a group of men calculated to inspire confidence among those interested in the ministry of the Methodist Church. And they worked together for 15 years before death made the first break in their ranks.

Nevertheless, a controversy over the "higher criticism" affecting the interpretation of the Bible was raging fiercely at this time, and even before classes began in the new school, the faculty came under fire from certain quarters. For some years charges of heresy were to be launched at members of the faculty, and there was even a threat to bring Bishop Candler to trial for his support of heretics. Himself a theological conservative, the Bishop was distinguished by his possession of a strong common-sense judgment. He was not by temperament a tolerant person, but paradoxically he had learned to practice toleration. And so, even though not infrequently in disagreement with what they taught, he stood as a shield and defender between the professors and the forces of intolerance within the Church that all tried to serve according to their lights.

The inevitable choice of a name for the seminary, the Candler School of Theology, was decided on in February 1915. A bronze bust of the Bishop by George Thomas Brewster, presented by the Emory College Class of 1893, was unveiled in the lobby of Theology Building on May 8, 1918. The move from Wesley Memorial to the just completed building on the raw new University campus had been made in fall 1916. Students were quartered in Dobbs Hall and took their meals in the dining room on the ground floor of Winship. With their arrival and the organization of the Lamar School of Law across the Quadrangle, Emory University was now on location.

Dr. Durham resigned the deanship in fall 1918 and Dr. Parker succeeded him on January 1, 1919. Some faculty changes were made necessary in the following years by resignations and deaths. Among the new appointees were two alumni of the School who have become veterans of the faculty: Boone M. Bowen '24T coming as Professor of Old Testament in 1930, and Arva C. Floyd '23, '24T, chosen as Acting Professor of Missions in 1934. Following the death of Dr. Durham in 1930 the beautiful little chapel in Theology Building which he had loved was dedicated to his memory.

In 1920 the Egyptian-Babylonian Museum was founded by a gift of Mr. John Manget. The original collections were gathered by Professor Shelton, who was with the American Scientific Expedition of that year. Among his acquisitions were Egyptian mummies and coffins, bronzes dating back to 1500 B.C., scarabs, amulets, and other objects, including earthenware jars from prehistoric times. From Babylonia-Assyria came cuneiform tablets, a brick inscribed with the name of Nebuchadnezzar II, conquerer of Jerusalem, a great roll of the Pentateuch from Nineveh written on 200 sheepskins, and a rare barrel cylinder of Nabopolassar from the royal palace at Babylon. To these were added a number of casts, among them the black obelisk of Shalmanezar, recording his victory over Israel, and the Rosetta Stone from the British Museum, the Code of Hammurabi and the Moabite Stone from the Louvre. Originally located on the first floor of Theology Building, the Museum has had a number of removes. The collections have been greatly expanded, with additions of a miscellaneous nature, including American ethnology and natural history. Most recently valuable additions have been made by the participation of the School of Theology through Professor Bowen and Professor Ben-Dor in archaeological expeditions to Israel. The University Museum under the directorship of Professor W. B. Baker is now located on the ground floor of Bishops Hall.

The course of study covered three years, or nine quarters, leading to the degree of Bachelor of Divinity or a certificate. Requirements for the B.D. included a college degree for entrance, courses in the original languages of the Bible, Hebrew and Greek (both languages until 1924, one only until 1931), a thesis, and an oral examination. Students without a college degree might obtain the certificate without the special requirements. Since 1931 Hebrew and Greek have been optional courses. For several years candidates for the degree were outnumbered by those seeking the certificate only. In 1924-25 with ninety-nine students registered, only fourteen received degrees. There was, however, a constant pressure to raise the standards of the School, this depending ultimately upon the Church setting higher academic requirements for entry into the annual conference. Dean Parker was especially active in the successful movement to bring this about. After 1934-35 the certificate was no longer offered, although provision was made for the admission of lay workers as special students.

The Candler School was active in all affairs of the Methodist Church, South, and the members of its faculty were recognized as leaders. In 1918 Dean Parker had been elected to the episcopacy, an office which he declined in order to continue in the field of education. On a later occasion he would not allow his friends to put him in nomination with election again certain. On the other hand, William T. Watkins '16, '39H, Professor of Church History, accepted election at the General Conference of 1938. It would be difficult to list the calls made upon the faculty for special services, lecture series, institutes, and the like. In the quadrennium 1934-38 Emory supplied leaders for ninety institutes, serving approximately 2,000 preachers.

The first Ministers Week was held in Winter Quarter 1935 in conjunction with Religious Emphasis Week, Dr. Lynn Harold Hough, Dean of Drew Theological Seminary, delivering the Sam P. Jones Lectures on Evangelism. Ministers Week has since been held annually without interruption, bringing religious leaders of international reputation as speakers on the endowed lectureships.

The first series of Sam Jones Lectures, founded by the family of the famous Georgia evangelist, was delivered in 1925. The Quillian Lectureship had been established at Emory College in 1897. Later foundations are the William Wallace Duncan and A. J. Jarrell Lectureships. After delivery the greater number of these lectures have had book publication. Ministers Week annually brings a large attendance of the clergy of the Southeast to the Emory campus, for whom a full program of professional and social occasions is arranged.

In 1937, Dr. Henry Burton Trimble, Professor of Homiletics since 1931, was appointed Dean, succeeding Dr. Parker, who had held the deanship for eighteen years. Dr. Trimble was one of those who led the Church, beginning in 1944, to make ministerial education one of the specified objectives for which funds were raised and allocated through the World Service Commission, a practice which soon produced a substantial annual grant for current operations of the Candler School of Theology. His policy of recruiting promising young scholars for the faculty was within a few years to make possible the extension of theological studies to the higher graduate degrees.

Five members of Emory University—President Cox, Dean Trimble, Dean Emeritus Parker, Dr. Smart, and Dr. John D. Lee, Assistant Professor of Church History—were present at the historic Unification Conference, held in Kansas City, Missouri, in May 1939. The Conference brought together again in one body under the name of The Methodist Church the elements of former divisions: the Methodist Episcopal Church (the Northern body), the Methodist Episcopal Church, South, separated in 1844 over the slavery issue involving Bishop J. O. Andrew, President of the Board of Trustees of Emory College, and the Methodist Protestant Church, separated on the issue of lay representation in 1828. The Declaration of Union was unanimously adopted on May 10. Bishop Candler, retired from office in the Southern Church in 1934, who had been an implacable and successful opponent of unification, accepted without approving the action. He is reported to have said: "Well it's done now, and I intend to go on loving my Church. I won't be here long. I'll be in heaven anyway before Unification gets to working good."

In 1939-40 there is noted an increasing emphasis on field work. Under the direction of Emmett S. Johnson guidance was given students in actual experience of a large variety of religious activities. The present Director of Field Education is G. Ross Freeman, who also serves as Assistant to the Dean.

In connection with the University's campaign for endowment, the clergy of the Southeastern Jurisdiction in 1940 sponsored a Parker Recognition Fund of $100,000. The intervention of World War II delayed collections, but on completion of the capital sum the Franklin N. Parker Chair of Systematic Theology was established, with Mack B. Stokes, a member of the faculty since 1941, named its first occupant in 1953. Since 1955 Professor Stokes has also served as Associate Dean.

Enrollments in the School of Theology held up well in the war years. In addition to regular work, the School carried on a Navy training program for chaplains. The first postwar year produced a staggering registration of 367 students, to be accommodated by facilities that had already been taxed by rather less than half that number. In 1945 also the Board of Trustees authorized an extension of theological studies for the degrees of Master of Religious Education and Master of Theology. The Doctor of Philosophy degree has been offered since 1958 in various fields of the Division of Religion of the Graduate School.

The Board of Missions in 1930 had provided 100 scholarships of $50 each to enable pastors in rural and industrial communities to attend a six-weeks summer course at Emory. In 1945 the first continuing summer short course was inaugurated, originally known as the Town and Country School, now renamed the Church and Community Workshop. In 1946 began the Approved Course of Study School for supply pastors, and the Workshop in Christian Education. Other short schools and workshops have been offered from time to time, the latest being the Seminar in Television Preaching, added in 1958 in coöperation with the Protestant Radio and Television Center. A Workshop in Pastoral Care employing video tape was held in the summer of 1965.

Ruel B. Gilbert Hall on Pierce Drive at Oxford Road, built with funds collected from Methodist sources and named for a generous donor, was occupied in 1948, furnishing forty-eight units for married students. In 1951 Wesley Hall, on Arkwright Drive near the railroad station, provided much needed quarters for unmarried men.

On the retirement of Dean Trimble in 1953, Dr. William Ragsdale Cannon was named to succeed him. In the following year Dean Emeritus Trimble was appointed Associate Director of Development for Church Affairs.

A progressive move at this time was the organization of the Committee of One Hundred, a group of Methodist laymen of the Southeastern Jurisdiction whose function is to maintain liaison between Emory University and the Church. The Committee was activated on the Emory campus on November 10, 1954. In 1955 the Committee established the Methodist Fund for Ministerial Education to provide essential financing for the Candler School of Theology, and sponsored the 1% Plan to secure continuing support for this fund from the churches of the Southeastern Jurisdiction. At first a voluntary project promoted largely by laymen, in 1960-61 the Plan produced a peak income of $71,191 under the leadership of E. D. Whisonant, Assistant Director of Development. The 1% Plan proved so acceptable and effective that in 1960 the Jurisdiction took it over, with half its income allocated to the seminaries at Emory and Duke on the basis of enrollments, and half retained by the Annual Conference for grants-in-aid to ministerial students. The realization of the ever-increasing need for educated pastors and the inability of young people to finance extended schooling has brought a gratifying response from the churches of the region. Since July 1963 the Reverend Charles A. Jackson '23 has carried on Emory's fund-raising work with the Methodist constituency.

Among interdenominational activities in which Emory University and the School of Theology are involved may be mentioned the establishment in 1953 of reciprocity with Columbia Theological Seminary, the Presbyterian institution in nearby Decatur. The agreement permits exchanges of both students and professors. Emory, representing the Methodist Church, joined with the Episcopal, United Lutheran, Presbyterian U. S., and Presbyterian U. S. A. Churches in founding the Protestant Radio and Television

Center on Clifton Road adjoining the campus. The Center was dedicated on January 16, 1955, in connection with the fourteenth annual Ministers Week. Members of the faculty of the School participate in numberless national and international conventions, institutes, and religious assemblies. Of special interest was Dean Cannon's appointment by the Methodist Church as one of its forty delegates to the third Assembly of the World Council of Churches in New Delhi in 1961, and his appointment by the World Methodist Council as one of its seven official observers at the third and fourth sessions of the Second Vatican Council in Rome in 1964 and 1965.

The International Greek New Testament Project, transferred from the University of Chicago, was installed at Emory in 1955 with Dr. Merrill M. Parvis as Director. Collation of extant versions of the Gospels has occupied the staff for the past ten years, and a specimen of the Gospel according to Luke for the examination and criticism of the international committee has been printed by the Oxford University Press.

In 1956 Mrs. Genevieve S. Shatford pledged $250,000 to establish the Almar H. Shatford Chair of Homiletics in memory of her late husband. The first Shatford Professor was A. Wilburn Beasley '23, '28G.

The construction of Bishops Hall across Kilgo Circle from the Old Theology Building at length relieved the overcrowding that had long hampered the work of the School, and permitted its expansion in various areas. A certain amount of remodeling of the former building was also accomplished. Funds for both projects were provided by the Church. Bishops Hall was consecrated on September 20, 1957. A convocation was held at which Dean Emeritus Luther A. Weigle of the Yale Divinity School was the speaker, and at which eight bishops of the Jurisdiction received the honorary degree of Doctor of Divinity, thus completing adoption by the University of all eleven heads of the Church in the area. Dedication ceremonies for the building were held eight years later, on January 21, 1965.

Besides a generous complement of classrooms and offices, Bishops Hall contains, on the main floor, a parlor furnished by friends of Bishop Roy Hunter Short '57H, the Bowden conference room, a memorial to the Reverend John M. Bowden of the North Georgia Conference provided by gifts of the family, the Moore conference room, furnished by friends of Bishop Arthur J. Moore '14, '34H, and a small meditation chapel furnished by Dean Cannon in memory of his mother. The auditorium on the top floor was designed by Professor Jordan for the special needs of the Department of Homiletics, including radio preaching.

The entire first floor of Theology Building exclusive of Durham Chapel was renovated for library use, and a range of offices was provided on the ground floor below the chapel. Much of the upper floor is now devoted to seminar rooms: the Barnett Memorial, dedicated to the late Professor Albert Edward Barnett '16, as a New Testament seminar room, and the Garber Suite, furnished by friends of Bishop Paul N. Garber '57H, for the sociology of religion. Here also is the Nolan B. Harmon Suite, furnished by friends of Bishop Harmon '19T, '57H, for the use of the International Greek New Testament Project. Extensive renovation of the Building, including reconditioning of the ground floor library stacks with a gift from the John L. and Mary Franklin Foundation, and the installation of air conditioning, was completed in the summer of 1965. The handsome pine-paneled room off the foyer was refinished and rearranged for the shelving and display of Emory's notable Wesleyana collection.

The School of Theology joined the observance of its semicentennial with the thirtieth annual Ministers Week on January 20-23, 1964. A large attendance daily filling Glenn Memorial heard a distinguished group of speakers on the general theme, "The Challenge of Contemporary Civilization to the Church." The Quillian Lectures were delivered by Dean Ernest Gordon of the Princeton University chapel. At the anniversary banquet that closed the session a tape recording was played of a conversation of older members of the faculty reminiscing on the early days of the School.

The original endowment of the School of Theology, $500,000 of Mr. Asa Candler's million-dollar donation, received no substantial addition until the organization of the Committee of One Hundred in 1954. Since then the endowment has been more than doubled by gifts in excess of $650,000. In almost the same time contributions for current operations have increased more than four-fold, from $80,000 in 1952-53 to $360,775 in 1964-65.

The Candler School of Theology, now the largest seminary of the Methodist Church, in 1964-65 enrolled 442 students, taught by a faculty of twenty-eight. More than 2,500 graduates fill every rôle in the leadership of the Church. It produces more Methodist pastors than any other seminary in the world. In the promotion of Christian scholarship and in devotion to the comprehensive needs of a living Church the Candler School has sought with all its growing resources to achieve the ends for which it was founded.

The School of Medicine
and the Hospitals

THE STORY of early medical education in Atlanta has been told so often and in such detail that it need be given here only in outline. On February 14, 1854, the General Assembly of Georgia granted a charter for the Atlanta Medical College. The first four-month session was held in the following year with Dr. John G. Westmoreland as Dean. The first building was erected on the future site of Grady Hospital in 1856. During the Civil War sessions were suspended, and the building was used as a Confederate hospital. On November 21, 1878, a rival institution, the Southern Medical College, was chartered, with Dr. William Perrin Nicolson as Dean. The two institutions, both proprietary, were merged in 1898 as the Atlanta College of Physicians and Surgeons, Dr. W. S. Kendrick, former Dean of Atlanta Medical, becoming Dean of the new foundation. Six years later, however, Dr. Kendrick withdrew to organize the Atlanta School of Medicine.

Although sessions had been lengthened, standards had been raised, and clinical instruction added to the curriculum, a committee from the Carnegie Foundation had visited the two institutions and had reported unfavorably on them. A consolidation aimed at improving the situation was agreed on, and in 1913 the College of Physicians and Surgeons and the School of Medicine united as the second Atlanta Medical College with Dr. William Simpson Elkin, of the former, chosen as Dean of the amalgamation. The American Medical Association had been putting all possible pressure on private medical schools to form mergers with universities, and when it was announced that Emory University was to be located in Atlanta, a committee of Atlanta Medical conferred with officials of the new institution to propose a union. On June 28, 1915, the trustees of Atlanta Medical College conveyed the school to Emory University, Dr. Elkin continuing as Dean of the division until 1925.

It was not until the completion in 1917 of the John P. Scott and

T. T. Fishburne laboratory and classroom buildings, Anatomy and Physiology, that the preclinical years of medical instruction were moved to the Druid Hills campus. Dobbs Hall served as dormitory for medical students. The new Wesley Memorial Hospital on the campus, opened at the close of December 1922, had been intended to furnish clinical facilities, but financial difficulties prevented this use of its wards. In 1920, however, the buildings of Atlanta Medical College had been transferred to the City of Atlanta for a Negro hospital, with the agreement that the medical faculty and students should attend its patients. Clinical teaching of the Emory School of Medicine was therefore concentrated at "Colored Grady" and the J. J. Gray Clinic, the latter completed in 1917.

Upon the entrance of the United States into World War I, the American Red Cross began to organize base hospital units for service overseas. The Emory unit was organized in the summer of 1917 by Dr. Edward Campbell Davis '30H, "federalized" on August 30, and mobilized at Camp Gordon, Georgia, April 2, 1918, under command of Lieutenant-Colonel S. U. Marietta, U.S.A.M.C. As Base Hospital 43, American Expeditionary Forces, the Emory Unit was activated, July 3, 1918, in Blois, France, where it was housed in more than a dozen large brick buildings, formerly hospitals and schools, scattered throughout the town. There was a total bed capacity of 2,400 by the time of the armistice. The Unit began with 35 medical and dental officers, most of them with Emory connections, the staff later increased to 52. Dr. Davis, Lieutenant-Colonel, M.C., was Medical Director, and Dr. Frank K. Boland '00M, Lieutenant-Colonel M.C., Chief of Surgical Service. The Unit comprised 200-291 enlisted men and 96 nurses. During the six months and eighteen days that the outfit functioned, 9,034 patients were treated, with a mortality of only a little more than one per cent. The Emory Unit was relieved of its duties on January 21, 1919. On February 20 Dr. C. W. Strickler '97M assumed command, being promoted from Major to Lieutenant-Colonel on March 1. Demobilization occurred at Camp Gordon on April 2.

The merger with Emory University had brought about a tightening of entrance requirements and a limitation of enrollments in the Medical School. In 1917, following an inspection, the School was accepted into the Association of American Medical Colleges. For the 1920-21 session the four classes totaled 214 students, and already qualified candidates were being turned away on account of the lack of laboratory facilities and the small faculty. In 1921 there was a teaching staff of 100, of whom only fourteen were full-time professors, instructors, and technicians, the others on volunteer, part-time appointments in the clinical branches. Within its self-imposed limitations the School was offering instruction recognized as of high quality.

$250,000 had been originally set aside by the University as endowment for the School of Medicine, and this sum had been slightly augmented by a campaign for funds among Atlanta doctors, dentists, and druggists. The School, nevertheless, was to remain in financial straits for many years, somewhat relieved in 1923 by a grant for operating expenses from the General Education Board.

In 1923 Dr. F. Phinizy Calhoun '04M, '54H, made a gift of $10,000 to found the Abner Wellborn Calhoun Medical Library, named in honor of his father, for thirty-eight years Professor of Ophthalmology and Otolyryngology in the Atlanta Medical College. In 1926 library endowment of $32,000 was provided by the Calhoun family.

Under the leadership of Dean Elkin, the Emory University Medical Alumni Association was organized in 1921. Dr. Frank K. Boland was elected its first President, and membership was opened to alumni of the Emory School of Medicine, to graduates of the schools that had preceded it, and to Emory alumni holding medical degrees from other institutions. Four years later the Association inaugurated the annual Postgraduate Clinics. In 1965 the Medical Alumni Association listed 2,553 members.

On the resignation of Dr. Elkin in 1925, Dr. Russell H. Oppenheimer became Dean of the Medical School. Dr. Oppenheimer, who had come to Emory in 1921, was serving as Superintendent of Wesley Memorial Hospital at the time of his appointment to the deanship. It may be safely assumed that by this time the organization of the School of Medicine had become fairly stabilized. The Register of 1925-26 lists the following as full professors: George Bunch Adams (Pathology), Jean George Bachmann '22G (Physiology), Homer Blincoe (Gross Anatomy), Edward Bates Block (Neurology and Psychiatry), Frank Kells Boland '00M (Surgery), Arthur Dermont Bush '01M (Pharmacology), Ferdinand Phinizy Calhoun '04 (Ophthalmology), James Le Roy Campbell '03M and William Stokes Goldsmith (Clinical Surgery), Paul Eugene Lineback (Micro- and Neuro-Anatomy), Joseph Llewellyn McGhee (Physiological Chemistry), James Edgar Paullin (Clinical Medicine), Weldon Edwards Person '01M (Clinical Surgery), Stewart Ralph Roberts '00M, '02 (Clinical Medicine), Cyrus Warren Strickler '97M (Principles and Practice of Medicine). Here and in the complete listing of the staff will be found, in addition to those of full-time teachers, the names of Atlanta's most eminent practitioners. A major improvement in clinical training was brought about in 1931 when the Grady authorities were persuaded to open the white wards for medical instruction on a limited basis.

In what had now been renamed the Emory University Hospital the Robert Winship Clinic for the study and treatment of neoplastic diseases was opened in 1937 with Dr. J. Elliott Scarborough Director. In 1939 the Department of Surgery received a grant of $250,000 from the Joseph B. Whitehead Foundation as the beginning of a much larger endowment to establish the Joseph Brown Whitehead Chair of Surgery. A similar sum to endow a Chair of Medicine was provided through the interest of Mr. Robert Woodruff, who had become the inspiration for much that was taking place to develop medical facilities and care in Atlanta.

In 1941 the Joseph B. Whitehead Foundation gave $550,000 to erect and equip the Conkey Pate Whitehead Surgical Pavilion. Before the completion of the project five years later, the Foundation, through the generosity of Mrs. Lettie Pate Evans, only woman member of Emory's Board of Trustees, mother of Conkey Pate Whitehead, had more than doubled the original gift. The Pavilion was dedicated on November 8, 1946, with Dr. Alfred Blalock, Professor of Surgery, Johns Hopkins University, delivering the dedicatory address. The exercises were directed by Daniel C. Elkin '20M, Whitehead Professor of Surgery, and Robert F.

Whitaker, Superintendent of the University Hospital.

In 1940 Dr. Luther C. Fischer '99M deeded the privately owned and operated Crawford W. Long Hospital to the University, the gift to become effective at his death. When this occurred in 1953, Emory took over the management, Dr. Wadley K. Glenn '33M succeeding Dr. Fischer in the direction. Crawford Long is a general hospital, including the Emily Winship Woodruff Maternity Center and the affiliated Jesse Parker Williams Hospital for Women. Located in downtown Atlanta, it serves private practitioners of the community, especially volunteer members of the clinical faculty of the Medical School, and carries on a graduate program for interns and residents.

The School of Medicine furnished an Emory Unit for World War II as it had for World War I. The 43rd General Hospital, organized by Dr. Ira A. Ferguson '23M about a faculty group, was activated on September 1, 1942, and sent for training to Camp Livingston, Louisiana. The Commanding Officer was Colonel Leroy D. Soper, U.S.A.M.C., Colonel Ferguson was Chief of Surgery, and Colonel R. Hugh Wood, Chief of Medicine. The Unit was "essentially Emory University Hospital transferred to the field."

Embarkation was delayed, and it was not until the end of October 1943 that the Unit was established at Oran, Algeria, where it remained until near the end of June 1944. On September 27, 1944, it was at Aix-en-Provence in France. Never working in as close association as in World War I, members of the Unit were frequently given assignments that took them away from their base, many of the officers seeing action with invasion troops in Italy and Southern France. Inactivation came on September 13, 1945. On May 30, 1946, the University honored the staffs of Emory Units I and II with a dinner at the Biltmore Hotel.

The School of Medicine had adopted an accelerated program for the war period, beginning the academic year in June and teaching around the calendar. The loss of faculty necessitated difficult adjustments, particularly in clinical assignments. In fall 1943 the School enrolled 170 Army trainees and 78 Navy trainees, with a single civilian. No freshman class was entered for summer 1945.

The first postwar class was graduated in March 1946, at which time the M.D. degree was granted for the first time to a woman, Dr. Elizabeth Gambrell '31G.

1943 was troubled by two controversies involving the School of Medicine. Oglethorpe University had undertaken to set up a medical school, and had sought to obtain clinical facilities at Grady Hospital. Emory necessarily opposed this request, since Grady could not accommodate two institutions, and Emory had earned its right to exclusive use by large expenditures for the improvement of facilities and staff. When it was further shown that Oglethorpe could not meet the educational standards of the American Medical Association, the petition was denied.

Shortly thereafter a wholesale attack was launched against the Emory School by the Secretary-Treasurer of the Medical Association of Georgia in the pages of its *Journal* and by circulation of reprints. The charges, unreasonably high standards of performance and favoritism, while utterly unfounded, were so serious and so widely disseminated that President White felt called upon to make a public reply. This cleared the air, and there was no further annoyance from that source.

In 1945 Dr. Eugene A. Stead, Jr., '28, '32M, since 1942 Professor of Medicine and Physician-in-Chief of Emory's division at Grady, succeeded Dr. Oppenheimer as Dean of the School of Medicine. Dr. Stead remained in the position only for a year, and was succeeded in 1946 by Dr. R. Hugh Wood, Physician-in-Chief of the Emory University Hospital. After recuperating from the illness that had caused his retirement from the deanship, Dr. Oppenheimer returned as Professor of Clinical Medicine, retiring in 1954 after thirty-three years of service to Emory.

The development of an outstanding medical center in Atlanta had been one of the proposals of the 1938 University Center report, and for years the plan was under constant discussion. The chief problem involved was the division of activities between the Emory University School of Medicine on the Druid Hills campus and the Grady Memorial Hospital in downtown Atlanta. The paramount question was the location of the administrative and research center of the Medical School, at that time divided between the campus and Grady Hospital. Although the addition of the Robert Winship Clinic for neoplastic diseases and the Conkey Pate Whitehead Surgical Pavilion to the Emory University Hospital considerably expanded campus teaching and research functions, nevertheless the Grady clinical facilities were considered virtually indispensable, and there was a strong sentiment for centralizing administrative and research activities at Grady. A report to the President by a blue-ribbon committee of the medical faculty recommended major development and direction on the campus, but the discussion continued in lively fashion until the Executive Committee of the Emory Board of Trustees in 1946 decided that the Medical School, although retaining its Grady division, should center and expand its functions primarily on the University campus.

The National Foundation for Infantile Paralysis in 1945 made the Emory Hospital a grant of $167,100 for a five-year program in physical medicine. Its threefold objective was to support research in neuro-muscular diseases, to train doctors and technicians, and to provide facilities for treatment. A special feature of the research program was the after-care of victims of poliomyelitis. The new Department of Physical Medicine was headed by Dr. Robert L. Bennett, Director of Physical Medicine at the Georgia Warm Springs Foundation, dividing his time between Emory and Warm Springs. The Department's main service unit is located on the ground floor of the Whitehead Surgical Pavilion. Since the expiration of the original grant the program has been carried on with University funds.

The School of Medicine has made every effort to meet the need for qualified practitioners, but applicants for admission to the Freshman class have consistently far exceeded the number who could be accepted. In 1947 there were 800 applicants. In that fall Emory College had an enrollment of 833 premedical students. In 1948 funds were contributed to allow expansion of laboratory and teaching facilities so that the entering medical class could be enlarged by twenty per cent, from the normal sixty to seventy-two, but there were 1,000 applications. The screening of applicants has become a demanding task of a special Admissions Committee.

Meanwhile, the expenses of a medical education have risen

steeply. The budget of the Medical School was less than $100,000 in 1931, ten years later was $150,000, grew to $840,000 in 1951, to $1,300,000 in 1961, and exceeded $2,200,000 in 1965. It was necessary that medical students bear a part of this increased cost. Tuition charges, which in 1931 had been $300, $337.50 in 1941, $600 in 1946, in 1951 had mounted to $800, to $1,000 in 1961, to $1,100 in 1965, and still the medical student pays less than a third of the cost of his education. More financial assistance is also available to medical students as, for instance, the James Edgar Paullin Scholarship Fund, established in 1950, the Cyrus W. Strickler Fund, and the William C. Warren Fund.

In 1951 the Emily and Ernest Woodruff Foundation made a grant for a medical research building, which was completed and put into partial use in 1952. The upper floors of the main section and the south wing were left unfinished until 1958. The Woodruff Memorial Building was dedicated in early winter 1952 with a series of five lectures on aspects of modern medicine addressed to laymen. In 1964 sixth and seventh floors were added to the south wing, and in 1965 a north wing was added with further grants from the original donor and contributions from Federal agencies. With the provision in Woodruff Memorial of adequate facilities, research has become a major activity of the School of Medicine. In 1950 Dr. Rolla E. Dyer, former Assistant Surgeon General, U. S. Public Health Service, Director of the National Institutes of Health, became Director of Research in the Robert Winship Clinic.

Burwell W. Humphrey took over as Superintendent of the Emory University Hospital in 1952. In the same year Boisfeuillet Jones was appointed to coördinate medical and health services.

Vigorous growth of Emory's work in health fields led to the establishment in 1953 of a Health Services Board composed of five Emory trustees under the chairmanship of James D. Robinson, Jr. '25. Boisfeuillet Jones was named Administrator of Health Services. Dr. Arthur P. Richardson, Professor of Pharmacology and Associate Dean of the School of Medicine, became the first Director of Basic Sciences in the Health Services, to carry out a most significant change in the preclinical teaching program.

Friends of Dr. Grady E. Clay '10 provided funds to strengthen the Department of Ophthalmology in the School of Medicine by establishing an eye clinic at Grady Hospital. The Grady Clay Memorial Eye Clinic, under Emory direction, was dedicated in September 1949. In 1960 the F. Phinizy Calhoun Chair of Ophthalmology was founded with a grant of $500,000, and in 1963 a laboratory for basic eye research was opened on the campus with Dr. Morton B. Waitzman in charge.

New headquarters for members of the Medical School at Grady Hospital and a center for clinical research were afforded by the erection of the Thomas K. Glenn Memorial Building. Built with contributions from the Wilbur Fisk Glenn Foundation and the Fulton-DeKalb Hospital Authority, it was named in honor of an early leader in the movement for an Atlanta medical center, the first Chairman of the Hospital Authority, and a long-time Emory trustee. Construction was begun in 1952, and it was occupied the next year.

Financial aid for the development of Emory's School of Medicine began to be received from many sources. For more than a quarter of a century it had demonstrated the ability of a small school with minimum funds to train physicians skilled in modern healing methods and to produce medical scientists who were winning wide reputations. It was evident that foundations had been laid on which an imposing edifice might be built. Among early grants was one of $500,000 in 1946 from the Federal Security Administration for medical research. In 1953 the Georgia Heart Association provided an annual subsidy of $12,000, to which the University added $3,000, for the establishment and maintenance of a chair of cardiovascular research. By the gift of Mrs. George C. Walters the Frances Winship Walters Chair of Pediatrics was founded in 1954 with an endowment of $435,268.

The most significant as well as most substantial single addition to the School's resources came also in 1954, when the Emily and Ernest Woodruff Foundation made a capital grant of $4,259,676, setting up a trust fund to provide operating income. Ten years later, the corpus of this endowment having attained a market value in excess of eleven million dollars, title of the fund was transferred to Emory and it became the Woodruff Endowment for

Medical Education.

In 1955 Emory University Hospital was granted $158,100 and Crawford Long $243,500 from the Ford Foundation. From the same source the School of Medicine was to receive $2,000,000 by 1958. The Commonwealth Fund made an award of $600,000 for the improvement of medical education. From the J. M. Tull Foundation $100,000 was received for fellowships for graduate students in the basic health sciences, which had begun a Ph.D. program in 1954. The first of several expendable grants from the John A. Hartford Fund of New York City was for research in burns and blood diseases.

The Atlanta Medical College, parent, or rather great-grandparent of Emory's School of Medicine, was chartered in 1854. A two-day centennial observance was held on the University campus, October 4-5, 1954. Among the visitors who signed the registers were alumni from all quarters, representatives of other schools of medicine, and delegates from medical organizations and societies. An attendance filling Glenn Memorial heard lectures by five internationally known medical men in the morning and afternoon of the first day. Class reunions, luncheons, a reception and banquet were scheduled for the guests of the University. The celebration was concluded on the second day with an academic procession and convocation. The convocation speaker was Dr. Allen Gregg, Vice-President and Medical Director of the Rockefeller Foundation, who discussed the commitments of the medical school of today and the obligations that exist between it and its community. Following the address honorary degrees were conferred on the speakers of the preceding day and on Dr. F. Phinizy Calhoun, Emory's distinguished veteran teacher and trustee.

In 1956 Dr. R. Hugh Wood resigned the deanship for reasons of health, and Dr. Arthur P. Richardson was appointed to the position. Dr. Evangeline Papageorge, Associate Professor of Biochemistry, was named Assistant Dean, and the following year was promoted to Associate Dean. Dr. Carl C. Pfeiffer, Professor of Pharmacology, succeeded Dr. Richardson as Director of the Division of Basic Health Sciences. In 1960 Dr. James A. Bain, Chairman of Pharmacology, was appointed to the directorship of the Division.

In 1952 the Emory University Clinic began its development, with Dean Wood as Director and seventeen physician members; its organization was completed the following year. The Clinic is a partnership of doctors of the clinical faculty engaged in private practice. Its establishment resulted from the need of the Medical School greatly to augment its teaching staff, yet to keep within the bounds of a relatively fixed budget. Members of the Clinic commit themselves to clinical teaching and research to at least twenty-five per cent of their time while providing self-support through private practice. Clinic members are "geographically full-time" members of the faculty by virtue of the location of their offices in a University building on the campus. They receive priority on beds in the University Hospital for their patients. They pay for all facilities afforded them for use in their private practice and also make a substantial financial contribution to the School. Similar clinics, to provide essential teachers, exist at most of the major American schools of medicine.

In 1954 a grant of $1,000,000 was made for a five-story Clinic building to be erected on Clifton Road across from the Hospital; construction began in May 1955. The center section and north wing were occupied in mid-1956, the south wing remaining "shelled in" until 1959. A back extension was added in 1963. On occupation of the building the Clinic consisted of thirty-four doctors; in fall 1965 the number had increased to 104. Dr. J. Elliott Scarborough became Director in 1956 on the resignation of Dean Wood.

From the beginning there had been opposition to the University Clinic from some Atlanta doctors. The charge was made that Emory was engaging in the corporate practice of medicine in unfair competition with the doctors of the community. Now the utmost care had been taken to make sure that the Medical School should exert no authority over patient care in the Clinic. Furthermore, patients from the Atlanta area are normally admitted only if they are sent there by their own physicians, and the greater number of patients come from outside the area. Attorneys for Emory and the Medical Association of Georgia advised on the organization of the Clinic, with the result that the state Association adopted a resolution declaring the Clinic both legally and ethically acceptable to the medical profession.

When the Chairman of the Department of Medicine sought to dictate procedures of the private practice of members of the Clinic, he was immediately relieved of the chairmanship. The case, however, was taken up by the Fulton County Medical Society, although, as a matter of internal policy of the School of Medicine, the Society had no jurisdiction. The affair was widely publicized and heatedly argued, but the University administration held to its decision, and three months later the principal in the controversy resigned.

So ended the first phase of the quarrel, which nevertheless at once built up to explosive violence. When Dean Richardson refers to 1956-57 as the "year of fire," the burning of the Administration Building in the early fall is not uppermost in his mind. In January the Chairman of Surgery submitted his resignation, and the Chairman of Obstetrics-Gynecology was informed that he would not be reappointed, the latter giving the news to the press. A member of the clinical staff in medicine followed with a public announcement of his intended resignation, "because of my concern about the future of medical education in Atlanta."

The second phase of the controversy now rapidly expanded. There had always been dissidents to the policy, determined in 1946, that medical education should be centered on the Druid Hills campus, even though Grady's clinical facilities should be retained. The four professors involved were chiefly concerned with the clinical program, and they were supported behind the scenes by others who resented the University's policy. There obviously could be no place on the Emory faculty for those who refused to go along with a decision of the University's governing body. Charges of Emory's maladministration at Grady, moreover, freely bandied through the newspapers, made it imperative that the University reply to them. Dean Richardson had publicly refuted all charges point by point, but still the controversy raged. Finally, on February 1 President White called a meeting of all the faculties, to which the press was invited, and made a strong statement of the University's position. On February 6 a full-page advertisement was run in both Atlanta papers informing the public of Emory's policies and programs for medical education.

Meanwhile it had become clear to the responsible heads of the Fulton-DeKalb Hospital Authority that Emory had gone far beyond its commitments to Grady, and that the Hospital and all who used its facilities had immeasurably benefited from the services of the Emory staff. On February 1 a joint Authority-University statement was issued confirming the relationship of Grady and the Medical School and affirming that no basic differences existed between them. The *Atlanta Constitution* about this time looked further into the matter, backed Emory's statement of its case, and in editorial comment stated that it was time the community realized its obligation equitably to assume the burden of patient care at Grady with a greater financial outlay.

This controversy was the most serious in which the School of Medicine has found itself engaged. The involutions and evolutions were more complicated than can be set forth in this brief account. It threatened permanent damage, but in the end it turned out more prosperously than could have been expected. A closer unity within the medical faculty was one result. Another was a clearer understanding between the School and the Grady authorities, establishing good mutual relations for the development that Grady was soon to undertake.

Meanwhile Atlanta's medical center, with Emory's School of Medicine at its heart, the product of long and devoted planning, was moving toward a notable development. The medical and teaching program of Lawson General Hospital, and on the discontinuance of that temporary facility, of Veterans Hospital 48 on Peachtree Road, was already supervised by the Emory School of Medicine. In 1946 it was announced that the Veterans Administration would build a $14,500,000, 580-bed hospital near the University, in which the Emory affiliation would be continued.

In 1946 also the U. S. Public Health Service announced its intention to build a Communicable Disease Center on a fifteen-acre tract donated by the University on Clifton Road just beyond the railroad bridge. In 1960 the Center, a $12,500,000, six-building plant, was completed and occupied. Shortly thereafter plans were made to double its size by 1966. Its professional staff of more than

400 members works closely with the faculty of the School of Medicine.

The Elks Aidmore Hospital for Convalescent Children, 72 beds, on Ridgewood Drive, a project of the Elks Clubs of Georgia, was occupied in 1954; an addition was completed in 1961.

The trustees of Henrietta Egleston Hospital for Children in 1956 signed an agreement of affiliation with Emory. Ground was broken for a $2,500,000, 100-bed plant on Clifton Road across from Physiology Building on October 11, 1957, and new Egleston was occupied in 1959.

Grady Memorial Hospital on January 28, 1958, moved into a magnificent new home. Erected at a cost of $26,000,000, a building of twenty-one stories with 1,069 beds, new Grady gives Atlanta a facility worthy of the South's most progressive city. In 1965 Emory rebuilt and greatly enlarged the former J. J. Gray Clinic, now Woodruff Memorial Research-Henry Woodruff Extension, as a major step to increase research by the medical faculty at Grady.

Most recently Emory has been contracted to furnish some psychiatric services and to direct the teaching and research programs for the Georgia Mental Health Institute. This facility of the Georgia Department of Public Health is located on the former Asa Candler, Jr. estate on Briarcliff Road. It became operative late in 1965.

Emory University Hospital undertook a thoroughgoing renovation in 1958 which, after six years and the expenditure of $4,750,000, brought the hospital completely up-to-date in its ability to serve patients and to function as a major facility in medical research and teaching. Also in 1958 Crawford Long Hospital began a $750,000 program of addition and change. A twenty-patient psychiatric ward was opened in the University Hospital in 1960. In 1964 the combined capacities of the two institutions for patient care were 803 beds, 68 bassinets.

Of the numerous grants received in recent years the following may be listed as furthering development in specific areas. In 1959, $193,000 was received from the John A. Hartford Foundation for research in chronic lung disease. In 1960, a U. S. Public Health

Service award of $396,000 was made for a clinical research center in the Emory University Hospital. The McAlister Chair of Preventive Medicine and Community Health was established in 1961 with an endowment of $250,000; Dr. Thomas F. Sellers '47, '50M, was named McAlister Professor. The first gift toward the Louis W. Orr Chair of Urology was made in 1961. In the same year Burroughs Wellcome made a grant of $75,000 for a clinical pharmacology section. A Federal grant in 1963 made possible the establishment of the Department of Biometry, under the chairmanship of Professor Malcolm E. Turner, Jr., offering work leading to the M.S. and Ph.D. degrees. The annual expenditure at Emory for research in medical and allied fields exceeds five million dollars and increases each year.

In July 1965 the Yerkes Regional Primate Research Center, of which Geoffrey S. Bourne, Professor of Anatomy, is Director, occupied its new quarters on the Emory campus and the field station near Lawrenceville with the transfer of the animals from Orange Park, Florida. The Yerkes, formerly emphasizing research in the behavioral sciences, has now expanded into programs dealing with problems in basic health sciences and the clinical medical sciences. The Center was dedicated on October 27, 1965.

A complete recounting of the history of the Emory University School of Medicine and of the development of medical service, teaching, and research in Atlanta would necessitate documentation of the contributions of the Woodruff family. Without the stimulation and inspiration, the thoughtful leadership and generosity of Mr. Robert Woodruff and his brother Mr. George Woodruff, people in this community and region would not yet have all the medical services now available to them.

It has been possible to give no more than a general summary of the part that the School of Medicine has played and is playing in the development of a great medical center. The progress of the idea, first given intensive study in the 'thirties, has been most impressive. In three decades Atlanta, with Emory's active participation in every move, has advanced to a foremost place in the nation's campaign for public health.

In fifty years as a division of Emory University, the School of

Medicine has made enormous contributions to the region and the nation through the training of doctors and other medical workers, and through its search for better ways to combat illness and disease. The scope of its activities has constantly increased, the development of its research placing it in the forefront of contemporary medical science. Its reputation has become national and international. The present teaching staff of the medical school includes nearly a thousand persons, among them leaders in almost every branch of the healing profession. Emory faculty and alumni have held high positions in many national and international organizations—the American Medical Association, the Federal Department of Health, Education, and Welfare, the National Institutes of Health, the Rockefeller Institute, the World Health Organization, and nearly every medical specialty society. Emory medical specialists have been called into consultation in many quarters of the world, and from many quarters of the world specialists come to Emory to observe programs and procedures and to take advantage of research facilities. The Emory University School of Medicine takes rank as one of the nation's most progressive centers of teaching, research, and service.

The Lamar School of Law

THE SCHOOL OF LAW began its first session on September 27, 1916, in the building on the main quadrangle designed for its occupancy, although for several years it was to share its facilities with departments of the College and the School of Business Administration. It was named for Lucius Quintus Cincinnatus Lamar (1825-1893), one of the most distinguished graduates of the old College at Oxford, Class of 1845, Secretary of the Interior in President Cleveland's first administration, and Associate Justice of the United States Supreme Court, 1888-1893. Its first separate endowment was for a Chair of Statute Law, named in honor of Superior Court Judge Richard H. Clark (1824-1896), who had collaborated in the first codification of Georgia laws. The greater part of this gift was made by Judge John S. Candler '80, '83G, '24H, as was the later endowment of a Chair of Common Law, named in honor of Chief Justice Thomas J. Simmons (1837-1905) of the Supreme Court of Georgia. In 1920 the endowment of the School of Law amounted to about $70,000.

In the first semester twenty-seven students were enrolled. William D. Thomson '95 had consented to serve as Acting Dean, and with him were associated Herschel W. Arant, who as Secretary of the Law Faculty was largely concerned with administration until his resignation in 1921, and Paul E. Bryan '07, full-time professors, and six Atlanta attorneys who held part-time appointments.

From the beginning the case study method of instruction was adopted. L. Q. C. Lamar had pioneered this method as Professor of Law at the University of Mississippi in 1867, and William Albert Keener '74 had been instrumental in its adoption at both Harvard and Columbia before the turn of the century. In the Lamar School of Law students are at once introduced to the principles and procedures of practice, over and above the theoretical presentation in textbooks, by the analysis of specimen cases and by participation in sessions of practice courts, as fully as possible approximating actual courts of law, in which every procedure from preparing briefs to giving final judgments are carried out by the students un-

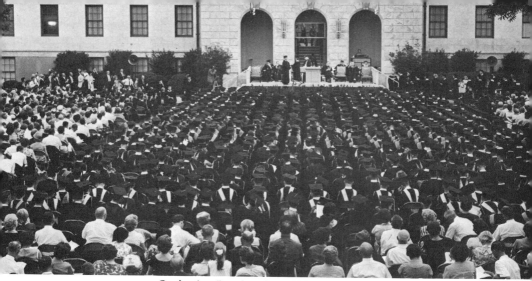

Graduation Exercises, June 1963

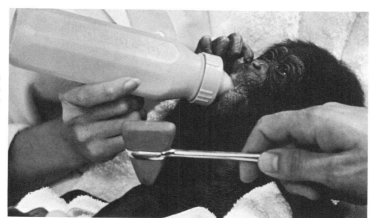

Atlanta, First-Born
at New Yerkes
Gets her Bottle

New and Old on Oxford Campus: Dickey, Stone, Dowman, Few

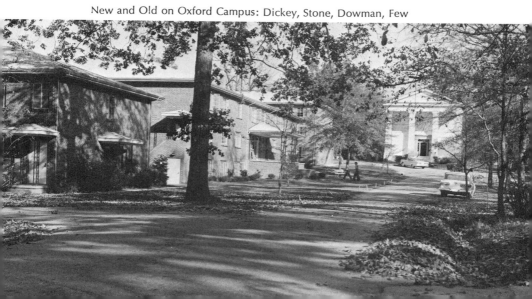

In the Woodruff building
medical students become
medical scientists

Page of 14th-Century
MS Bible,
Charles H. Candler
Collection

Books of the Joel Chandler Harris Collection

Christmas Carol Concert, Glenn Memorial

der the critical eyes of the faculty.

In 1919, Samuel Cole Williams, sometime Associate Justice of the Supreme Court of Tennessee, a Southern historian whose fine personal collection of Tennesseeana is now in the Emory University Library, was elected Dean. During his administration the faculty was enlarged, one of the additions being Henry M. Quillian '13, who remained in service until 1961. In 1920 the Lamar School was admitted to membership in the Association of American Law Schools. In 1923 the Council on Legal Education and Admissions to the Bar of the American Bar Association, making a classification of law schools, awarded Emory "Class A" rating, a distinction shared in the Southeast at that time with only the University of Virginia and Washington and Lee University. During the war years the draft had reduced the student body almost to the vanishing point, but after the war enrollments picked up, so that in the 'twenties attendance rose to an average of sixty.

Dean Williams resigned in 1924, and for the ensuing year Professor Bryan served as Acting Dean. In the fall of 1925 Charles J. Hilkey took over the deanship, which he held for twenty-three years until his retirement in 1948. A widely recognized legal scholar, Dr. Hilkey had extensive experience in the teaching of law, from 1918 to 1923 serving as Dean of the Drake University College of Law, Des Moines, Iowa. For the year prior to his Emory appointment he had engaged in private practice in Des Moines.

In the last years of Dean Hilkey's administration the enrollment of the School of Law was to rise to above 300. But in the depression of the 'thirties it fell below fifty, and in the years of World War II only the Evening Division continued to function. The Evening Division had been his own creation. Operating since 1941, it has offered fully accredited work, for the most part under the regular full-time faculty. The chief difference between Day and Evening Divisions has been that in the latter, since it was impracticable for the students to take full-time work, time in residence for the three-year course leading to the LL.B. degree normally extended to four and one-half years.

A high standard of legal training had been resolved on from

the foundation of the Lamar School of Law. For many years the Catalogue carried the following statement:

In establishing the law school, the trustees of the University have realized that there can be no excuse for its existence if it is to do no more than simply increase by one the number of law schools of the type which already exists in the South. These schools are now over-supplying in numbers the demand for lawyers. The legal profession is undoubtedly overcrowded numerically, while the demand for properly trained lawyers continues under-supplied. To provide at home a supply for this real need and to lead other Southern schools to adopt a program which will enable them to assist therein are the ultimate and larger objects which have led to the establishment of this school.

Dean Hilkey worked tirelessly for the raising of standards both of legal training and for admission to the Georgia bar. Emory joined with the University of Georgia and Mercer University in forming the Association of Georgia Law Schools. On a rotating basis one of the deans is an *ex officio* member of the Board of Governors of the Georgia Bar Association. In 1938, when summer enrollments had seriously fallen off, the three schools organized a combined Summer Session to meet at each in successive seasons. The pressures of World War II brought this plan to an end in 1941, since when the Association has made problems of legal education its major concern.

On the resignation of Dean Hilkey in 1948, W. D. Thomson again served for a year as Acting Dean, with Professor William H. Agnor '35, '37L, Secretary of the Law Faculty, handling routine matters of administration. Professor Maurice S. Culp took over from June 1949 to January 1950, when William M. Hepburn assumed the deanship. Dean Hepburn was the son of Charles McGuffey Hepburn, sometime Dean of Law and Professor of Law at Indiana University, author of *Cases on the Law of Torts,* the third edition of which edited by his son appeared in 1954. Dean Hepburn was also a nationally recognized authority on labor law, his services frequently called upon by agencies having to do with labor relations. For twenty years a member of the faculty of the University of Alabama Law School, he had served as its dean since 1944.

In spring 1952 appeared the first number of the *Journal of Public Law,* a semiannual publication edited by advanced law students under the general direction of a faculty committee.

The *Journal* is an international review devoted to law, government and politics, and its contributors are philosophers, historians, economists, political and social scientists, as well as lawyers and legal scholars.

Notable issues have been Vol. 3, No. 1 (Spring 1954), *Segregation in the Public Schools,* Vol. 3, No. 2 (Fall 1954), *Law and Medicine,* a symposium of 480 pages, and Vol. 13, No. 2 (1964), *Religion and the Constitution.* A Student Editorial Board also supervises a program of student writing for the *Georgia Bar Journal,* a quarterly published by the Georgia Bar Association.

Every spring since 1950 the Student Bar Association has sponsored a Law Day. This serves as a local observance of Law Day-U. S. A., as homecoming day for alumni, and "senior day" for the students. The program includes the presentation of final arguments in the Case Club Competition, a barbecue at noon, an address by a distinguished guest, and an evening banquet and dance at which honors and awards are presented. Law Day speakers have included former Assistant Attorney General of the United States Thurman Arnold, guest at the first Law Day, Morris F. Ernst, James A. Farley, Mr. Justice Tom Clark of the Supreme Court of the United States, Attorney General Nicholas de B. Katzenbach, and presidents of the American Bar Association.

The Bureau of Legal Research and Service, established in 1951, has sponsored numerous special institutes for members of the bar, in 1956-57, for instance, Anatomy for Lawyers, Corporation Workshop, Taxation for Beginners, and Income Tax Problems, in 1958, Patent Law.

On the death of Dean Hepburn in 1960, Professor G. Stanley Joslin served as Acting Dean until the appointment of Dean Ben F. Johnson '39L in 1961. A member of the Law School faculty since 1946 after private practice in Atlanta and a tour of duty in the Navy, Dean Johnson also served as a special Assistant Attorney General for the State of Georgia, and in 1962 was elected to the State Senate from the 42nd District.

Student organizations include Lamar Inn of Phi Delta Phi international legal fraternity, chartered 1923, and Keener Chapter of Phi Alpha Delta legal fraternity, installed 1928, inactive 1936-1946, reactivated 1946. The Case Club supervises Moot Court Competitions; final arguments are heard on Law Day, and the winning team represents Emory in the Regional Moot Court Competition, the winner of which in turn goes to the National Moot Court Competition held annually in New York. In fourteen years of interschool competitions Emory has been represented in the finals six times. The Student Bar Association is a charter member of the American Law Student Association, organized in 1948. The Bryan Society was founded in 1951 to recognize outstanding scholastic achievement. Its name honors Professor Paul E. Bryan, a member of the faculty from the founding of the School until his retirement in 1953.

On the whole, life in the Lamar School of Law is a serious business, as it is generally in the graduate divisions of the University. The finally impending bar examinations offer small inducement to promiscuous high jinks. But from time to time original comic interludes have been included in the program of Law Day, as the mock trial in 1950. For some years there was a Saturday Easter egg hunt, for which on occasion Professor Quillian impersonated Peter Rabbit himself. The "money egg" furnished the means and the obligation to the finder to treat the whole gang to Cokes at Jeffares' drug store on the corner. Students of Professor Quillian's course in Contracts will also recall the annual sale of his watch, an object lesson as enlivening as enlightening.

The School of Law has offered the LL.B. and LL.M. degrees, the latter dating from 1955, the regular LL.B. course occupying three years, and the LL.M. requiring three quarters further residence. From 1936-37 through 1950-51 an honors course was offered leading to the J.D. (Juris Doctor, Doctor of Law) degree, which was conferred on fifty-two graduates of the School in that period. Admission requirements have varied; in 1964 three years of college work were necessary for enrollment in the LL.B. program. A combination degree, A.B. in Law, was provided for a student who entered with three years of college credits and successfully completed forty-six quarter hours of law courses. Beginning Fall Quarter 1966 an undergraduate baccalaureate degree will be required for admission. Beginning in June 1967, the basic professional degree will be the J.D., the advanced degree remaining the LL.M. In recent years enrollments have fluctuated in the neighborhood of 250, with a rise in 1963-64 to 330.

A Law School Alumni Association was organized in 1941. Disrupted by World War II, reorganization was effected in 1950 as a division of the Alumni Association of the University. With an inclusive membership, it has vigorously promoted all the activities and interests of the Lamar School of Law. Breakfasts or luncheons are arranged at every important bar association meeting, and an alumni directory is published periodically.

Alumni of the School of Law during the past fifteen years have achieved positions of leadership in the local and regional bar. Active in all legal affairs, Emory men have been presidents of the Atlanta Lawyers Club, the Atlanta Bar Association, the Georgia Bar Association, and the American Bar Association. As the School attains greater age it is certain that its dignities will increase in direct ratio.

The Library School—
Division of Librarianship

WITH THE FOUNDING of the Atlanta Public Library in 1899 by a gift from Andrew Carnegie, an apprentice class in librarianship was formed to supply trained assistants. Women who had received this training were soon in such demand that it was found advisable to set up the class as a regular school for librarians. Mr. Carnegie was appealed to, and with his subvention of $4,000 a year for three years the Southern Library School came into being in fall 1904.

On April 9, 1907, it was incorporated as the Carnegie Library Training School of Atlanta, its patron agreeing to give $4,500 annually to continue the School indefinitely. Miss Tommie Dora Barker '09L.S., '30H, became Director in 1915, and under her administration application was made to affiliate with Emory University. This was brought about in November 1925, with classes continuing in the Carnegie Library in downtown Atlanta.

The move to the Asa Griggs Candler Library on the Emory campus occurred in fall 1930. A subvention of $50,000 each from the Carnegie Corporation and the Julius Rosenwald Fund, to be paid over the five years 1930-35, conditioned on matching by the University with assurance of the permanence of the School, completed its organization as the Library School of Emory University. Miss Clara Howard was appointed Dean, serving until 1935.

In its beginnings the Library School had been something more than a professional training agency. It had contributed a wide range of services to libraries of the Southeast in the years of their rapid development. Its later rôle was to meet their need for highly qualified staff members. From its affiliation with the University it required a college degree for admission, and in 1926 it was accredited by the Board of Education for Librarianship of the American Library Association as a junior undergraduate library school. In the following year it was accredited as a graduate library school, granting the degree of Bachelor of Arts in Library Science.

This record makes it the oldest of the American Library Association accredited schools in the Southeast. Accreditation was renewed under the new standards of the A. L..A. in 1954, and continuation was granted in 1964. When the School was moved to the Emory campus men were enrolled in its courses.

On the death of Dean Howard in December 1935, Miss Lydia E. Gooding became Acting Dean, serving until the July following. Miss Barker then again took charge, as Dean until 1948, and as Director of the Division of Librarianship when it became a part of the Graduate School in that year, until 1954. Miss Evalene Jackson '29 L.S. was named Director in 1954, holding the position for ten years. In fall 1965 the directorship was assumed by A. Venable Lawson '50G.

Until 1948 a second bachelor's degree had been conferred by the School, even though its work was postgraduate. As a division of the Graduate School those completing their studies are awarded master's degrees. A grant of $100,000 by the Carnegie Corporation in October 1940 had greatly strengthened its resources.

Besides training in the basic techniques of library administration, book selection, cataloguing and classification, and reference, the curriculum devotes special attention to library materials and specialized areas of service. Courses for school libraries have been long established; more recently a summer course for medical librarians has been organized, under the direction of Miss Mildred Jordan '30L.S., '42G, of the School of Medicine. A large collection of professional books, pamphlets, and periodicals adjoins the classrooms of the Division.

Enrollments for the regular academic year have varied from fifty to seventy-five with women students in the majority but with an increasing male registration. Graduates have never equalled the number of appointments open to them as American education has placed greater and greater emphasis on the library as its vital center and as business and industry have developed research collections. Alumni of the School and the Division are found occupying key positions in libraries across the nation.

The School of Dentistry

SOUTHERN DENTAL COLLEGE was founded in Atlanta in 1887 as a department of the Southern Medical College, and it continued the connection in the successive mergers of that institution until 1915, when Atlanta Medical College became the Emory University School of Medicine. Dr. L. D. Carpenter, the first Dean, was succeeded in 1896 by Dr. Sheppard W. Foster, Professor of Oral Pathology. In 1892 a rival school, Atlanta Dental College, like its predecessor a proprietary foundation but independent of a medical connection, was established, with Dr. William C. Wardlaw as Dean, succeeded in its first year by Dr. William Crenshaw. A merger of the two was effected in 1917 under the name of the Atlanta-Southern Dental College. Dr. Sheppard W. Foster was chosen as President and Dr. Thomas P. Hinman '91 (Southern) received the appointment as Dean. In 1926 the School moved from the former premises of Southern Dental, adjacent to Grady Memorial Hospital, to a new building erected at the corner of Forrest Avenue and Courtland Street that it has continued to occupy until the present.

In March 1926 the School, which up to this time had been a private stockholder corporation, became an eleemosynary institution for the advancement of dentistry. Following this change of status it was rated Class A by the Dental Educational Council of America.

Atlanta-Southern and its precedent schools exerted a strong influence in the Southeast, especially in Georgia, Florida, Alabama, and the Carolinas, where the greater number of alumni were located for practice. Until recently the latter states have not had dental schools of their own. The faculties and alumni were distinguished for their receptivity to new ideas and techniques, and their contributions to modern dental science were widely recognized. Dr. Hinman in 1913 founded the Atlanta Midwinter Clinic, later renamed in his honor the Thomas P. Hinman Dental Meeting, which draws an ever-increasing annual attendance. He was elected President of the National Dental Association for 1922. In

1925 Lambda chapter of Omicron Kappa Upsilon, national honor society of dentistry, was installed at Atlanta-Southern. In 1926 Dr. Foster served as President of the American Dental Association, in which year he presided over the meeting of the World Dental Congress. The library of the School of Dentistry is named in affectionate memory of "Uncle Shep."

In the will of Dr. DeLos L. Hill '03 (Southern), a professor in both Atlanta and Atlanta-Southern, provision was made for the establishment of a children's clinic as a memorial to his son who had died in boyhood. At this time no school in the South taught dentistry for children. Shortly following Dr. Hill's death, Mrs. Hill, anticipating the terms of the bequest, in September 1931 turned over the sum of $50,000 so that the DeLos L. Hill, Jr., Memorial Dental Clinic for Children might be organized without delay. Mrs. Hill made additional gifts in 1937 and 1950, and at her death in January 1958 the balance of the Hill estate was placed in an endowment for the support of the Department of Pedodontics and the Memorial Clinic. Dr. Hill, a prominent figure in national dentistry, first Secretary of the American Association of Dental Schools, inspired a deep loyalty to the profession in his wife. For many years a regular attendant at dental meetings, she was a President of the Woman's Auxiliary of the A.D.A. But the chief rôle of the woman universally known as "Mother" Hill was that of patroness of her husband's School and particularly of Psi Omega fraternity.

Early in the nineteen-hundreds independent dental as well as medical schools were seeking to form university connections. Atlanta-Southern's first proposal of affiliation with Emory University was rejected, since problems of Emory's internal organization at the time made it impracticable. The proposal was renewed later, and on June 2, 1944, the Emory Board of Trustees approved the merger. The petition of Atlanta-Southern Dental College to become an "integral part of Emory University" was granted by the Fulton Superior Court on September 15, 1944. By the decree all property of Atlanta-Southern was transferred to Emory, including buildings of the Dental School, equipment, securities, and donated funds. Officials and faculty of the School became members of the staff and faculty of the University, and its 3,693 living alumni became members of the Emory alumni body. Ralph Roy Byrnes, Dean of Atlanta-Southern since 1931, became the first Dean of the Emory University School of Dentistry, serving until 1948.

On the resignation of Dr. Byrnes, Dr. John E. Buhler, of the Temple University School of Dentistry, was appointed to the deanship, which he occupied until 1961. In 1949 the Dental School began to participate with the Medical School in the program of the Board of Control for Southern Regional Education for the training of dental and medical candidates from the Southern states. Organized by the Southern Governors Conference under a compact ratified by twelve Southern states, its purpose was to aid the states, especially those lacking dental and medical schools, to secure practitioners adequate to the needs of their populations.

Shortly after taking office, however, Dean Buhler had stated: "Our physical facilities are inadequate in terms of teaching. The advances made in dentistry in the past decade or so indicate a strong need for a new dental building to be located on the main University campus and to work in connection with the Emory University Hospital and School of Medicine." In 1950 a general renovation of the Dental Building was accomplished, but the problem of securing adequate facilities for the sorely pressed School of Dentistry has not yet been solved, though the solution now appears near at hand. Some amelioration of the situation was achieved by the transfer of basic science courses to the Druid Hills campus, so that the Dental Building could be given over to clinical subjects.

The School of Dentistry was honored by the choice of its alumnus, Dr. Oren A. Oliver '09D, President of the American Dental Association 1941-42, as the June 1949 commencement speaker for the professional and graduate divisions, at which time an honorary LL.D. was conferred on him. Dr. Oliver, a distinguished orthodontist of Nashville, in July 1952 was elected President of the Federation Dentaire Internationale.

Following the death in December 1951 of Dr. Joseph D. Osborne '11D, who "during his lifetime of outstanding professional service . . . exerted a singularly strong and continuing influence in stimulating the advancement of knowledge and skills in the clinical and preclinical sciences essential to the modern dental practice," his friends donated more than $100,000 to equip the large general adult clinic, which was named in his honor, the Joseph D. Osborne Memorial Clinic.

In 1951 an annual series of alumni seminars on dental problems was begun, and in 1952 postgraduate short courses were instituted. On May 16, 1952, the School of Dentistry, that at this time, as a result of the recent adoption of more rigid standards than those of twenty-five years earlier, was on the list of institutions "provisionally approved," was voted full approval by the Council on Dental Education, accrediting agency of the American Dental Association.

Some unpleasantness developed in 1961, when it was charged that a disproportionately large number of Jewish students in the Dental School had been failed in their work. President Martin made a personal investigation, after which he stated his belief that there had been no "willful or intentional discrimination." Dean Buhler's resignation coming at this time, it was rumored that his leaving was the direct result of the unfavorable publicity that the School had received. This charge also Dr. Martin dismissed as "pure coincidence."

Dr. Buhler was succeeded in the deanship in June 1961 by Dr. George H. Moulton, since 1955 Professor of Crown and Bridge Dentistry. Dr. Moulton in 1939 was commissioned as a U. S. Army dental officer, serving in World War II with the 88th Infantry Division. After the war he was assigned to Walter Reed Army Medical Center and Hospital, where he became President Truman's personal dentist.

The minimum requirement for admission to the School of Dentistry is two full years of work in an accredited college of arts and sciences. In addition to prescribed laboratory science courses, electives in the humanities and social sciences are recommended so that the dental candidate may acquire a broad cultural background. The professional course occupies four years, the major part of the first year devoted to courses in the Division of Basic Health Sciences on the Druid Hills campus. The major portion of the second year is given to dental studies in the Dental School Building, and the third and fourth years are devoted primarily to clinical practice. For graduation with the degree of Doctor of Dental Surgery it is necessary that the student shall have passed the National Board Examinations.

The program of graduate study is "designed particularly for individuals interested in careers in graduate education and for dentists who intend to qualify for the various dental specialty boards." The degree of Master of Science in Dentistry since 1961 is offered in oral pathology, periodontia, orthodontia, pedodontia, crown and bridge prosthetics, prosthetic dentistry, operative dentistry, and oral surgery. A minimum of two full-time academic years is required, each candidate undertaking an individual research problem and writing a thesis based on it. The program in orthodontia, however, requires a minimum of three full-time academic years. Postgraduate programs of twenty-four and nine months tenure are also offered, for which certificates are awarded on satisfactory completion of the courses.

Research occupies an important place in the activities of the School of Dentistry. Carried on in four separate laboratories—the Physiology Laboratory, the Virus Tissue Culture Laboratory, the New Physiology Laboratory, and the Bowman Dental Research Laboratory, the latter, completed in September 1964, especially equipped for handling radioactive isotopes, autoradiography, and histochemistry—as well as in the various clinics within the School and in coöperative projects, faculty members and graduate students are engaged in clinical and basic studies extending the bounds of dental science. Further development in this field only waits on enlarged physical facilities and financial support.

Under coöperative arrangements made by Emory University the School of Dentistry now provides dental services for the hospitals and other health services of the Atlanta area. This plan achieves a further extension of clinical training and graduate research to the benefit both of the community and the School.

The Bulletin of the School of Dentistry for 1965-66 lists an active faculty of 102 members, of whom twenty-seven are full-time.

Enrollment for 1964-65 was 286. Both teaching and research have long been handicapped to a degree by the inadequacy of existing facilities, in spite of which work of the highest quality in step with modern dental progress has been accomplished. More than five years of intensive study have resulted in detailed plans for a building for the Dental School to be located on the University campus which will make adequate provision for teaching, clinical service, and research.

The School of Nursing

WHEN WESLEY MEMORIAL HOSPITAL was opened in August 1905 in the "Calico House," on the southeast corner of Auburn Avenue and Courtland Street, a Training School for Nurses was established to serve its fifty patients. At first, classroom teaching was minimal, the two-years course consisting chiefly of practical training, but there was a gradual improvement in theoretical instruction. Miss Alberta Dozier became Superintendent of Nurses in 1907, in which position she was to continue until 1923, the year after Wesley Memorial Hospital on the Emory University campus received its first patients.

The training course continued in the new hospital with instruction participated in by members of the medical faculty. Graduating classes were awarded their certificates at the June commencement exercises of the University, at which times the white-capped nurses occupied the front rows of the assembly. The School of Nursing was assigned quarters in the hospital building until 1929, when it was moved to the beautifully appointed Florence Candler Harris Home for Nurses.

In December 1942 a survey of Emory University and the Atlanta community to determine the adequacy of resources for a university school of nursing was conducted for the U. S. Public Health Service by Miss Julia M. Miller. In September 1943 Miss Miller was appointed Director of the School of Nursing, and plans proceeded rapidly for raising it to collegiate level. The new curriculum was established in 1944, and Miss Miller was named Dean.

The Emory University School of Nursing continued to offer a diploma program until 1952, when the last students under this plan were graduated. The basic four-year program, awarding the degree of Bachelor of Science in Nursing, required two years of general education in a college of arts and sciences for admission. Since 1951 in the basic professional curriculum, instruction in science relevant to nursing has been provided by the Division of Basic Health Sciences. In a testing program reported in the *Emory Alumnus* for June 1945, the 101 matriculants of the School proved to be above the national average.

Nurses in training in 1943 increased in numbers from prewar ninety to 165, the larger enrollment due to a government-financed program similar to the V-12 program. Members of the U. S. Cadet Nurse Corps made a colorful addition to the campus in their smartly tailored blue uniforms and distinctive Montgomery berets. In their exacting schedule the visit of the handsome movie star Tyrone Power created a brief but thrilling interlude.

The story of Emory University Hospital and its School of Nursing from their beginnings was told by Mrs. Maybelle Jones Dewey in the volume, *Until Now,* published in 1947. Mrs. Dewey, an enthusiastic and tireless worker with the Woman's Auxiliary, brought together from all available sources accounts of the early days of the related institutions as a tribute "to the nurses past, present, and future of the Emory University School of Nursing."

Following the resignation early in 1950 of Dean Julia Miller to accept a position with the National Nursing Accrediting Service, Miss Ada Fort was named to succeed her.

Harris Hall requiring all of its space for dormitory use, in 1953 the offices of the School of Nursing were moved to the Professional Building on Clifton Road, on the present site of Henrietta Egleston Children's Hospital, and classrooms were transferred to the University Hospital. Grants from the Kellogg Foundation and the Commonwealth Fund in 1954 permitted the School to move into a graduate program offering the degree of Master of Nursing. Emory was one of six institutions chosen by these sponsors working with the Southern Regional Education Board for the advancement of nursing education. In that year all undergraduate students were regularly registered in the College of Arts and Sciences. An irrevocable trust fund of $10,000 was established for the School of Nursing in 1957 by Mrs. Stephens (Anita Benteen) Mitchell '34N, the first endowment received by the School. In 1959 the basic professional program was changed to three academic years following two years of general education. The first male student was admitted to the School, in the graduate program, in 1962.

Another move was made necessary in 1957, when the School occupied Annex B in the Fishburne area. It is expected that a new building will be constructed in the near future, finally bringing wanderings to an end and providing the School with complete modern facilities for its work.

A visit by Mrs. Mary Clark Rockefeller in April 1959 led to the organization of the Associates of the Emory University School of Nursing, a group of women drawn from the region served by the School active in the promotion of its work. The first President of the Associates was Mrs. Henry L. Bowden.

The School of Nursing is fully accredited by the Board of Review for Baccalaureate and Higher Degree Programs of the National League of Nursing. The basic curriculum is also accredited for preparing nurses for beginning positions in public health nursing. Graduates meet the requirements for state board examinations for licensure. The Women's Division of Christian Service of the Board of Missions of the Methodist Church in 1963 endorsed the School of Nursing "as an institution which makes an essential contribution to the Christian way of life." Alpha Epsilon Chapter of the honorary nursing sorority Sigma Theta Tau was installed on April 13, 1964.

Of the $500,000 annual budget of the School of Nursing approximately half comes from government grants in support of specific programs central to the ongoing curriculum. Complete support of undergraduate and graduate programs of psychiatric nursing, for instance, is furnished by the National Institutes of Health.

A large attendance of loyal alumnae celebrated the semicentennial of the School of Nursing on April 1-2, 1955. Some who were present had observed its progress from a small in-service training center to the present University division with diversified curriculum imparting the professional knowledge and skills to keep patient care fully abreast of modern medical science. In their classrooms and in the hospitals of a great urban medical center students of the Emory School of Nursing are given the theoretical and practical preparation to fit them for every requirement of their high calling. In sick-rooms throughout the world 1,300 graduates of the School are giving devoted service in the cause of health.

Oxford and Valdosta
Junior Colleges

THE EMORY UNIVERSITY ACADEMY was established at Oxford in September 1915 as a replacement for the College which was eventually to be transferred to the Atlanta campus. The first Principal, 1915-16, was Robert C. Mizell '11. Three principals followed before the organization of the Junior College: A. M. Hughlett, 1916-18, J. A. Sharp '92, 1918-22, A. W. Rees, 1922-29. The curriculum offered was a standard college preparatory course. The enrollment for the Academy in 1916-17 was seventy-four, and though it did not greatly increase in size, with only one dormitory and with other facilities shared with the College, by 1918 Chancellor Candler was impatient to move the latter. When this was accomplished in the early summer of 1919, the Academy took over.

The Academy did not prove self-sustaining, but alumni sentiment was unanimously opposed to the abandonment of the old campus. Plans were therefore formed to set up a junior college at Oxford. After World War I, however, the plant was in a badly run-down condition, and extensive reconditioning was imperative. For this a gift of $10,000 was secured from J. Fred Allen '95, which with other smaller gifts made it possible to ready the buildings for junior college classes in September 1929. Hugh A. Woodward '01, '29G, was appointed Associate Dean of Emory-at-Oxford, serving from 1929 to 1934, directing both Junior College and Academy. In the first year there were 101 students enrolled in the latter and sixty-three in the former division.

Historic Old Church, adjoining the campus, in 1932 had suffered from long neglect. In this edifice the College commencement exercises of former times had been held, from its pulpit had preached the leaders of Southern Methodism, and famous orators —among other, Alexander H. Stephens, John B. Gordon, L. Q. C. Lamar '45, Henry W. Grady—had addressed students and townspeople since its dedication in June 1841. The old timbers were sound, and Bishop Candler undertook as a labor of love and piety the restoration of this monument to his Church and his College. By generous contributions from alumni the work was completed, and on June 4, 1933, the church was rededicated by its preserver. But fifteen years later destruction again threatened. Then the North Georgia Conference under the leadership of Bishop Arthur J. Moore '14, '34H, took decisive action, and it may be hoped that Old Church with its memories of the past has been finally saved for posterity.

Hugh Woodward was succeeded as Associate Dean by George S. Roach '11, who served from 1934 to 1945, followed by Virgil Y. C. Eady '36G, who is now Dean and Division Executive of Oxford College. In December 1947 Emory-at-Oxford was accredited as a four-year junior college by the Southern Association of Colleges and Secondary Schools. Careful planning had preceded this development of the curriculum, which was to include the last two years of high school and the first two years of college. The Academy now began to be phased out. In 1948-49 the net total enrollment at Oxford was 192; with the introduction of the four-year Junior College in fall 1950, the enrollment rose slightly to 201.

It had been anticipated that extensive plant improvement was called for if the new plan was to be successful. A beginning was made in 1956 with the erection of Dickey Hall, named for the last President at Oxford, a fifty-two bed dormitory. Further additions were completed in 1957, made possible by gifts of $50,000 each by Mr. and Mrs. Albert S. Mitchell of Mobile. In this year also the North and South Georgia Conferences launched campaigns to raise funds in support of Methodist colleges in the state.

The building program was continued in 1960 with the construction of Bonnell and Stone Halls, named in honor of professors of Old Emory College, and Dowman Hall, named for the eleventh President, in 1961. These were men's dormitories, together accommodating 180 students. Pierce Science Hall, although built as late as the administration of President Dickey, was already superannuated, and was replaced in 1962 with a modern structure retaining the name of its predecessor.

In Fall Quarter 1964 the enrollment of what by action of the

Board of Trustees was now officially designated Oxford College had risen to 426, with a faculty of thirty-four. While still considered an institution for men, a few women day students had been admitted for several years. The Junior College did not become fully coeducational until dormitory rooms for women could be provided in Haygood Hall, where they have been housed since 1955. A complex of a new residence hall for women together with a cafeteria and an infirmary is planned to be ready in fall 1966. With this and with the contemplated repair and renovation of older buildings the Oxford plant will more effectively serve the institution of which it is the oldest division.

The spring Homecoming Day still brings back alumni of the Old College on annual pilgrimage. The return of Vice-President Alben W. Barkley in June 1949 for reunion with the Class of 1900 will long be remembered. But now alumni of the younger foundation join with the veterans under the campus trees, and the new generation looks with pride upon the present as with honor to the past.

Municipal pride inspired civic leaders of Valdosta in South Georgia, already the location of Georgia State Women's College, to petition Emory University to establish there a divisional junior college for men. The offer, made in June 1927, included a forty-three-acre site in the northern suburbs, an administration building —an all-purpose instructional facility—furnishings and equipment, at a cost of $150,000, and $200,000 endowment. The idea of situating a "feeder" division in this area was approved by the Emory Trustees, and the offer was accepted.

On September 26, 1928, Emory Junior College at Valdosta opened its first term with exercises attended by a large gathering of enthusiastic Valdostans. Fifty students were registered for Fall Quarter. A faculty and staff of seven was headed by William B. Stubbs '19, Associate Dean of the College of Arts and Sciences. The privately owned "College Inn," adjoining the campus, was rented for dormitory use, and some students found lodgings in Valdosta homes. In 1931 a dormitory, Sophomore Hall, was added to the plant. The only other addition in the first period of operation was the Centennial Swimming Pool in 1936.

[183]

In 1937 Associate Dean Stubbs joined the University faculty in Atlanta, and he was succeeded at Valdosta by A. Hollis Edens '30. The work at this division, largely consisting of required basic courses, was of a high quality, and students going on to the junior class on the University campus gave a generally good account of their training, but the student body did not grow appreciably. In the fourteen years 1928-42 the average enrollment was sixty-one, with a high point of seventy-nine in 1939-40. With the coming of World War II it was thought necessary in 1942 to close the Junior College "for the duration," and faculty and students were transferred to Atlanta.

After the war Emory-at-Valdosta was reopened in September 1946, with Eugene D. Whisonant as Associate Dean and Division Executive. An additional dormitory, "Swamp Hall," and a recreation hall-gymnasium were provided by securing surplus army buildings. In 1951 Freshman Hall was erected. With returning veterans taking advantage of the "G.I. Bill of Rights" the enrollment rose in fall 1947 to 247, but with their departure attendance fell to near its former average. Through the years the majority of students were engaged in preparation for the professions, chiefly medicine and dentistry.

When in the fall of 1950 the former Georgia State Woman's College became coeducational, it soon clearly appeared that the Junior College would not flourish with the resulting competition. In spring 1953 the enrollment stood at sixty-five. Faced with continuing annual deficits, the Emory University Trustees offered its Valdosta plant to the University System of Georgia. The gift was accepted by the Regents on May 13, 1953, as an addition to Valdosta State College, as G.S.W.C. had been renamed, and Emory's South Georgia division ceased operation.

The Libraries

THE EMORY UNIVERSITY LIBRARIES consist of eight divisions: the Asa Griggs Candler Library, the Library of the School of Business Administration, the Sheppard W. Foster Dental Library, the Library of the Lamar School of Law, the Library of the Division of Librarianship, the A. W. Calhoun Medical Library, the Library of the Candler School of Theology, and the Oxford College Library. Their combined resources on June 30, 1965, were 823,609 volumes, besides miscellaneous items, including 80,195 manuscripts, to the number of approximately a quarter of a million.

When Emory College moved to the Atlanta campus, the library was consigned to the Theology Building, with Miss Eva Wrigley '07LS serving as Librarian from October 1919. Reading room, stack, and office space were meagerly provided in Theology basement in summer 1920, the book collections being chiefly those brought from the Candler Library at Oxford. During succeeding years books continued to be brought up in installments from Oxford, leaving there, however, a basic collection suitable to the needs of the Academy. In March 1921 failing health compelled Miss Wrigley's resignation, and she was followed in the librarianship by Miss Margaret Jemison '14LS, who was to hold the office until 1954, and in whose long term the Library was to be brought to a service of modern efficiency.

At the Commencement meeting of 1924 the Board of Trustees authorized a library building to cost $400,000, a sum provided by a gift of Mr. Asa G. Candler. The site was changed, from the central location indicated in the Hornbostel layout, to the east end of the main quadrangle, previously assigned to the Administration Building. James Hinton, Professor of English, was sent on a tour of university libraries to gather ideas, and by his advice Edward L. Tilton of New York, a specialist in library building, was chosen as architect. Ground was broken in February 1925, and the completed building, named, over the donor's protest, the Asa Griggs Candler Library, was dedicated on February 26, 1926. Mr. Tilton had designed an impressive marble-clad structure, that appeared sufficiently commodious for a long future. Three levels of stacks provided space for an estimated 325,000 volumes, and a lofty reading room, extending the length of the second floor, furnished accommodations for a considerably larger student body than the College was to enroll for twenty years. The ground and first floors were immediately occupied by administrative offices of the University and the Museum, the former to continue in possession until the erection of the Administration Building in 1955. A large room on the top floor was used as a faculty club room until the installation of the Library School on the Emory campus in 1930.

Professor Hinton, who had been the moving spirit in library planning, was named Director of Libraries in 1926, in which position he served until his death in 1929, when the office fell vacant until 1954. In 1933, Thomas H. English, Professor of English, was appointed Chairman of the Library Committee. In that year was received the first grant for the purchase of books from the Lewis H. Beck Foundation of Atlanta. The financial stringency of the depression years had cut deeply into the Library budget, and enlargement of the collections had come to a virtual standstill. With the receipt of a generous subvention from the Beck Foundation began a vigorous building of library resources, and to its continuing assistance through the years since 1933 must be chiefly attributed the development of reference and research materials that at length made possible the expansion of the graduate program. An unpredictable but fortunate result of the meagerness of book funds in the early years of the University Library had been a high selectivity in its acquisitions, so that when its budget was increased, it was able to build on a firm foundation of the really indispensable works in most areas. Miss Jemison's buying trips to Northern book markets, and especially her journey to European centers in spring 1950, made large additions to Emory's research collections. On the European tour she purchased 4,274 volumes, including long runs of important periodicals and rare individual titles.

One of the projects contained in the plan of a University Center was the establishment of a union catalogue of books in the Atlanta-Athens area. A grant of $55,250 by the General Education Board on November 30, 1939, set this plan in operation. A portion of the grant was to be devoted to completing the cataloguing of other libraries of the Center. In 1943 the Union Catalogue, still far from representing current holdings of the some dozen and a half coöperating libraries, was opened to users, with card files at Emory and the University of Georgia. After a promising beginning, enthusiasm lagged, and in the early 'fifties it seemed that the project might be abandoned. New life was given it by a reorganization completed in 1955, at which time the Athens catalogue was discontinued, centering services in the Emory University Library, since when it has grown steadily and fully proved its unique value to increasing numbers of researchers. During the three-month period January-March 1965 there were 1,044 users, and 2,111 titles were "searched." In 1964 the Union Catalogue contained approximately 780,000 author cards representing several times that number of volumes, 75,608 from twenty-one institutions having been added in 1963-64.

In 1954, Guy R. Lyle was appointed Director of Libraries. Mr. Lyle was brought to Emory from Louisiana State University, where he had served as Director of Libraries since 1944. A native of Canada, a graduate of the University of Alberta, which was to award him an honorary LL.D. in 1964, with a varied experience as librarian and teacher of librarianship, he is widely recognized as an authority on college library administration. At this time a new Library Policy Committee was organized as a committee of the University Senate.

When in spring 1955 administrative officers were moved to the new Administration Building at the west end of the quadrangle, the interior of the Library building underwent complete remodeling and renovation. Crowding had become so desperate that even with full occupancy it was not expected that the new provision for collections and services would allow the Library to function efficiently for a long future. Nevertheless, by taking over all space vacated in the ground and first floors, and by making two floors of the former two-story circulation foyer and reading room to accommodate a Science Library on the upper floor, all departments were allowed critically needed expansion. The entrance lobby was furnished as an exhibition area, and leading from its left was sit-

[187]

uated the Special Collections suite, with the first room set apart as the Candler Memorial. In the Memorial Room are placed manuscripts and memorabilia of the Candler family of Emory donors, especially of Mr. Asa Griggs Candler, Bishop Warren Akin Candler, and Mr. Charles Howard Candler. In wall cases is shelved Mr. Howard Candler's private collection of rare books, which was placed in the Library by Mrs. Candler shortly after her husband's death.

Less than ten years have elapsed since the thoroughgoing reorganization was completed, but already facilities have proved inadequate to expanding book collections, augmented services, and increased University enrollments. A solution of the problem will be the erection of a Library for Advanced Studies, to serve as a center for graduate and other research, the older building to continue in use as the undergraduate library with the stacks devoted to book storage, uses for which it will be eminently suited with a minimum of remodeling. Preliminary plans for the Library for Advanced Studies were drawn up in 1964, and in the University's program for physical development it holds top priority. Already envisaged as a necessary future development is the establishment of a science library to be placed in the science complex also in preliminary planning. This would house all the mathematics and science collections in a central location convenient to seminar rooms, laboratories, and offices.

The Library's oldest endowment for book purchases is the Akin Fund, established in 1908 with a gift of $5,000 by the family of John Wesley Akin '77. The principal is augmented yearly by 20% of the income, and on August 31, 1965 its total value was $9,179.09. The income is expended for books for the Department of English. The Eva McDonald Memorial Endowment was established in 1923 with a gift of $10,000 by Mrs. Dora McDonald, of Cuthbert, Georgia, in memory of her daughter. Its income is devoted to books in the social sciences. The McCandless Fund was established in 1927 in memory of the pioneer Southern teacher, Mrs. Frances Coleman McCandless, by her son, Dr. J. M. McCandless. Generous annual gifts were succeeded in 1942 by an endowment of $10,000 for the purchase of books in the field of education. A marble bust of Mrs. McCandless from the studio of Gutzon Borglum stands in the catalogue area. Annual grants from the Lewis H. Beck Foundation 1933-1965 total $276,353.87. Formerly devoted to a wide range of works for reference and research, the Beck grants are now employed as a fund for buying costly research materials for which departmental budgets are inadequate. Titles for general reading are purchased from the interest on $5,000, bequeathed the Library by William Danner Thomson '95. Other endowments are the Barnes Fund, 1947, for general purchases, the Cullen B. Gosnell Fund, a memorial established by colleagues and students, for books on state and municipal government, and the Ruth Candler Lovett Memorial, with a principal of approximately $25,000, for English literature before 1900 with priority to eighteenth-century and Restoration items.

Annual gifts have been received from, among others, the Class of 1907, DVS senior honor society, Kappa Delta Epsilon educational sorority, and David Chewning '41, the latter to build a collection of writings by and about Presidents of the United States. Following the death of Professor Hinton in 1929, memorial gifts provided a small but carefully selected collection for recreational reading, hopefully intended as the foundation for a "browsing room," a project that had been near his heart from the first planning of the Library. Annual memorial gifts from the Emory Woman's Club have permitted recognition of a wide diversity of bookish interests.

The first important accession to Special Collections after the occupation of the Asa Griggs Candler Library was a deposit in 1927 of manuscripts and correspondence of Joel Chandler Harris '02H by his children. Since the original consignment, the collection has grown steadily by additions made by the family and other donors and by purchase, so that now it includes more than 6,000 pieces of literary manuscript, large blocks of correspondence, a nearly complete series of first and later editions, photographs and book illustrations, and ana. Title to deposits made by the Harris family was transferred to Emory in 1942. A culminating addition was the presentation in 1963 of the personal library and papers of

Julian LaRose Harris, the eldest son, and Julia Collier Harris, the biographer of her father-in-law. Besides extremely valuable Joel Chandler Harris items, the collection comprises a large number of letters from literary, artistic, and political contemporaries, presentation copies of books, and first editions. A group of portrait miniatures by Lucy Stanton, the distinguished artist in this medium, is a charming inclusion.

Other Southern authors are represented: by manuscripts and scrapbooks of Frank L. Stanton, the gift of Percy Megahee '15, '18L, son-in-law of the poet, with additions from other sources; literary manuscripts and correspondence of Mary Noailles Murfree ("Charles Egbert Craddock"), presented by her sister, Miss Fanny Murfree, of Murfreesboro, Tennessee; typescripts of the books of Howard W. Odum '04, '31H; papers and memorabilia of Henry W. Grady, the gift of the Grady family through Professor Raymond B. Nixon '25, author of *Henry W. Grady: Spokesman of the New South,* 1943; and manuscripts, books, and memorabilia of Maurice Thompson, from the estate of the author of *Alice of Old Vincennes,* the gift of Mr. Frank E. Davis of Atlanta, 1959. A nearly complete series of editions of *Gone With the Wind,* with a small group of correspondence of Margaret Mitchell, has been obtained through gift and purchase.

The Keith M. Read Confederate Collection was purchased in 1938. This consists of manuscripts, Confederate imprints, and other books, with miscellaneous materials, comprising approximately 15,000 items gathered by the Savannah collector. In 1910 Emory College had received from the estate of Captain Robert E. Park '62 his extensive Confederate library. The Park and Read Collections, together with constant accessions by gift and purchase, have made Emory's holdings both of primary and secondary sources exceptionally strong for study and research in the Southern Confederacy. One notable acquisition is a large group of papers of Alexander H. Stephens, including his prison diary, a gift-purchase secured from the estate in 1946 through Granger Hansell '23.

The Tracy W. McGregor Collection of Rare Americana came to the Library in 1934-40 by means of an annual grant matched by the University. The Judge Samuel C. Williams Library of Tennesseeana and Southern Americana, a gift-purchase of 1948, added 2,576 titles. The map collection of Mr. Ivan Allen in 1957, with continuing additions, is especially useful for its series of rare maps of the Southern regions of the United States.

Among several large collections of personal papers, those of Bishop Warren A. Candler and of Charles Howard Candler call for particular mention.

The Library of the Candler School of Theology, housed in the Theology Building, in 1965 reported 75,626 volumes. Miss Elizabeth Royer has been Librarian since 1934. During her administration a continuing project has been the building of complete files of conference minutes, board and commission reports, and periodicals of American and British Methodism. A paneled room on the first floor is devoted to Wesleyana, consisting of the Thursfield Smith Collection, purchased in England in 1911 by Bishop Candler, with large additions by gift of various donors. In the memorial room hangs a portrait of John Wesley in his old age painted from life by Henry Edridge. A large and important series of papers of the Wesley family, including John Wesley's Georgia journal in shorthand, and of other early Methodist leaders is deposited in the Special Collections division of the Asa Griggs Candler Library.

When the Atlanta Medical College became the Medical School of Emory University and occupied the buildings on the Druid Hills Campus, book collections were distributed among the offices. In October 1923 members of the Calhoun family provided an endowment for a Medical Library, named for Dr. Abner Wellborn Calhoun (1845-1910), the distinguished ophthalmologist, a member of the Atlanta Medical College from 1872 until his death. Miss M. Myrtle Tye was appointed Medical Librarian in 1923, a position she held until 1933, during which time the collections were organized and greatly augmented. In 1931 the Library was moved to the third floor of the west wing of the Emory University Hospital. Besides larger quarters for books and services, space was provided for an A. W. Calhoun Memorial Room. In 1933 Miss Mildred Jordan '30LS, '42G, became Medical Librarian. On completion of the Woodruff Memorial Research Building, the Library was moved in July 1952 to its present more commodious quarters. The late Dr. F. Phinizy Calhoun '04M, '54H, longtime member of the Emory Board of Trustees, son of Dr. A. W. Calhoun, has been the Library's chief benefactor, his continuing interest insuring its development as a facility of regional rather than of narrow institutional usefulness. Special endowments include the Fitten Fund for books and periodicals dealing with diseases of the chest, and the Qualman Fund for books on hematology.

The Medical Library in 1965 contained 66,171 volumes, of which approximately three-quarters were journal files. Nearly a thousand periodicals are received currently. Besides working collections of books and periodicals, the Library contains a collection of rare medical works, including Vesalius's *De Humani Corporis Fabrica* (Basel, 1543) and Beaumont's *Experiments and Observations on the Gastric Juice* (Plattsburg, 1833), and a small medical museum. A basic collection, designated as the Grady Branch, is placed in the Thomas K. Glenn Memorial Building opposite the Grady Memorial Hospital in downtown Atlanta.

In 1916 the Law Library contained approximately 5,000 volumes; its crowded shelves now hold approximately 56,000 volumes.

> This includes a complete collection of the statutes and reported decisions of the courts of all states, a substantial collection of the reports and decisions of federal and state administrative agencies, a representative collection of English and Canadian legal materials, and the commonly used digests, encyclopedias, loose-leaf services, periodicals and treatises.

The collections have received valuable additions from several private law libraries, and a large number of duplicates from the law library of Columbia University.

The Library of the Division of Librarianship, with 21,850 volumes, is devoted primarily to technical publications, including library reports. The Clyde Pettus Collection on the History of the Book was purchased with a fund contributed by alumni and friends of Miss Pettus '27G as a tribute on her retirement in 1957. The Hilda P. Holme Collection, received by bequest of the Baltimore collector, comprises more than 1,500 titles, mainly in children's literature, the history of the book, and the fine arts.

The Sheppard W. Foster Library, 14,439 volumes, is located on the third floor of the School of Dentistry Building in downtown Atlanta. Currently it receives 340 periodicals in dental, medical, and allied fields.

The Library of the School of Business Administration, 13,139 volumes, is located on the top floor of the Rich Memorial Building. It contains a comprehensive collection of business and economics periodicals, including corporation reports.

The Candler Library of Oxford College contains 11,724 volumes chosen to fill the needs for study and reference of a junior college of liberal arts and sciences.

The intellectual life of the University centers in the Asa Griggs Candler Library and the six divisional libraries of the Atlanta complex. They function as a unit insofar as their resources are equally available to all members of the University, and their collections are catalogued together in the Asa Griggs Candler Library. But their use is not confined to students, faculty, and alumni of Emory University, even though it is obviously necessary to preserve priority of rights. Largely consulted by members of the Atlanta Medical Center and the Atlanta-Athens University Center, generous provision is made for community and regional use. Finally, with the growth, diversification, and distinction of its acquisitions, it has responded more widely to the needs of scholars at a distance through interlibrary loan. With the contemplated threefold organization of undergraduate library, Library for Advanced Studies, and science library, and the continued enrichment of collections, her libraries should play a leading rôle in placing Emory among the great American institutions of learning.

ACTIVITIES

Dooley and the Frolics Queen, 1958

Sigma Chi's Lawn Display,
"Polynesian Holiday,"
Dooley's Frolics 1961

The Coke Lounge, Alumni Memorial Building

Coaching Session, Upper Athletic Field and Field House

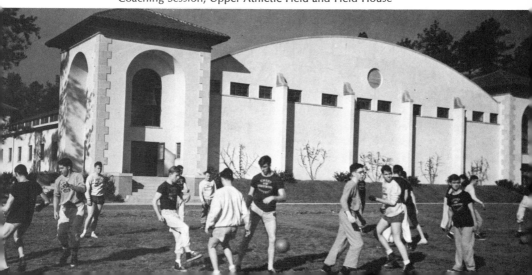

Jennie Tourel Sings in Alumni Memorial

Secretary of State Dean Rusk
at Special Convocation,

Soccer Match,
Emory vs. Vanderbilt

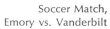

Charter Day Dinner
in Field House, 1964

Student Affairs

CAMPUS POLITICS was not unknown at Oxford, but it had been largely confined to class organization and the activities of the literary societies. For the most part students had been content to leave larger matters with faculty and administration, employing petition and more informal means to make their wishes known in matters of more personal concern. But by the time that the College removed to Atlanta student self-government had made great headway across the nation, and Emory joined in the movement.

When the first Student Government was organized in 1919, with W. B. Stubbs as Chairman of the Executive Council (*de facto* President of the Student Body), four sub-councils were constituted: Athletics, Publications, Debate, and Music, with provision for "any other council necessary for the welfare of the students." The organization's concept of its purpose is shown in its makeup of three men from each of the four Schools—Liberal Arts, Law, Medicine, and Theology—and its resolve to "emphasize not one particular school but the entire University."

Whatever larger ends had been originally conceived, the main business of the Council soon became the appropriation of funds derived from the student activities fee to the various recognized activities. At the time of its organization the Council had charge of allocating the $6.00 per student per year student activities fund. Within five years the fee had been raised to $10.00 per year, and representation on the Council was changed to membership in proportion to enrollment in the schools.

Activities supported by the student activities fee were the three publications—*Campus, Phoenix,* and *Wheel*—, athletics, debate, and the Glee Club. The entire athletic program was considered to be extracurricular, and as such to be paid for by the students. The fee was collected by the University, but the budget was determined by the Council.

In 1927 the students voted to request an increase of $2.50 per year in order to strengthen the athletics program. When the Board of Trustees gave their approval, they also accepted a petition from the Lecture Association to add another $1.00 per year for this activity. After the latter increase the student activities fee remained at $4.50 per quarter ($13.50 per academic year) for over twenty years. Through the years athletics received around 30% of the resulting budget and the *Campus* around 25%; the other activities got along on the remainder.

For these twenty years the Student Activities Council thought of itself primarily as the trustees of the student activities fund. Their budgets reflected student opinion. At times there were complaints from the medical students, particularly those at Grady, that they received nothing for their fee except the publications. Time and again the Council and the administration tried to do something to meet the needs of these students. Tennis courts were built at Grady—to become the site for a new building. On two occasions lounges were built or furnished, only to have them taken over for other purposes, once as interns' quarters and the second time as a laboratory. But the attempts to meet the needs of students through means other than the organized activities were sporadic and occasional.

The Chairman of the Student Activities Council was thought of as President of the Student Body, but the Council did not think of itself as having authority over the various other student government organizations that arose to meet specific needs: the Honor Councils in the various schools; the Traffic Court, inaugurated by the Student Council but left autonomous; the Student Bar Association, and other school and class organizations; the Interfraternity Council.

The coming of the V-12 Program in 1943 made the work of the Student Council difficult for a time. The Navy paid tuition and an adjusted health fee, but not an activities fee. Activity cards were put on sale at $5.00 per "trimester," but until Commander McCann "urged" the trainees to purchase them, the student activities fund was in difficulty. Thereafter 90% or more of the trainees followed the Commander's "suggestion."

After World War II student government on a University-wide basis became aimless and confused. There seem to have been two reasons. First, the student activities fee was absorbed into a single tuition and fees charge when tuition was increased in 1949. Second, the National Student Federation began to challenge the Student Council to speak for the student body on national and international issues.

When activities began to receive funds from an appropriation in the University budget, the sense of being trustees of the students' money was taken from the Council. It no longer dealt with a set amount, but felt obligated to wheedle as much money as possible from the University. The cost of the greatly expanded athletic program and the salaries of directors of activities, however, have now been absorbed by the University.

In the early 'fifties the Council changed its name to the Student Government Association, but paid little attention to local campus affairs. Most of its energy was spent on debating membership in the National Student Federation, which was being tagged "pro-Communist." In 1953 Emory pulled out of the N. S. F. To replace it, under the leadership of Gilbert Turner '53B representatives of six Southern universities met here in the fall of 1954 and organized the Southern University Student Government Association. The Association has thrived, but Emory's interest in it has waned through the years.

With the removal of its primary function and the growing self-consciousness and self-concern of the various schools, the S. G. A. turned more and more to College affairs. Most of its active members were College students, and the College had no separate organization. This was remedied, however, in 1955 with the formation of a College Council that in the last decade has grown in strength and importance.

The Student Government Association, now renamed the Student Senate, with less concern for budgets, turned to playing politics. In the spring of 1955 a law student decided to see what a tub-thumping, gallus-snapping, whoop-em-up campaign would do on a "sophisticated" campus. Winning the election, he worked hard to put life and dignity into the Student Senate, which was floundering to define its function.

Otherwise student government has developed and prospered. The Interfraternity Council has demonstrated responsible leadership for years. With their admission to the College in 1953, the women established House Councils to set up and enforce regulations for residence hall living. The original Inter-Club Council in 1959 became the Panhellenic Council; from the beginning its officers have shown a serious and mature attitude. The men's Residence Hall Councils, while handicapped by the greater turnover of residents than in the women's dormitories, have developed sound procedures and traditions. The College Council is fast becoming a valuable instrument for communication and leadership in its area of activity.

As the schools of the University have gained stature, each has developed strong and responsible student organizations that work *with* its separate faculty and administrative officers but *for* its students. With the exception of the Graduate School, among whose members there is no strong group consciousness, more and more responsibility is being borne by students.

University-wide student government is not lacking. The Traffic Court, that necessary evil, takes its unpleasant work seriously. The Publications and Finance Committees of the Student Senate have no easy task in supervising publications and other larger campus activities. In recent years a Student Center Board has made real progress toward the planning and control of such programs for the University community as the Creative Arts Series, Cinema Wednesday, Saturday Night Movie, intercollegiate sports tournaments, and lectures.

Although student self-government on the Emory campus has had its ups and its downs, as indicated, among other evidences, by constant revision of its written constitution, it has been and is a popular activity, playing a useful rôle in the informal curriculum of the University.

Various musical organizations had flourished briefly on the Oxford campus but no longer existed when in 1917 the Emory College Glee Club was revived by Christian F. Hamff, Professor of German. In a concert on March 8, 1918, this group gave the Emory *Alma Mater* its first public rendition. The words of the song were written by J. Marvin Rast '18 to the tune of Cornell

University's "Far Above Cayuga's Waters," which in turn had been borrowed from the old sentimental favorite, "Annie Lisle."

In 1920 direction of the Glee Club was taken over by Malcolm H. Dewey, Professor of Romance Languages, who was to continue in charge until 1957. Dr. Dewey began at once to enlarge and diversify Emory's musical activities. In 1921 he organized the "Little Symphony." Beginning with sixteen instruments, it grew by 1925 to include thirty, for twenty years presenting a classical repertory with vocal and instrumental soloists. On January 31, 1921, the first Stunt Night combined a popular musical program with vaudeville skits devised by the undergraduates. A growing reputation persuaded "The South's Sweetest Singers," so styled by James Dombrowsky '23, to undertake extended tours, in December 1922 traveling to Florida and Cuba, and giving their first Washington concert on March 25, 1925. On this occasion President and Mrs. Coolidge were in attendance. On November 24, 1933, the Glee Club sang for President Franklin D. Roosevelt at the dedication of Georgia Hall, Warm Springs. Presenting a repertory of classical choral music and specializing in Negro spirituals in Dr. Dewey's own distinctive arrangements, annual tours were to carry the Glee Club along the Atlantic seaboard from Miami to New York, to Nassau, Bahamas, and San Juan, Puerto Rico.

The first program of Christmas carols, which became an annual event with an overflow attendance of both town and gown, was given in Atlanta's First Presbyterian Church on December 13, 1925. Since the completion of Glenn Memorial in 1931, the Christmas concerts have been presented on the Emory campus.

An epoch-making event in the history of the Glee Club was its first transatlantic tour, June-September 1926. In England there were concerts at various resort cities, and in London in Queen's Hall, with a week's engagement at the Coliseum, the first-ranking variety house. Everywhere the singers won applause from concert-goers and critics. In addition to public appearances they were entertained by, among others, the English-Speaking Union, by Lady Astor, the Lord Mayor of London, and the Duke of Manchester. Three years later a second tour took the Glee Club again to London, where they were engaged for a two-weeks stand at the Coliseum, and passing over to the Continent, they sang for a week at Mille Colonnes, Amsterdam. They left behind them two dozen records of their repertory, including spirituals, produced by the Metropole Gramophone Company. The Third European tour was delayed until the summer of 1953, when the Glee Club visited ten countries, sang sixty-five concerts, and made a two-weeks tour of Army and Air Force installations in West Germany.

It would be almost impossible to exaggerate the enthusiastic reception encountered by the student group throughout their singing tours, or the pleasures enjoyed by them in foreign scenes and personal contacts. An incident of particular interest was a friendship made on the second visit to England. They were heard in Norwich by Mr. Ernest S. Howlett, a retired elderly gentleman of that city, who was so pleased with their performance that he followed them on successive engagements, introduced himself, and quickly won their esteem. In 1929 he came to America and spent more than a year in close association with his new-made friends. On his return to England he designed the coat of arms since used by the Glee Club, and he continued to keep in touch with his American hosts until his death, brought about by privations suffered during World War II.

Among engagements at home should be especially noted the Glee Club's two concerts in New York's Town Hall, the first on March 27, 1952, the second on March 22, 1956. On both occasions highly complimentary notices appeared in the metropolitan press.

A close fellowship holds old members together, inspiring frequent reunions, the most notable of them being the Twenty-Fifth Anniversary Reunion, June 7-8, 1946, of which Chess Lagomarsino '26 was Chairman. These have continued since Dr. Dewey's retirement, members of former years coming from all quarters to sing the old choruses and to exchange reminiscences. A scrapbook record in twenty-two volumes, compiled by Dr. Dewey, was placed in the Emory University Library in 1964.

With the coming of coeducation the Emory Woman's Chorale was organized, Fall Quarter 1954, with Mrs. Bayne Smith Director; its first concert was given on May 13, 1955. Combined with the Glee Club as the Emory University Chorus, 125 voices, it sang under Robert Smith's direction at the Warm Springs twentieth anniversary celebration on January 2, 1958, and was featured on Dave Garroway's NBC-TV "Today" show.

Under various directors, including Edward A. Kane '28, a well-remembered soloist of the 'twenties, the Glee Club carried on until the appointment of William Lemonds as Director of Choral Music in 1963.

Dr. Lemonds trains and conducts both the men's Glee Club and the Woman's Chorale, combining them for large musical performances. For smaller works the Emory Chamber Singers of eighteen voices are chosen from the Glee Club and Chorale. In 1965 the Chamber Singers were invited to make an album for the Methodist Church in the "Hymn of the Month" series. Dr. Lemonds also organized the Atlanta Chamber Orchestra, Emory University, playing complete concerts and accompanying choral groups. An ambitious and highly successful undertaking was the Southeastern première on May 11, 1965, of Benjamin Britten's *War Requiem,* originally written for the dedication of England's Coventry Cathedral. For this the full resources of Glee Club, Chorale, and Chamber Orchestra were employed, augmented with members of the Atlanta Symphony and professional soloists.

In 1963 the Emory Glee Club became a member of the Intercollegiate Music Council, a national organization of forty-two college groups. On May 12-14, 1965, Emory was host to its national convention, on the last evening of which the glee clubs of Emory, Sewanee, Davidson, and Georgia Tech presented "Men in Concert" in Glenn Memorial Auditorium. Dr. Lemonds has promoted faculty and community as well as student musical activities, carrying on the artistic tradition for which Emory has been most noted in the past.

The *Phoenix,* which had begun publication on the Oxford campus in 1886, was brought to Atlanta with the College. For something less than two decades it enjoyed a late flourishing period, with editors who took its literary function quite seriously. It is surprising how much verse of a really fair quality appeared in its pages, a certain distinction being given it by the early work of, among others, Ernest Hartsock '25, '27G, and James E. Warren, Jr. '30, '41G. A Fiftieth Anniversary number, edited by Frederick Lagerquist '35, '37L, appeared in May 1935. The magazine, which had formerly had monthly issues, was now a quarterly, and it was becoming more and more difficult to fill even twenty-odd pages with literary materials. Subsequent editors embarked on various imitative experiments, featuring rather callow and tasteless humor. Student interest was rapidly declining, so that in the financial stringency of the war years there appeared to be no reason for struggling to keep the *Phoenix* alive. From Winter 1943 to Winter 1946 the magazine suspended publication. After the war, however, there was an undergraduate demand for its revival, readily acceded to by the Student Activities Council. The *Phoenix,* justifying its name, sprang to life again and actually regained a measure of popularity, but its successive editors, alternating between designs for a literary and a humor magazine or a combination of the two, have never won for it the standing that it possessed in earlier years. Attempts have been made by the campus literati, despairing of the *Phoenix,* to create a purely literary medium, but as yet their efforts have received little substantial support.

The *Emory Wheel,* Volume 1, Number 1, appeared on December 12, 1919, Ernest Rogers '20 Editor. From its beginning the student newspaper, published weekly throughout the academic year, has been the accepted organ of the campus, chronicling University activities, giving voice to student opinion, and propagandizing for all sorts of causes. In early issues it encroached on the literary preserve of the *Phoenix,* printing columns of verse, and it quite absorbed the former function of the magazine as commentator on campus issues. The *Wheel* from the first assumed a complete freedom of expression, which the Dean of the College was reluctant to grant, and from time to time outspoken and rash editors have found themselves at odds with the administration. But through the years the generally serious and sound policies of the paper have more than made up for certain evidences of irresponsibility, mainly the effect of youthful exuberance, and its boast of being "The South's Most Independent Collegiate Newspaper" has been fairly earned. From 1926 to 1952, during his headship of the Department of Journalism, Professor Raymond B. Nixon as faculty adviser gave a professional tone to the publication, which under purely amateur direction has not been lost since. In its own field it has gathered twenty-six all-American citations. From an apprenticeship on the *Wheel* a large number of its editors have gone on to high positions in journalism. Its founder has won a large following as feature writer and columnist on the *Atlanta Journal*. Francis W. Carpenter '28 is Director of News Services, the United States Mission to the United Nations; Warren S. Duffie '38 is at the United Press International Bureau, Washington, D. C.; Rhea Eskew '48 is Southern Division Manager of United Press International; Claude Sitton '49 is National News Director of the New York *Times*. The list of editors contains many others who have won distinction in fields of public service. No extracurricular activity has more fully brought out the abilities of Emory students than the *Wheel*, nor provided more useful training for future careers.

The *Campus* annual appeared at the end of the first year after the College's arrival in Atlanta. A yearbook had been published at Oxford under various titles, and the new venture was largely devoted to the College, though it included sections devoted to the other schools. As the University has grown, the coverage of the *Campus* has become more and more inclusive, so that it is now an indispensable record, mainly pictorial, of all University activities, as well as the class album to which the old grad will return in after years to refresh his memory of early companionships. Although in many respects following a standardized pattern for college and university annuals across the nation, its lavishness in format and illustration, especially in its employment of color, has given it a rather special distinction. A long-time feature has been "Dooley's Diary," a calendar of campus gossip as from the pen of the patron of the student frolics. Problems of production have made it extremely difficult to bring out the yearbook on a set schedule, so that it is almost traditional that the distribution of the *Campus* should be weeks or months delayed beyond the close of the academic year. The finished product, however, has usually been worth waiting for.

Phi Gamma and Few Literary Societies came to Atlanta with Emory College. They had been chartered at least as early as 1839. The societies had their own buildings at Oxford which are still standing, and the outstanding orator or debater was a "B.M.O.C."

On the Atlanta campus the literary societies continued to meet weekly for a decade or so. Under the direction of Professor Nolan A. Goodyear a varsity team continued the tradition of intercollegiate debating. The *Emory Wheel* of May 6, 1924, reports a victory over "an ancient forensic rival, Trinity College," the North Carolina Methodist college which in that year became Duke University.

The decade from 1925 to 1935 was Emory's golden era of debating. In 1925 debaters came from Oxford University to meet our Southern Debate Champions. Teams from British universities, from Oxford, Ireland, London, and Cambridge, visited the campus almost every year. In 1935 an Emory team consisting of Robert Elliott and Robert Wiggins represented the National Student Federation of America in Europe. This was a time when an international debate drew an audience that comfortably filled Glenn Memorial, and the participants were powers on the campus because of their forensic ability.

But while intercollegiate debating throve, the literary societies dwindled away; in 1931 they voluntarily disbanded. Revived in 1937, in 1939, just a century after their founding, they were permanently dissolved.

When Professor Goodyear resigned from direction in the late 'thirties, freshman and varsity debaters were coached by fellow students. A Debate Forum was organized with faculty advisers and a faculty Debate Council, but interest in the activity, depending entirely on student leadership, was varied and unreliable. One year a Birmingham-Southern team arrived on the campus and was unable to find either opponents or audience.

Wartime restrictions virtually ended intercollegiate trips, and with them much of the motivation for debating. In its postwar revival the earlier audiences have disappeared. In the 'sixties no one is surprised to find a debate "chaired" by an alarm clock and arguments addressed to an audience of from one to three judges.

Postwar reorganization, however, was brought about in 1946, and when, two years later, George A. Neely came as Assistant Professor of Speech with an assignment to coach debate, the activity grew in size and strength. In academic 1950-51 the Debate Forum changed its name to the Barkley Forum, in honor of Vice-President Alben W. Barkley '00. This year also saw the inauguration of the Barkley Forum High School Debate Tournament. A donation was secured making it possible to offer Emory scholarships as prizes. The Tournament proved valuable in recruiting, and was given assistance by the Director of Admissions.

Professor Neely transferring to the School of Theology in 1952, coaching of debaters for some years was done by graduate and professional students with occasional faculty assistance. The Forum had enough momentum, nevertheless, to organize the Southeastern University Tournament on our campus in 1953.

In 1961 Mr. Glenn Pelham, a Georgia State Senator and member of the Governor's Commission on Higher Education, began to coach the Barkley Forum debaters. Since Mr. Pelham's coming, the Forum has become one of the most successful debating organizations in the country, as witness the impressive collection of trophies on display in the Alumni Memorial Building.

Drama was the last extracurricular activity to come to Emory. The traditional interdict of the Methodist Church on the theater was successfully invoked by Bishop Candler whenever the question of permitting the formation of a student dramatic club was brought before the Trustees. Nevertheless original play skits were included in the mixed bills of the Glee Club as early as 1924.

In the Glee Club's Extravaganza of December 1928 Booth Tarkington's one-act *The Trysting Place,* under the direction of Professor Thomas H. English, was introduced in the second half of the program, and this was the beginning of the Emory Players. Their first full-length production was *Seven Keys to Baldpate,* by George M. Cohan, staged in the Emory Auditorium on May 16, 1929. Goldsmith's *She Stoops to Conquer* was transferred to the auditorium of the Druid Hills School in 1930, and *The Yellow Jacket,* "a Chinese play done in a Chinese manner," by Hazelton and Benrimo, packed the auditorium of the Atlanta Woman's Club on January 30, 1931. The last of the annual productions directed by Professor English was Oscar Wilde's *The Importance of Being Earnest,* played for two nights, May 4 and 6, 1933, in the Emory Auditorium.

In 1934 Professor Garland G. Smith, of the Department of English, was persuaded to accept the direction of the Players, and for the next five years there were three productions annually. Professor Smith sought his repertory among plays of the contemporary theater, taking particular care to choose pieces adapted to the talents at his command. Many of the women's rôles were filled by members of Agnes Scott's Blackfriars. His first production was George M. Cohan's *Broadway Jones.* With *The Fool,* by Channing Pollock, in fall 1934 the Players moved into Glenn Memorial Auditorium. Leading parts in this play were taken by Sam Shiver '32, '38G, and Gatewood Workman '29, '31G. Especially successful offerings were Booth Tarkington's *Clarence* and *The Man from Home* and Moss Hart's and George S. Kaufman's *You Can't Take It With You.* Among the excellent student actors of this period George Downing '38 and Marcus Bartlett '39 deserve special mention.

Although the Players continued to function, there was no permanent director until 1943, when Edith Russell took over with the technical assistance of her husband, H. R. Harrington, the University's Superintendent of Grounds and Buildings. In summer 1943 she directed an elaborate production of Maxwell Anderson's *Valley Forge* in the Amphitheater.

In fall 1948 George A. Neely joined the College faculty as Assistant Professor of Speech and Director of the Emory Players. In his charge the organization enjoyed its longest period of steady development. In 1952 he moved to the lobby of the Alumni Memorial Building, where he established a "theater in the round." Among many successful productions may be noted *On Borrowed Time,* starring Dean E. H. Rece as Gramps and Jimmy Rouse, son of an English professor, as Pud. Mr. Neely was relieved of direction for the year 1955-56, and after resuming it for 1956-57, he resigned to become a full-time faculty member of the School of Theology.

Part-time direction has held the organization together, with good work done under difficult conditions. Following the removal of campus food services to Cox Hall, renovation of the old Auditorium, now a part of Alumni Memorial, in some respects improved the situation of the Players. But until an auditorium specially equipped for theatrical requirements is built, they must continue to struggle with inadequate facilities. With the provision of a theater, a full-time professional director should raise the status of the Players to a leading campus activity.

There have been numerous other dramatic ventures on the campus besides the Emory Players. One of the most notable was a performance of Shakespeare's *A Comedy of Errors,* presented on an Elizabethan stage in the Amphitheater. This was a feature of a Shakespeare Day celebration, under the direction of Professor John C. Stephens, Jr., on April 14, 1954. From 1956 to 1958 the Emory Opera Theater, with the guidance of Professor Chappell White, produced Puccini's *Gianni Schicci* and *Il Tabarro, The Rose and the Ring,* and *The Beggar's Opera.*

Dramatic interest at Emory has never languished, and it is remarkable what has been accomplished through the years with makeshift facilities and constantly changing, usually amateur, direction.

Religious Life

EMORY COLLEGE brought to the University a long tradition of close ties with the Methodist Church with mores rooted in those ties. Until the College came to Atlanta, all students were required to attend daily morning prayers, described as "a service of scripture reading, prayers, and hymns," and to attend church services "each Sabbath." Classes were held on Saturday but not on Monday, to avoid the necessity of study on Sunday. The Y.M.C.A. held weekly devotional meetings, organized study groups, and contained a strong "Student Volunteer Band." The students, who were "not allowed to leave Oxford without the consent of both of the parents and the President," were expected to exemplify high Christian ideals. From all accounts, nevertheless, it would appear that the expectation fell somewhat short of full realization.

The Oxford traditions were established at the University with little modification. The only immediate changes were to specify the church attendance rule as one service each Sunday and to require attendance at morning prayers only of students resident on campus. If it seems strange that the customs of small and isolated Oxford could be so easily transplanted to Atlanta, it must be remembered that the new campus was a small and isolated community. It took the city more than a decade to grow out to the campus.

That the atmosphere of Oxford did permeate the University campus is shown by the "great Durham revival" of February 1921. The student Y.M.C.A. organized and promoted a revival each year. In 1921 the Reverend Plato T. Durham, first Dean of the Candler School of Theology, widely known for his oratorical talent, was the preacher. When it was announced that he would occupy the pulpit, the Student Activities Council endorsed the meetings and the *Wheel* editorially urged attendance. The students came, and the campus was shaken by a "great awakening." Prayer groups were formed in dormitories and fraternity houses. Students went into the woods to pray; many spent most of the night in prayer.

The revival was University-wide. When Dr. Durham had reached the last of the scheduled sermons, the medical students, fifty of whom "came out for Christ and Christian service," persuaded him to continue the meetings for a second week.

The revival pattern continued for a few years, but never again resulted in the fervor of the Durham Revival. In the middle 'twenties Emory students were caught up in the nation-wide interest in the Student Volunteer Movement sponsored by the Y.M.C.A. They attended state and national conferences, particularly the Blue Ridge Conferences held in North Carolina in the summers. As a result a number of Emory students went to the mission field.

For the first two decades of the University the student organization concerned with religious life and activities was the Y.M.C.A. In the 'thirties activities became more campus-centered and ties with the national body weakened. In the early 'thirties the University created the office of Director of Religious and Social Life. The words "and Social" in the title reflect the carry-over of the recreational aspect of the Y.M.C.A. program. In 1937 the name of the organization was changed to the Emory Christian Association, indicating its independence of national ties.

In the late 'twenties the annual revival became Religious Emphasis Week, scheduled in Winter Quarter. After trying out several kinds of programs, the first week with a single preacher in a series of morning services was held in 1929, and this pattern was maintained for more than thirty years.

The first preacher was a young Emory B.D. from North Carolina, G. Ray Jordan '20T. For the first decade young preachers were sought for Religious Emphasis Week, because it was felt that they would best understand the student viewpoint. Eventually the students demanded the best preacher available, regardless of age. In 1935 Dean Lynn Harold Hough, of Drew Theological Seminary, was brought to Emory. Others of similar stature were sought, and in 1938 Dr. George A. Buttrick was scheduled. The ministers of the region were invited to hear these eminent preachers, and so began Ministers Week. Within a few years the Quillian, the Jarrell, and the Sam Jones Lectures were incorporated in the program, and ministers attended in such numbers that students were virtually squeezed out. Religious Emphasis Week was then moved to Fall Quarter in order to retain its original student-centered purpose.

As the size and complexity of the student body increased, the requirements as to attendance on religious services were modified. By 1924 the stated rule was only that "Every student of the University is expected to attend divine worship once each week." Soon this expectation was no longer expressed in the printed regulations. Midweek chapel exercises were continued, in spite of inadequate assembly halls and scheduling difficulties. When Glenn Memorial became available in 1933, the pattern of required chapel on Fridays at ten o'clock for all University students was established and remained in effect until World War II. Cancelled for the V-12 years, because servicemen could not be required to attend, compulsory chapel was restored in 1946. At that time, however, the College student body was so large that the Lower Division filled the auditorium, and only freshmen and sophomores were required to attend. This regulation held until 1958, when voluntary worship at ten on Wednesdays was inaugurated. This has now been discontinued, and an eleven o'clock service on Sunday in Durham Chapel of the Theology Building has been substituted. Professor Jack S. Boozer '40, '42T, of the Department of Bible and Religion, who was deeply concerned with the problem of student worship, accepted the appointment as Acting Chaplain for 1965-66.

The story of required chapel would not be complete without paying tribute to Dr. Wyatt Aiken Smart, who was in fact Chaplain to the University long before he received the title in 1944. The *Wheel* editorial of November 20, 1930, which said, "We can't buck regular chapel, but why such boring speakers?" was not the last such "gripe" from the student body. And when a student was asked to make a suggestion, he usually replied, "Let Dr. Smart speak every week." He did preach frequently, and always in the vernacular and to the situation of the campus. He also brought many challenging speakers to the Glenn pulpit, noteworthy among whom was Richard B. Harrison, who was in Atlanta playing the part of "de Lawd" in *The Green Pastures*. He was the first Negro to speak in Glenn Memorial. Atlanta's leading ministers were invited to address the students, and more than once Rabbi David

Marx of the Jewish Temple.

Required study of the Bible has continued over the years to be a feature of the undergraduate curriculum. The Oxford pattern of requiring every student to take one hour of Bible study each week through four years was abandoned after the first year on the Atlanta campus. Successive changes led in the late 'twenties to the development of a course in Biblical Introduction of five hours a week through one quarter. The pattern of one course in the Bible required of all students has lasted through all revisions of the College curriculum. While the title has varied and the effort has been made to keep the content abreast of developing scholarship, the basic approach has not changed. Meanwhile elective courses in the Department of Bible and Religion have increased in number and have been well-received.

The Emory Christian Association, since 1962 the Emory Religious Association, is the central organization through which the specialized religious groups coöperate for campus-wide activities. The development of denominational groups was rapid in the early 'forties. At first only two, the Young People's Department of Glenn Memorial Church, Methodist, and the Baptist Student Union were represented on the E. C. A. Council. Four years later six groups had representatives in the Council: the Baptist Student Union, the Newman Club (Catholic), the Canterbury Club (Episcopal), the Jewish Student Forum, the Methodist Student Movement, and the Presbyterian Student Association. All of these groups had been organized at the instigation and with the help of the Director of Religious Life, whose responsibilities have never been limited to any one group. Since 1944 the Office of Director has been filled by Samuel L. Laird '33, '44T, '50G.

In the late 'fifties and early 'sixties the various denominations began to place ministers or other adult leaders on the campuses of church-related colleges and universities, following the pattern already established at state institutions. Emory's religious program has been strengthened by the addition of a number of full-time and part-time workers of exceptional ability who have come with the full approval and coöperation of the University. In the varying ministry of their faiths they have nevertheless shown a fine

[213]

ecumenical spirit rooted in a common concern for the spiritual welfare of our students.

On the occupation of the Druid Hills campus a congregation of the Methodist Church was established in the chapel of the Theology Building. The membership was largely composed of the University families with some student attendance. In 1933 services were transferred to the new Glenn Memorial, and in 1940 the facilities of Glenn Memorial Church were greatly enlarged by the erection of the Church School Building. With the growth of the community around the campus the congregation has come to include a larger proportion of non-University than University members, and Glenn has taken on the status of the church of the Emory community rather than of Emory University. It shares student attendance on equal terms with Atlanta's other churches.

A chronicle of events, programs, and organizations affords only a surface picture of Emory's religious life. Granted that any attempt to describe religious life in depth is subjective, nevertheless the attempt should be made.

No doubt the sophisticates of the 'sixties would charge the Emory of 1915 with moralistic pietism and provincialism. Its early regulations, based on the Discipline of the Methodist Episcopal Church, South, did indeed contain elements of legalistic piety. Dancing off campus was not approved until 1933, and dancing on campus came only in 1941. Drinking has continued to be frowned on, though smoking has been condemned only by M.D.'s of the present era. Emory has inevitably reflected its time and place in history.

But Emory in some important respects has been ahead of its time. Some have called this being "radical." Some have called it a disregard for the responsibilities of leadership. Fifty years give enough perspective to suggest that usually Emory has been far enough ahead to lead and not too far to lose its following. The story of Emory's leadership when the racial problem in education became critical may validate this claim.

The College which came up from Oxford had a commitment to God and man deeper than its unabashed commitment to the Southern Methodist Church. When the Trustees stated in the bylaws that the University "is designed to be a profoundly religious institution without being narrowly sectarian. It proposes to encourage freedom of thought as liberal as the limitations of truth, while maintaining unwavering devotion to the faith once for all delivered to the saints," they were stating a solemn pledge and a heartfelt obligation.

Through the years the concerns of students have reflected and intensified the concerns of the world around them. In the revival era they had their Durham Revival. In the time of the social gospel, they were concerned about the racial issue, the plight of the tenant farmer, and while the clouds of war were only gathering, they embraced pacificism. When war came, all of the hundreds of ardent pacifists, except two, went to war. After the war, they came back in a hurry to finish their education, and to ask questions, deeper and more fundamental questions than before. When the racial problem became practical rather than theoretical, students took sides and some took action. And many students in these days are wrestling with the questions of "identity" and "alienation."

Some still feel that Emory is radical and some that it is too conservative. But the dilemma of the student, spiritual, moral, or intellectual, is one that ultimately he must himself resolve; the rôle of the faculty is only that of sympathetic and enlightened guidance, not coercion. President White's words of 1951 are the enduring statement of the philosophy of education for which Emory stands:

We cannot forget that religious faith, in God and in man, alone can justify educational or any other human endeavor. . . . We must find a way to put God at the center of the educative process . . . . At its heart and in its purpose, Emory is Christian and will remain so.

Athletics and Physical Education

IN THE 'EIGHTIES baseball was the leading intercollegiate sport. The game was popular on the Oxford campus, and for a few years Emory engaged in unsuccessful competition with the University of Georgia. The excitement roused and the absence of the team and student spectators from Oxford, always frowned on by the authorities, brought about the first pronouncement on intercollegiate contests. On June 6, 1891, the Board of Trustees passed a resolution against "match games," which was only modified later on petition from the student body by permission to join with other institutions of the state in one field day.

At the same time there was an awareness on the part of President Candler and the administrative officers of the benefit to be derived from physical exercise in the development of the well-rounded individual. In 1889 a ball field was cleared on the western border of the campus, and the old technology building was repaired and equipped as a gymnasium. In 1898 Frank Clyde Brown was appointed Adjunct Professor of Languages and Director of Gymnasium, under whose direction two hours of physical exercise per week was required of every student. He is credited with what was perhaps the first intramural system of athletics in America. Coach Fielding Yost of the University of Michigan is quoted as saying that "a little college down in Georgia" and Miami University, Oxford, Ohio, pioneered intramural sports programs. From the 'nineties football and the annual ten-mile relay race were the leading events of the autumn sports calendar. The academic classes and the student rooming houses were the units of competition, with members of the faculty acting as team coaches. The rural location of the College, its isolation from city attractions, had much to do with the success of the program.

In 1907 the J. P. Williams Athletic Hall, described as a facility unequalled in the South, encouraged the development of gymnastic exercises, whose exhibition became a feature of later commencements.

When Emory came to Atlanta, an active campaign for inter-collegiate competition was begun. The *Emory Wheel* in its first year displayed at its masthead, "For a Greater Emory and Inter-collegiate Athletics." The slogan was dropped after a time, but it has reappeared sporadically with variations. In 1921 Ray K. Smathers '22L was appointed Director of Athletics. He founded the Pyramid honor club, whose motto was "For Greater Emory and Athletics." Its members demonstrated in white robes around a bonfire, somewhat in the manner of the Ku Klux Klan, their pur-pose being to arouse a student-wide demand for intercollegiate con-tests. Smathers resigned at the beginning of Winter Quarter 1923, and the Pyramid is not heard from after 1925.

Bishop Candler, while Chancellor and afterwards as a member of the Board, spoke strongly against intercollegiate sports, which he regarded as "evil and only evil." His arguments dealt with the disruptions of academic routine, with expense, and chiefly with the immoral aspects of intercollegiate competition. There was no restraint in his utterances. His influence had kept the Trustees of the College from giving any serious consideration to appeals for a change of policy, and as University Chancellor his views continued to be accepted, whatever may have been the private opinions of some Board members.

Eventually three track meets were allowed at home, this form of competition chosen because it allowed more students to partici-pate than other games. Coach Smathers also organized a cross-country race, in which Emory was usually the winner until its dis-continuance in 1928. At first the only facilities provided were the upper athletic field and the basement of Winship Hall.

From 1923 to 1928 James G. Lester, Department of Engineer-ing, served as Director of Athletics. Then began "a period in which the program of intramural athletics was to experience its greatest and most thorough development." During the summer of 1923 a temporary basketball court was erected in the woods west of Dobbs Hall, financed largely with student funds. Up until this time all basketball games had been held at the Atlanta Y.M.C.A. or at the Wesley Memorial Church courts. An outdoor swimming pool was constructed in 1927. In the same year the temporary dining hall was renovated and remodeled as a student activities and athletic building. These facilities were nothing more than makeshifts, but they were forced to serve for twenty-five years.

Members of the faculty continued as volunteer coaches, to whom it is impossible to give too much credit for the success of the intramural system. Coaching aid was also furnished by members of the staff of the Reserve Officers Training Corps from 1919 to 1930, particularly by Captain, now General, Thomas S. Arms, who prepared Gordon Logan for entrance in the pre-Olympian decathlon trials of 1925 and 1926, when Logan placed one position away from the Olympic team. Athletic scholarships were also offered for graduate student assistants.

From 1928 to 1931 Ralph L. Fitts was Director of Athletics, with Frank Kopf as his assistant. In 1929 appeared Bulletin 23, *American College Athletics,* of the Carnegie Foundation for the Advancement of Teaching, which severely criticized overemphasis on intercollegiate competition, and found place for commending Emory's policy of "athletics for all" and its encouragement of "carry-over" sports. A new rule of compulsory freshman participation in physical exercise required the construction of more tennis courts and an additional playing field. Intramural football, basketball, and baseball by this time were accompanied by intercollegiate cross-country, golf, swimming, tennis, track, and wrestling. Track was abolished by student vote in 1930, to be reinstated in 1945. From 1923 to 1955 there was an annual pushball contest between freshmen and sophomores, which was finally abolished because of resulting disorder and injuries suffered by participants. Financing of the athletic program by student fees and book store profits remained altogether inadequate, but a fine spirit of coöperation in the student body made up for many deficiencies.

Dr. Howard J. Savage, Acting Secretary of the Carnegie Foundation, author of Bulletin 23, visited Emory in March 1931 to observe the University's system and to offer suggestions for its improvement. With the appointment of Jeff D. McCord '16 in that year as first full-time Director of Athletics the University moved a step forward in the promotion of its program of physical education. The basketball court was sided in and stoves were installed,

[218]

so that matches could be played and watched in some degree of comfort. The swimming pool was inclosed for year-round use, with the addition of dressing rooms and heating and filtration systems. The athletic fields were reconditioned, and three new tennis courts were built.

In his 1932 Report to the Board of Trustees President Cox was able to note progress:

> Thanks to the capable and enthusiastic leadership of our new full-time athletic director, Mr. Jeff McCord, more students have participated in athletics, more contests have been staged, and more forms of sports have been provided for the benefit of the students. Seventy percent of the students participated in athletics during 1931-32, as compared with fifty-four percent in 1930-31 and forty-nine percent in 1929-30.

National publicity was given to the Emory program by means of a radio debate on the NBC Blue Network, April 18, 1936, in which a team from Emory debated a team from Catholic University of Washington on the subject, intramural *vs.* intercollegiate sports.

The Athletic Department of 1931-42 presided over an organization of six major sports—baseball, basketball, boxing, football, swimming, tennis—and twelve minor sports—touch football, volleyball, bowling, wrestling, diamond ball, horseshoes, cross-country, ping-pong, badminton, golf, track and field, water basketball. A rather complex system of participation points, team awards, and individual trophies was instituted by McCord. The E Club was composed of members elected from letter men on the campus.

As early as 1924 there had been proposals for the erection of a combined student activities building and gymnasium, but the project developed slowly. Nevertheless, by the end of 1941 about $125,000 had been subscribed for this purpose, but with the entry of the United States into World War II nothing could be done immediately. Encouraged by the armed services, greater stress was put upon athletics and physical fitness by all colleges and universities in the nation. In 1942 Vice-President White made strong recommendations to the Trustees for the radical improvement of Emory's program, embracing finances, personnel, and physical facilities. At this time preliminary plans for a gymnasium were drawn by J. G. Lester with the advice and assistance of O. R. Quayle, J. B. Peebles, and J. D. McCord, which were placed in the hands of a professional architect for development.

In June 1942 Thomas E. McDonough, Chairman of the Department of Health and Physical Education, Eastern Kentucky State Teachers College, was named Professor of Physical Education. Edward J. Shea '44G was brought from the Atlanta Athletic Club as Instructor of Physical Education. Mr. McCord continued for a short while in charge of intramurals; on his resignation Mr. McDonough assumed full charge as Director of Athletics.

Under McDonough the Department of Physical Education adopted a new program based on the recognition by the University of the new Department as one of its educational functions and an increased budget furnished entirely by the University. It involved a decided step-up in the intensity of all its activities, a greater use of existing facilities, and a more thorough study of the needs of the individual student for physical fitness. Physical education was made a requirement for the lower division of the College.

The work of the Department was somewhat complicated by the establishment on the campus of the V-12 program of the United States Navy and Marine Corps with its more than 650 trainees. Staff assistance was furnished by one Navy officer and six Navy Chief Specialists.

In order to give greater attention to the medical needs of students, Dr. Jacob D. Farris, formerly of Eastern Kentucky State Teachers College, in 1944 was appointed University Physician and Director of Student Health. His duties were to provide better and more hygienic living conditions for students, to recommend personal remedial exercises for students requiring them to the Department of Physical Education, and to provide hospitalization for all student illnesses except those of a chronic nature. Dr. Farris resigning in 1947, in 1950 Dr. Wiley Roy Mason, Jr., was appointed Director of Student Health.

At the war's end it was determined that there could be no further delay in providing fit facilities for physical education. The plan of a combined student activities center and gymnasium was discarded. The University now undertook to finance the latter project, and the Alumni Association assumed responsibility for the former. From a fabricator of airplane hangars in Oklahoma City Business Manager George Mew made the advantageous purchase of a steel frame, which was erected adjacent to the upper athletic field and roofed by the manufacturer. The building was completed under the direction of a local architect. The Field House was occupied in fall 1948, and the swimming pool at the west end went into use the following year. In its new, carefully planned quarters a full program of physical education could now be developed with an augmented staff.

The requirement of three hours of physical education classes a week for six quarters was made for the lower division of the College, for which in 1951 limited academic credit was allowed. Activities for freshmen and sophomores now include archery, badminton, bait casting, basic skills, basketball, camping and outdoor education, folk games, fundamentals of movement, golf, gymnastics, handball, modern dance, riflery, soccer, softball, speedball, survival swimming (drown-proofing), tennis, touch football, track and field, tumbling, volleyball, water ballet, water crafts, weight training, and wrestling. More than 1,200 men and women participate in these activities each quarter. Ten outdoor and ten gymnasium teaching stations are used in handling this group.

The Board of Trustees' "Statement of Policy on Athletics and Physical Education" of October 16, 1945, with which Mr. McDonough and his staff are in cordial agreement, reaffirmed Emory's historic ban on high-pressure sports for public entertainment. This policy of non-participation in the major intercollegiate sports—football, basketball, and baseball—has made Emory almost unique among American institutions of higher education. Its stand has puzzled observers and has been a source of some dissatisfaction and occasional agitation among alumni and students. Emory gets no publicity on the sports pages of the newspapers. It is safe to say, however, that the situation is now generally accepted, that there are many who take pride in the fact that the University has developed strength without the aid of such publicity, and that the policy is the envy of many a college administrator.

At a dinner at the University of Chicago honoring Dr. Ernest C. Colwell, who was resigning the presidency there to return to Emory, one of the speakers congratulated him on going to an institution that "had followed Chicago's example" in abandoning football. Colwell took great delight in pointing out that just the reverse was true, and that Chicago had in effect followed Emory's example; Emory had never had to abandon football, because Emory had never put a "varsity" team on the field.

Nevertheless, Emory's teams engage in intercollegiate competition on and off the campus in soccer, swimming, tennis, track and field, and wrestling. There is, however, no anticipated intercollegiate program for women. Emory holds memberships in the Amateur Athletic Union and the National Collegiate Athletic Association. The Director and his staff have been active in these and other organizations, have held office, and have published many articles in the professional journals.

The Department of Physical Education has exerted a strong influence on high schools and smaller colleges of the southeastern United States through the sponsorship of track and field meets, swimming, handball, and wrestling tournaments, and other activities. The Havalanta (Havana-Atlanta) swimming meets added an international flavor to the program for ten years before Castro. In the 'forties Mr. Shea as swimming coach trained a remarkable string of champions among Atlanta high school boys and girls. Under E. J. Smyke, Aquatic Director since 1949, the Southeastern Swimming and Diving Championship for Boys and Girls, sponsored by the University and the Northside Kiwanis Club of Atlanta, in 1965 completed its sixteenth season with more than 400 entrants.

Emory's program of physical education and intramural sports has brought many observers to the campus, and features of the system have been adopted at a number of other institutions. Members of the staff are constantly called upon as consultants.

Under Mr. McDonough's chairmanship the physical plant of the Department has been greatly expanded. The most recent additions are a twelve-acre athletic field on the western border of the campus and four hard-surfaced tennis courts. Nevertheless, with the growth of the student body, and especially the number of women students, there is pressing need for more gymnasium space, more locker rooms, and other facilities. With their provision the continued efficiency of Emory's unique program of physical education should be ensured.

Public Cultural Activities

EMORY ANNUALLY PRESENTS a full program of cultural events to many of which the public is invited or freely admitted. Student activities—debates, concerts, plays—have drawn a large attendance from the Atlanta community, as have conferences and institutes with faculty direction and participation, as the Institute of Citizenship. The events of the Centennial of 1936 brought large audiences to the campus, as have visits by such dignitaries as Marshal Foch in December 1921, Vice-President Barkley in June 1949, and Secretary of State Dean Rusk in April 1961.

Special programs are frequently arranged for school children. For several years Pi Alpha, chemistry honor society, held an open house with scientific exhibits and demonstrations. The events of Language Day have attracted large numbers of high school students, and workshops sponsored by undergraduate organizations furnish guidance for leaders in high school activities. Throughout the year pupils from the public schools visit the Museum for conducted lecture tours of the collections.

From 1922 to 1944 an annual lecture series was presented on the campus under the auspices of the Student Lecture Association with Professor Ross H. McLean as Director. The series was supported by a student activities fee and by the sale of tickets of admission to the faculty and general public. From season to season leading lights of the platform were brought to Emory, among them the poets Vachel Lindsay and Carl Sandburg, Thomas Mann the novelist, the scientific popularizer Julian Huxley, the undersea explorer William Beebe, and the German "Sea Eagle" of World War I, Count von Luckner. Cornelia Otis Skinner and E. H. Sothern gave dramatic readings. A performance by the Abbey Theatre Company of Dublin, Ireland, was sponsored at the Erlanger Theater. Among musical events were concerts by the Curtis and Roth string quartets and the Don Cossack Chorus. A lecture-demonstration of magic by John Mulholland will not be forgotten by those whom he mystified and charmed.

Since the Navy V-12 unit could be assessed no activities fee, the lecture series came to a wartime halt. Resumed in 1945 under the direction of John A. Griffin, a somewhat leaner program was offered for a time. In recent years, however, without a pre-arranged schedule, constant visits of notables have diversified the public offerings of the University. The appearance of the British statesman Clement Atlee on January 11, 1957, and of Barbara Ward, an international authority on Western culture, on January 27, 1965, were especially memorable occasions.

Under the auspices of the University Center, scholars of many disciplines deliver lectures on their specialized subjects at Emory and the other institutions of the Center. The Walter Turner Candler Lectures in the humanities, inaugurated in 1952, and the John Gordon Stipe Memorial Lectures in Spanish culture, begun in 1954, have permanently enriched the University's schedule.

Discussions of public affairs have at times taxed Glenn Memorial beyond its utmost capacity. On March 7, 1962, Linus Pauling, Nobel prize-winner in chemistry from Caltech, spoke on the relationship of science to world peace. Two other occasions were the Buckley-Abram debate on October 18, 1962, and the report on the world situation by NBC news-bureau chiefs on January 3, 1963. The former, sponsored by a student conservative group, brought together William F. Buckley, editor of the *National Review,* a leading organ of conservatism, and Morris Abram, the Atlanta attorney, closely identified with the liberal principles of the New Frontier. The latter event anticipated the national telecast, "Great Decisions of 1963," and featured nine well-known foreign correspondents of the National Broadcasting Company, with Merrill Mueller moderating the panel.

Since 1950-51, under the generous patronage of Mrs. Charles Howard Candler, Emory has enjoyed an annual concert series of the utmost distinction. It was inaugurated on the evening of October 27, 1950, dedicating the Music Appreciation Room of the Alumni Memorial Building to the memory of Lieutenant Goodrich C. White, Jr. In succeeding seasons the greatest artists of the concert stage have appeared before audiences of Emory students and faculty and an invited list of Atlanta friends of the University. The foyer of Alumni Memorial was soon found too small for the attendance, and later programs have mostly been presented in Glenn Memorial. Among the offerings of the University Concert Series the following are representative: instrumental ensembles, the Budapest String Quartet and the Virtuosi di Roma; vocalists, Jussi Björling, Jerome Hines, and Lois Marshall; pianists Gina Bachauer, Guiomar Novaes, and Luboshutz and Nemenoff; the Robert Shaw Chorale performing Bach's *B Minor Mass,* and the Branko Krasmanovich Chorus of Jugoslavia; the Salzburg Marionette Theatre in Mozart's *Magic Flute.* Perhaps most enthusiastically received of all was an evening of dramatic readings by Charles Laughton.

The Fine Arts Department of the University presents concerts of chamber music at intervals, giving an opportunity of hearing the wonderful repertory for small ensembles most inadequately represented in the Atlanta musical season. A notable presentation was a performance of Bach's *Musical Offering* on April 4, 1965.

Quite recently popular programs under the auspices of the Emory Students Creative Arts Festival have included ballet, folk singers, and jazz bands.

In all these offerings the first consideration has been to enrich the cultural experience of Emory students. The attempt has been made to secure such variety of talents that sound scholarship, informed citizenship, and aesthetic appreciation may be promoted in the young people for whom the lecturers and concert artists are brought to the campus. It is Emory's privilege to make most of its offerings available also to the Atlanta community, but until a larger auditorium is built it will not always be possible to issue general invitations to the public.

The Alumni Association

IT WAS LONG AGO REALIZED that an alumni association was an effective means of continuing and localizing the good fellowship established in the companionship of young men and women during their academic years. More recently such associations have been recognized as reservoirs of loyalty representing stored-up power to be drawn on to maintain and strengthen American colleges and universities. The sentiment that once largely flowed to waste is now turned to practical use, without diminishing but, indeed, in most cases intensifying the feeling of fraternity among graduate bodies.

Emory College had an informally organized Alumni Association as early as 1880. Its most important contribution was to add three Alumni Trustees to the Board of Trustees in 1886. Encouraged by President Cox, plans for an Alumni Association of Emory University were developed in 1922, and an organization meeting was held on February 23, 1923. At this meeting Judge John S. Candler '80, '83G, '24H, was elected President and James A. Dombrowsky '23, Secretary. The Committee on Constitution and Bylaws, with Thomas W. Connally '02 Chairman, organized the Association around an Alumni Council. As organ of the Association the *Emory News Letter* was originated by Registrar J. Gordon Stipe '07, the first number dated February 1923, continued by twelve later issues.

A program was developed rapidly. In September of the same year the Alumni Office was opened in Physics Building, one of the first tasks undertaken being to compile full and detailed alumni rolls. It should be noted that as previously existing schools (Medicine, Nursing, Library, Dentistry) have become divisions of Emory University, their alumni have been added to the official rolls. The term "alumnus" is interpreted to mean a person who has satisfactorily completed the work of one academic year in any of the divisions of the University. The first local Emory Club was organized fall 1923 in Tampa, Florida. At the first meeting of the Alumni Council, December 18, an Alumni Loyalty Fund was instituted. The Atlanta Emory Club was founded at a "Benefactors' Day" dinner on January 25, 1924. Henceforth the anniversary day of granting its charter to the University was to be observed under various names by an alumni banquet.

The first meeting of the Association as the entire body of alumni, however, took place on June 8, 1925. A year later the College and University Associations merged to form a unified organization. On and about an annual Alumni Day, on a date usually just preceding June Commencement, class reunions of the schools have been organized, together with a meeting of the Alumni Association and other events. For the alumni of old Emory College an Oxford pilgrimage has returned them to the scenes of their undergraduate days. Attendance has grown steadily through the years, and the occasion has been employed to exhibit the physical growth of the University and to explain current administrative policies.

Although the personnel of the Alumni Office has frequently changed, its history is one of continually increased activity and improved efficiency. The second member of the permanent staff was Miss Elizabeth Chappell (after five years Mrs. James R. Duncan), who, entering upon her duties in June 1924, was to remain the keystone of the alumni arch for thirty-seven years to the day. With James Dombrowsky as Editor, Volume 1, Number 1 of the *Emory Alumnus* appeared in November of the same year. In May 1926 the *Alumni History and Directory of Emory University* was published. A new *Alumni Association Directory,* containing the names of 23,437 Alumni Association members, listed alphabetically, by classes, and geographically, was published late in 1965.

Following Mr. Dombrowsky's resignation in 1926, in Spring of 1927 Raymond B. Nixon '25 was chosen as *Alumnus* Editor and Acting Secretary, and four years later Robert F. Whitaker '26, '27L, was appointed Alumni Secretary. In 1934-43 the Alumni Association conducted scholarship contests that brought some scores of promising graduates of Southeastern high schools to Emory.

Under the auspices of the Association a committee headed by Robert C. Mizell '11 perfected plans for the observance of the centennial year of the College. The ten-day program, December 4-13, 1936, featured conferences and public addresses, concluding with a convocation at which honorary degrees were conferred on outstanding alumni. *A History of Emory University 1836-1936,* by Henry Morton Bullock '24, '25T, for the first time brought together an authoritative account from their founding of the various schools comprising the University.

In April 1941 Chess Abernathy, Jr. '34 accepted the positions of Alumni Secretary and Editor of the *Alumnus*. When Mr. Abernathy was called up for service in the Army in October 1942, Elizabeth Duncan took over as Acting Secretary, with Mr. Whitaker, now Assistant to the President, assuming chief responsibility for the *Alumnus*. During the years of World War II "Miss Bessie" performed the heroic task of keeping in touch with Emory servicemen in all theatres. The enthusiastic response that she evoked from men at the front worked powerfully to strengthen ties of Emory loyalty. At the Charter Day dinner of 1946 she and W. D. Thomson '95, Executive Vice-President of the Board of Trustees, were presented the first Alumni Awards of Honor. Three years later she was made Alumni Secretary, in which position she carried on an enormous correspondence by which the section of personal notes in the *Alumnus* was greatly amplified.

With the March 1946 issue of the *Alumnus* Randolph L. Fort '29, '30G, assumed the editorship. Mr. Fort, with a varied experience in journalism, his college major, had been Red Cross war correspondent in North Africa, Sicily, and Italy, and after a period of rest and recuperation he moved to Puerto Rico, where he edited the daily English-language newspaper and served as Caribbean press and public-relations executive for Pan American World Airways. In 1948 in addition to editing the *Alumnus,* he became Director of the University Publications Office.

The work of the Alumni Association from its organization had been supported by annual dues and subscriptions. In addition there had been an Alumni Loyalty Fund, the proceeds of which were used in promotional activities for the University for which no account was provided in the annual budget. When the University took over financing of the Alumni Office as an administrative division, membership dues were abolished, and the Emory Loyalty Fund was organized as a program of annual giving to augment the resources of the University in all divisions. Annual giving had already proved its worth as "living endowment" in a number of American private institutions of learning, especially in the "Ivy League," and from its inauguration at Emory it demonstrated the willingness of alumni to become a source of regular financial support. In its first year 1949-50, the new Loyalty Fund produced $14,879.59, and in the fifteen years since, with only slight variations in the pattern, there have been constant increases in amounts given, in number of donors, and the percentage of alumni participation. More than a third of Emory's alumni are now participating. In 1961, Waldo Sowell '37B, Committee Chairman, introduced the "Emory Challenge," by which a group of alumni pledged to increase their normal contributions in direct relation to increase of participation in the year's campaign. The Challenge for 1964-65 was a pledge of $100,000 to encourage gifts bringing the Loyalty Fund to a peak of $500,000. The challenge was met and surpassed, 8,725 donors, 37.3% of the number solicited, bringing the year's total to $506,670.

For many years it was keenly realized that there was no adequate center provided for athletics and other student activities. Makeshifts existed, temporary facilities that it was hoped would be soon replaced. As early as 1924, Norman C. Miller '93, Chairman of the Finance Committee of the Alumni Association, had proposed raising funds for an Alumni Memorial Building, combining a gymnasium and a student union. Attempts were made then and later to get the project under way, and in successive drives sums were collected toward that end, which, however, proved inadequate to the purpose. So matters stood, until in May 1947 it was determined to launch an all-out capital campaign for the erection of the long-delayed and critically needed facility. Plans no longer united gymnasium and union building, the University having undertaken to build the former if the Association would provide the latter accommodation. When pledges and collections approached the estimated cost, a groundbreaking ceremony was held on April 18, 1949. Construction beginning at once, within a year the student center was ready for occupancy. On March 6, 1950, the Alumni Office moved into its new quarters, for the first time enjoying ample space for its expanded and ever-expanding activities. The dedication was held on April 14, 1956, at which were present more than one hundred relatives of Emory alumni who had died in World Wars I and II and the Korean War, whose heroic sacrifice the building memorializes. The entire cost of the Alumni Memorial and its furnishings was $650,000.

In 1950 Walter R. Davis, Jr. '34, following Chess Abernathy's decision to return to the field of journalism, was appointed Alumni Director, in which position he has since played a leading rôle in all activities of the Association except its magazine. In April 1960 Ray P. Gandy '55 was added to the staff as Alumni Field Secretary, and in September 1962 he became Associate Alumni Director. Dr. H. Prentice Miller '27, '28G, Dean of the Lower Division of the College, who for several years had served as liaison officer on a part-time basis, especially in soliciting for the building fund and for scholarships, on September 1, 1960, became Dean of Alumni, working in close association with Walt Davis and the Alumni Council.

The death of Randy Fort on February 22, 1962, brought to a close one of the most distinguished careers in academic journalism. Under his editorship the *Emory Alumnus* achieved national recognition for its full and imaginative presentation of all aspects of the life of the University. The 25th Anniversary Number of November 1949 was an especially notable production, its one hundred pages containing a mine of information about the University and its Alumni Association lavishly illustrated. At the 1960 annual conference of the American Alumni Council the *Alumnus* received both the Robert Sibley Award for the "most distinguished magazine of the year" and the Alumni Service Award. During the sixteen years of Randy Fort's editorship he had gathered no less than fifty-five awards in American Alumni Council competition. The file of the magazine is an almost inexhaustible mine of information about Emory and its people in this era.

Succeeding as Acting Editor was Mrs. Pat Malone '62G, with Mrs. Marjorie Duncan Assistant Editor, both having been feature writers for the magazine. Two years later, Virgil A. Hartley '54, a journalism major with a varied experience as newspaper and magazine editor, was appointed Editor of the *Alumnus* and Director of Publications. On the completion of Volume 40 of the *Alumnus* the name was changed to the *Emory Magazine,* with some expansion of its function as official organ of the University.

FIFTY YEARS —
AND BEYOND

Fifty Years — and Beyond

FIFTY YEARS is truly a brief span of time in the life of an institution to whose conception the idea of permanence is basic. Taking College and University together, Emory's history covers little more than a century and a quarter. In comparison with the ancient universities of Europe, and even with the more venerable foundations of our own land, Emory may appear scarcely to have arrived at the years of discretion. It is nevertheless to be noted that in the world of academe as in all other areas of life the past half-century has been one of unprecedented change and development. Whereas older institutions have reached their present status by a process of slow growth, our university came into being at a time of rapid and radical transformation, and took as its starting place the point that its predecessors had labored long to arrive at. Emory is old enough to have a tradition of past achievement and young enough not to be shackled by a tradition.

In its beginnings the idea in the minds of its founders was that of a modern university. The transfer of the name of an older center of learning from Oxford to Atlanta was a moral as well as a physical fact. The preservation of past values is also a part of progress, but their symbols are not the values themselves, and the new college was something more than a continuation of the old. As each division took its place in the university complex its function was defined in terms of the modern age to whose service it was committed.

The university, indeed, is today the world's prime service institution. In moments of disaffection its critics refer to it as an ivory tower. It is a tower, whatever the material of which it is constructed—an observation tower—from which to survey the world. Here the student, for how brief a period, may contemplate the scene in which, how soon, he must be actively engaged, and learn something of its complexity. Here the scholar may observe conditions in a time of accelerating change and devise means by which the present generation may come to terms with it. In the middle ages two ways of life were distinguished, the active and the contemplative, with the university devoted to the latter. In our day the university brings the two together, making the contemplative a preparation for the active life.

On our campus young people are taught to live in the modern world. They are made acquainted with the enduring ideas of the past, and they are trained in the higher vocations whose efficient performance depends on active intellects. And so Emory serves its students that they may serve the world.

But service to the world is not enough. In an era of increasing automation it is vitally important that human beings do not degenerate into automata. Emory is dedicated to the elevation of the life of the mind and the life of the spirit above all outward activities, however worthy and however necessary. It seeks to impress upon its students values of the inner life that enrich and give meaning to all other facets of human existence.

Emory University was founded by a Christian Church and remains in perpetuity an institution of that Church. The spirit of religion, though not the dogma of a sect, is pervasive throughout its policies and procedures. At its center is a college of the liberal arts and sciences, whose spirit carries on into the professional schools and enhances their vocational objectives. This, then, is Emory's educational aim for the young men and women given briefly to its charge: to endow them with knowledge and skills that will render them useful to their time and place, and to develop their inner resources so that theirs shall be the more abundant life.

Emory's educational philosophy may be defined as an imaginative conservatism. It has preserved an awareness of proven disciplines and established values, with a full realization that changing conditions may necessitate modification in their employment. Constant curricular change is a case in point. Courses of study in the basic curricula have retained the same heads, but content and emphasis vary from academic year to academic year. Emory does not seek after educational novelties; it does not push into advanced positions from which after a few terms it must beat a retreat. It has taken Pope's maxim to heart:

> Be not the first by whom the new are tried,
> Nor yet the last to lay the old aside.

Nevertheless the University has not lagged in the rear of educational progress, and in its various divisions it has boldly taken the lead in adapting its resources to clearly discerned emerging needs.

Recognition in academic circles came with remarkable promptness after the University's projection in 1914-15.

For reasons that are not clear, Emory College, prior to its becoming a part of Emory University, had not affiliated with the Southern Association of Colleges and Secondary Schools, the regional accrediting agency; nor, for that matter, had the College belonged even to the Georgia Association of Colleges. In 1917, however, Emory University became a member of the Southern Association. In the years since, Emory's representatives have been active in the Association's affairs, serving continuously on its commissions, holding important offices.

Emory was placed on the approved list of the Association of American Universities in 1924, even though its library was at that time miserably housed in the basement of Theology Building, and the Association places particular emphasis on adequate library facilities. It is clear from the report of the official visitor of the A.A.U. that he was impressed by the quality of the faculty, and by the obvious firm commitment to educational standards that were in no small degree setting the pace for other institutions in the region.

A chapter of Phi Beta Kappa was established in 1929, and a chapter of Sigma Xi in 1944.

In 1935 the Southern University Conference was organized with Emory as one of its initial members. This organization was described as including "only institutions of acceptable educational standing . . . limited to colleges of liberal arts and universities including colleges of liberal arts." The Conference did not propose to become another accrediting agency. Its purpose was to provide opportunity for the discussion of problems of common concern to institutions of comparable interests and ideals. Membership was to be by invitation only. A later definition of the qualifications for membership specifies: "Preference is to be given to colleges or universities whose influence in the educational world is distinctly on the side of promoting and maintaining *high standards*. These standards should be evident in the admitting and training of its students and in the general reputation which the institution has in this country for educational excellence." In the Southern University Conference Emory's representatives have participated in the programs, served on important committees, and held offices, including the presidency.

While Emory has not attained membership in the Association of American Universities (with a total membership of forty-three institutions of the United States and Canada), for two decades or more it has participated on equal terms with Virginia, Duke, North Carolina, Vanderbilt, Rice, Tulane, and Texas in important programs for the upgrading of higher education in the South. It was one of the coördinating centers in a program supported (1946-52) by the Carnegie Foundation providing opportunity for faculty members in selected liberal arts colleges to carry on research while still teaching. Since 1952 it has been a member of the Council of Southern Universities directing the Southern Fellowships Fund, supported by the General Education Board, which has provided fellowships and grants-in-aid to college teachers, actual and prospective, for the completion of doctoral studies. The records indicate that some 750 college faculty members will have attained their doctorates with the help of the Fund.

In 1965 Emory accepted an invitation to membership in the International Association of Universities. This organization, founded in 1950 with financial support from UNESCO, consists of over 400 universities from eighty-seven nations, including seventy-four from the United States. With a permanent secretariat in Paris, the Association holds general meetings at five-year intervals in world centers. The 1965 meeting was held in Tokyo, with President Atwood in attendance.

Emory University is yet too young to have a long roll of alumni who have achieved highest distinction. Yet it has every reason to take pride in the men and women who have made their mark in virtually every profession, besides the hundreds and thousands who exemplify the finest qualities of useful citizenship. If few names can be cited of those who have achieved the uppermost ranks in government, and fewer in the creative arts, there are almost no other spheres of human endeavor in which they have not taken positions of leadership. Emory's scholars have made noteworthy contributions to knowledge in many fields. Every school has its roll of honor, which should lengthen with the years.

It is possible to list more than a score of colleges and universities whose presidents have been or now are alumni of Emory. Most of these are in the South; a few are in other regions. The list includes three tax-supported universities as well as, more typically, private and church-related colleges.

Institutions on whose faculties Emory alumni have served with distinction include Harvard, Yale, Columbia, Chicago, California, Stanford, Johns Hopkins, Rochester, Duke, North Carolina, Wisconsin, Minnesota, Union Theological Seminary. And this is to say nothing of alumni on the staffs of smaller and less well-known colleges throughout the country.

Two Emory alumni have been appointed Harmsworth Professors of American History at Oxford University; in 1965-66 this distinguished chair is filled by a current member of the Emory faculty.

Attendance of Emory faculty is taken for granted at the annual meetings of learned societies in all disciplines, where they and alumni of the University regularly appear on the programs. In recent years participation in international congresses has become frequent. Emory representatives have filled virtually every office of the regional professional societies, and they have held the presidency of great national organizations—the American Medical Association, the American Academy of Surgeons, the American Dental Association, the American Library Association, the National Education Association, and others. Emory professors and administrators have been called to Washington to serve on committees dealing with the problems of both war and peace. A member of the history faculty appointed to the President's Civil War Centennial Commission was sent on lecture tours all over the nation and to European centers.

In addition to the University's contributions of personnel to higher education, mention must be made of the hundreds of school superintendencies, principalships, and elementary and high school teaching positions filled by Emory graduates. In many instances those individuals have exercised notable leadership in their communities; probably there is no more loyal group to be found in the entire alumni body.

Since 1915 fifteen Emory alumni have been elected to the episcopacy of the Methodist Church, and two have been made bishops of the Protestant Episcopal Church. Emory alumni minister to congregations of many faiths throughout the South and elsewhere.

In preceding chapters the attempt has been made to indicate Emory's contributions to community cultural and intellectual activities, to the professions, and to business. The University, within the scope of an educational institution, has sought to realize and to meet the various and complex needs of its place and time. It does not work alone, but in coöperation with the other agencies of social and cultural progress. In this large partnership Emory has accomplished much; it aspires to greater accomplishments. It can be said with assurance that Emory's influence has consistently been exercised and felt in behalf of quality in education and integrity in educational claims and practices. Emory's will to usefulness is great; as its funds and other resources increase, its usefulness to the community, to the region, to the nation, will be notably expanded.

An institution of higher learning must move forward with the march of intellectual and social progress. New duties devolve on it with changing times, new opportunities present themselves. Physical facilities must be expanded or replaced, and personnel must be enlarged and given remuneration in accordance with the changing economic situation. Much of this continuous development is accomplished in a steady adaption of resources to needs from year to year. But the larger projects that require great financial outlays can seldom be achieved from the relatively fixed normal income of a private institution.

It therefore follows that universities such as Emory, which receive no routine support from public funds, must from time to time make special appeals to their constituencies for the means to provide expanded physical facilities and increased endowment to support their educational opportunities and commitments. Such appeals are based on programs for development arising from exhaustive study of ways and means, extending over long periods of time, and designed to provide those services which are most needed in its sphere of influence.

For more than a decade Emory has been engaged in preparing a program for development upon which depend both its academic standing and the extension of its services to the community and region. Every item in the program has been subjected to the closest scrutiny; there has been constant modification and clarification of detail. This planning has been participated in by the University faculties, the administrative officers, the Board of Trustees, the Board of Visitors, and alumni leaders. The time has come when the program can confidently be presented to friends of the University, to philanthropic foundations, and to government agencies as a sound and balanced statement of basic resources needed by Emory to fulfill the opportunities and obligations it faces.

The primary service of a university is to contribute to the general culture and the specialized knowledge which are the marks of an advancing civilization. Atlanta, the great urban center of the Southeastern region, is a most logical place for a great university to serve as one essential instrument for the progress of the region. To its city and to its region Emory offers a facility which will produce the educated citizenry capable of discharging the functions of an enlightened society.

Among the physical facilities projected are a Library for Advanced Studies, a Science Center, and a Fine Arts Building. These additions will not only provide for the special services indicated for each, but will relieve serious overcrowding in existing buildings that has hampered both teaching and research in the College and the Graduate School. The bringing together of the Departments of Chemistry, Physics, and Mathematics in a Science Center will inaugurate a new day of basic training and reseach in areas of major contemporary progress. The Departments of Art and Music have already contributed richly to student and community life, but until the present they have been ill-equipped to realize their potentialities.

[241]

The community and regional value of the professional schools—of business, dentistry, law, medicine, nursing, and theology—can hardly be exaggerated. The expansion, even the maintenance, of their capacities for service, however, depends on the improvement of and addition to their physical plants. The shifts to which these and other divisions have been forced in order to carry on and advance their programs, have been heroic, but the law of diminishing returns, if it has not already set in, cannot long be fended off. Thus Emory's plans call for a complete new plant for the School of Dentistry, located on the campus; for substantial new Medical School facilities, also on the campus; for a building to house the growing School of Nursing, something it has never had; and for major additions to the Law School's plant.

Among the needs for a healthy and happy student life is an addition to the gymnasium and playing fields. Emory's distinctive program of physical education should not be allowed to deteriorate.

While there has been a considerable amount of recent building on the campus of Oxford College, the older structures, several of them of historical importance, are in a state of disrepair, and there must be some replacements. The old chapel, Seney Hall, and Candler Library require extensive restoration, and a new gymnasium should be built. A new dining room and a modern women's residence hall will greatly facilitate Oxford's work.

This is but an incomplete statement of needed physical facilities. The account in its entirety mounts to several millions of dollars.

A university must have more income than tuition fees and the normal flow of donations received from alumni and friends. A permanent endowment is required to provide a good portion of teachers' salaries, of scholarships, and of plant maintenance, equipment and supplies. And the endowment must be continually strengthened to take care of these permanent and basic needs which grow as the academic program is enlarged and as costs rise. If Emory is to be a great institution, greatly serving its community, it must on occasion make extraordinary appeals for support from those who will benefit from its activities in ever-increasing measure.

And so a program for development has been announced in Emory's semicentennial year, coupled with a campaign for funds, that will enable it to carry on and to improve the work and progress of the half-century that this history relates. The multimillion-dollar capital sum sought will make a long step toward the growth projected for the next ten years, a period in which there is clear indication that the tasks assigned by the public to educational institutions across the nation will be enormously increased. If Emory is to perform its share of the work, many public-spirited and far-seeing friends must lend their support. Then when fifty years hence the University's full century is completed, Emory will have attained the greatness to which it is surely destined.

APPENDIXES

Buildings

(This list includes all major permanent buildings, excluding minor service and temporary facilities, belonging to the University.)

1915* Butler Street Medical Building

1916 Theology Building (renovated 1957, 1965)

1916 Law Building (ground floor excavated 1950)

1916 Dobbs Hall (renovation and addition 1962)

1916 Winship Hall (renovation 1962)

1917 John P. Scott Laboratory of Anatomy

1917 T. T. Fishburne Laboratory of Physiology

1917 Chemistry Building (completed 1927)

1917 J. J. Gray Clinic, Grady Memorial Hospital (renovated and rebuilt, 1965, as Woodruff Memorial Research—Henry Woodruff Extension)

1919 Physics Building

1919 Alabama Hall

1922 Wesley Memorial (Emory University) Hospital, Lucy Elizabeth Memorial Pavilion

1923 Heating Plant

1923 L. C. Fishburne Building

1926 Asa Griggs Candler Library (remodeled 1957)

1927 Dining Hall-Auditorium (Student Activities Building) (addition 1950; reconverted 1961)

1928 Fraternity Row: Sigma Alpha Epsilon (burned out and rebuilt 1932; addition 1956)

1929 Florence Candler Harris Home for Nurses (Harris Hall) (addition 1954)

1930 Fraternity Row: Sigma Chi, Kappa Alpha, Chi Phi (Tom Connally Hall—burned 1946, rebuilt 1947; addition 1957)

1931 Wilbur Fisk Glenn Memorial Auditorium-Church (renovated 1962)

1937 Haygood-Hopkins Memorial Gateway

1938 Fraternity Row: Delta Tau Delta (addition 1964), Alpha Tau Omega (addition 1957), Sigma Nu

1940* Crawford W. Long Memorial Hospital

1940 Fraternity Row: Phi Delta Theta (burned out, remodeled 1959)

1940 McTyeire Hall

1940 Glenn Memorial Church School

1941 Fraternity Row: Pi Kappa Alpha

1943* W. D. Thomson House

1944* Uppergate House

1944* School of Dentistry, Forrest Avenue and Courtland Street (renovated 1950)

1946 Conkey Pate Whitehead Surgical Pavilion

1947 Rich Memorial Building, School of Business Administration

1947 Ruel B. Gilbert Hall, William D. Thomson Hall

1949 Field House

* Year of transfer to Emory University

1949   Fraternity Row: Sigma Pi (1962, Phi Gamma Delta)
1950   Alumni Memorial Building
1950   Fraternity Row: Alpha Epsilon Pi (addition 1957)
1950   Geology Field Camp, Ringgold (addition 1957)
1951   Geology Building
1951   Biology Building (addition 1962) ; Greenhouse, 1953
1951   Emory Park Apartments 1 and 2
1951   History Building
1951   Basic Science (now Psychology) Building
1951   Wesley Hall
1951   Fraternity Row: Beta Theta Pi, Tau Epsilon Phi
1952   Woodruff Memorial Building (completed 1958) (sixth and seventh floors added to south wing 1964)
1955   Administration Building
1955   Longstreet Hall, Means Hall
1956   Parking Deck
1956   Clinic Building (completed 1959, addition 1963)
1957   Mizell Memorial Stairway
1957   Bishops Hall
1958   Shop
1958   James R. Thomas, Isaac S. Hopkins, Luther M. Smith Halls
1959   Clifton Court Apartments
1960   Harvey W. Cox Hall (food services)
1963*   Lullwater House (President's home)
1964   Hospital renovation
1964   Graduate and Professional Housing Center
1965   Saunders Hall
1965   Yerkes Regional Primate Research Center
1965   Primate Research Center Field Station, Gwinnett County
1965   North Wing, Woodruff Memorial Building

* Year of transfer to Emory University

Fields of Study in which Degrees Are Offered, 1965

Bachelor of Arts, with major in:

Art	Education	History	Political Science
Bible and Religion	English	Latin	Psychology
Biology	French	Mathematics	Russian
Chemistry	Geology	Music	Sociology
Economics	German	Philosophy	Spanish
	Greek	Physics	

Bachelor of Science, with major in:

Biology	Geology	Physics
Chemistry	Mathematics	

Bachelor of Business Administration

Bachelor of Science in Nursing

Master of Arts, with major in:

Anatomy	Chemistry	English	Physics
Biochemistry	Classics	Geology	Political Science
Microbiology	Comparative	History	Psychology
Pharmacology	Literature	Librarianship	Religion
Physiology	Economics	Mathematics	Romance
Biology	Education	Philosophy	Languages
			Sociology

Master of Science, with major in:

Anatomy	Microbiology	Biology	Mathematics
Biochemistry	Pharmacology	Chemistry	Physics
Biometry	Physiology	Geology	

Master of Arts in Teaching, with major in:

Chemistry	English	History	Religion
Education	General Science	Political Science	Romance
			Languages

Master of Education

Master of Business Administration

Master of Librarianship

Master of Nursing

Master of Christian Education

Bachelor of Divinity

Bachelor of Laws

Master of Laws

Master of Science in Dentistry

Doctor of Dental Surgery

Doctor of Medicine

Doctor of Philosophy, with major in:

Anatomy	Pharmacology	English	Philosophy
Biochemistry	Physiology	History	Political Science
Biometry	Biology	Liberal Arts	Psychology
Microbiology	Chemistry	Mathematics	Religion
			Sociology

Summary of Enrollment 1964-65

College of Arts and Sciences	2470
School of Business Administration	136
School of Dentistry	313
Graduate School of Arts and Sciences	957
School of Law	366
School of Medicine	304
School of Nursing	173
School of Theology	442
Full-time students Atlanta Campus	5161
AATES Registrants (in-service Education)	195
Oxford College	488
GRAND TOTAL	5844

Degrees Conferred, Academic Year 1964-65

	Dec. 1964	Mar. 1965	June 1965	Aug. 1965	TOTAL
Bachelor of Arts	33	62	275	56	426
Bachelor of Science	—	3	16	7	26
Bachelor of Arts in Law	—	1	8	3	12
Bachelor of Business Adm.	—	3	19	2	24
Bachelor of Science, Nursing	—	—	39	12	51
Total Undergraduate	33	69	357	80	539
Master of Arts	6	3	17	23	49
Master of Science	4	4	8	13	29
Master of Arts, Teaching	—	2	8	39	49
Master of Education	1	1	—	11	13
Master of Business Adm.	—	—	26	—	26
Master of Librarianship	8	—	8	17	33
Master of Nursing	3	2	4	30	39
Master of Christian Educ.	—	1	8	1	10
Bachelor of Divinity	6	11	87	15	119
Bachelor of Laws	16	9	28	6	59
Master of Laws	—	—	—	—	—
Master of Science, Dentistry	—	—	4	—	4
Doctor of Dental Surgery	2	—	59	—	61
Doctor of Medicine	—	—	70	1	71
Doctor of Philosophy	5	8	11	11	35
Total Graduate and Professional	51	41	338	167	597
GRAND TOTAL	84	110	695	247	1136

Total for 1963-1964 academic year	1095
Total for 1962-1963 academic year	1070
Total for 1961-1962 academic year	939

Trustees of Emory University 1915 - 1965

Plato T. Durham
Atlanta
A. Hollis Edens '28, '38G, '49H
North Carolina
T. D. Ellis '93, '07H
Georgia
Lettie Pate Evans
Virginia
Luther C. Fischer '99M
Atlanta
T. T. Fishburne
Virginia
H. R. Fitzgerald
Virginia
G. T. Fitzhugh
Tennessee
Aubrey F. Folts '25, '27L
Tennessee
L. W. Foreman '01
Georgia
Marvin A. Franklin '15, '57H
Mississippi
J. Stewart French '08H
Tennessee
George R. Gibbons '00
Pennsylvania
Thomas K. Glenn '43H
Atlanta
Wadley R. Glenn '33M
Atlanta
J. J. Gray, Jr.
Tennessee
L. D. Hamilton
Tennessee
Granger Hansell '23, '24L
Atlanta
Paul Hardin, Jr. '27T
South Carolina
Nolan B. Harmon '19T, '57H
Virginia
Costen J. Harrell '57H
Virginia
L. Bryant Harrell '03
Georgia
Luther A. Harrell '13, '19T, '56H
Georgia
Hal F. Hentz '04, '36H
Atlanta

H. Warner Hill '80
Atlanta
E. W. Hines
Kentucky
Spessard L. Holland '12, '43H
Florida
Earl G. Hunt '46T
North Carolina
James M. Jackson
Florida
I. C. Jenkins '96, '36H
Florida
Edgar H. Johnson '91, '42H
Atlanta
Boisfeuillet Jones '34, '37L
Atlanta
John C. Kilgo
North Carolina
A. J. Lamar
Tennessee
L. M. Lipscomb
Mississippi
Harry Y. McCord, Jr. '09
Atlanta
L. P. McCord
Florida
J. H. McCoy '17H
Alabama
J. F. McCrackin
Georgia
J. A. McCullough
Maryland
James A. Mackay '40, '47L
Georgia
T. G. McLeod
South Carolina
W. F. McMurry
Missouri
Edgar R. Malone
Florida
James C. Malone
Atlanta
Thomas O. Marshall '09
Georgia
John E. Mathews, Jr. '42
Florida
Nathan L. Miller
Alabama

Norman C. Miller '93
    Atlanta
Robert C. Mizell '11
    Atlanta
Arthur J. Moore '14, '34H
    Atlanta
Thomas W. Moore '00
    Atlanta
B. Hart Moss
    South Carolina
William B. Murrah
    Tennessee
Walter H. Neal
    North Carolina
W. M. Nixon
    Atlanta
Howard W. Odum '04, '31H
    North Carolina
H. E. W. Palmer '72
    Atlanta
M. M. Parks '92
    Georgia
F. J. Prettyman
    Washington, D. C.
J. Harris Purks, Jr. '23, '57H
    North Carolina
Stewart R. Roberts '00M, '02
    Atlanta
James D. Robinson, Jr. '25
    Atlanta
Lester Rumble '15T, '21T, '35H
    Atlanta
Donald S. Russell
    South Carolina
J. P. Scott
    Louisiana
Roy H. Short '57H
    Tennessee
J. C. Smith
    South Carolina
John Owen Smith '64H
    Atlanta
Waldo Sowell '37B
    Atlanta

J. Adger Stewart
    Kentucky
Peter Stokes
    South Carolina
Harry H. Stone '80, '83H
    Georgia
Harry Stone Strozier '05
    Georgia
Lee Talley '23
    Atlanta
Samuel Tate
    Georgia
Lavens M. Thomas
    Tennessee
W. G. M. Thomas
    Tennessee
William Danner Thomson '95
    Atlanta
Charles E. Thwaite, Jr.
    Atlanta
Charles M. Trammell '07
    Washington, D. C.
Pollard Turman '34, '35L
    Atlanta
D. Abbott Turner
    Georgia
William B. Turner
    Georgia
William C. Warren, Jr. '20, '22M
    Atlanta
William T. Watkins '16, '39H
    Atlanta
John Wesley Weekes '24, '27L
    Georgia
W. Emory Williams '32
    Illinois
J. H. Wilson
    Alabama
Charles T. Winship '26
    Atlanta
George W. Woodruff
    Atlanta
Robert W. Woodruff '12
    Atlanta

Recipients of Honorary Degrees

(Positions noted are those held at time of the conferring of degrees)

1915   James Edward Dickey '91, *LL.D.*: President, Emory College
1917   James Henry McCoy, *LL.D.*: Bishop, M. E. Church, S.
        William Bartley Taylor, *D.D.*: Methodist Minister, Tennessee
1918   Bennett Battle Ross, *LL.D.*: Dean, Alabama Polytechnic Institute
1919   Joseph Elmore Cockrell, *LL.D.*: Lawyer and Banker, Texas; Emory
        Trustee
        Charles John Prescott, *D.D.*: President, Newrington College, New
        South Wales, Australia
1920   William Edward Dodd, *LL.D.*: Professor of History, University of
        Chicago
        Henry Burnell Faber, *Sc.D.*: Professor of Chemistry, Columbia
        University
        George Allen Morgan, Sr., *D.D.*: Methodist Minister, Tennessee
1921   William Henry LaPrade, Jr. '97, *D.D.*: Methodist Minister,
        Georgia
        William Fletcher Quillian '01, *D.D.*: President, Wesleyan College
1924   John Slaughter Candler '80, '83G, *LL.D.*: Associate Justice,
        Supreme Court of Georgia; Emory Trustee
        Charles Gideon Hounshell, *D.D.*: Secretary, Board of Missions,
        M. E. Church, S.
1925   William Simpson Elkin, *LL.D.*: Dean, Emory University School of
        Medicine
        Lewis Davies Lowe, '99, *D.D.*: Methodist Minister, Florida
        Guy Everett Snavely, *LL.D.*: President, Birmingham-Southern
        College
1926   David Martin Key, *LL.D.*: President, Millsaps College
1927   William Peter King '93, '96G, *D.D.*: Methodist Minister, Georgia;
        Editor, *Christian Advocate*
        Alfred Mann Pierce '95, *D.D.*: Methodist Minister, Georgia; Editor,
        Wesleyan Christian Advocate
1928   Joseph Anderson Thomas '84, *D.D.*: Methodist Minister, Georgia
        Marion Luther Brittain '86, *LL.D.*: President, Georgia School of
        Technology
        Samuel Candler Dobbs, *LL.D.*: Philanthropist; Emory Trustee
1930   John Ernest Rattenbury, *D.D.*: British Methodist Minister
        Edward Campbell Davis, *LL.D.*: Physician; Co-founder, Crawford
        Long Memorial Hospital
        Tommie Dora Barker '09LS, *Litt.D.*: Director, Library School,
        Carnegie Library of Atlanta
1931   Elzy Dee Jennings, *LL.D.*: British Methodist Minister
        Howard Washington Odum '04, *LL.D.*: Kenan Professor of
        Sociology, University of North Carolina
        Orville Augustus Park, *LL.D.*: Lawyer, Macon, Georgia
1932   Lawton Bryan Evans '80, *LL.D.*: Superintendent Augusta and
        Richmond County (Georgia) Schools

[254]

1933   Theodore Henley Jack, *LL.D.*: President Randolph-Macon Woman's College

1934   Embree Hoss Blackard '21, '22T, *D.D.*: Methodist Minister, Baltimore

Arthur James Moore '14, *D.D.*: Bishop, M. E. Church S.

Walter Harvey Moore '19T, *D.D.*: President, Granberry College, Brazil

Ivan Lee Holt, *D.D.*: Methodist Minister, St. Louis

1935   Warren Akin Candler '75, '78H, '88H, '97H, *L.H.D.*: Bishop, M. E. Church, S.

Lester Rumble '15, '21T, *D.D.*: Methodist Minister, Georgia

Harmon White Caldwell, *LL.D.*: President, University of Georgia

1936   Paul Bentley Kern, *LL.D.*: Bishop, M. E. Church, S.

John William Langdale, *Litt.D.*: Book Editor, Methodist Church

Dumas Malone '10, *Litt.D.*: Editor in Chief, *Dictionary of American Biography;* Director, Harvard University Press

1936   *Degrees conferred at convocation celebrating Centennial of Emory*
Dec.   *College*

Thomas Franklin Abercrombie '03M, *ScD.*: Director, Georgia State Department of Health

Hal Fitzgerald Hentz '04, *LL.D.*: Architect

Isaac Cheyney Jenkins '96, *D.D.*: Methodist Minister, Florida; Emory Trustee

Edwin Dart Lambright '94, *Litt.D.*: Editor, Tampa (Florida) *Tribune*

Kemp Malone '07, *Litt.D.*: Professor of English, Johns Hopkins University

Thomas Milton Rivers '09, *Sc.D.*: Medical Scientist, Rockefeller Institute

William Holcombe Thomas '87, *LL.D.*: Associate Justice, Supreme Court of Alabama

1938   Raymond Ross Paty '21, *LL.D.*: President, Birmingham-Southern College

1939   William Turner Watkins '16, *D.D.*: Bishop, M. E. Church, S.

James Ross McCain, *LL.D.*: President, Agnes Scott College

1940   John Wallace Rustin '21, '23L, '24T, *D.D.*: Methodist Minister, Washington, D. C.

Willis Anderson Sutton '03, '03L, *LL.D.*: Superintendent of Schools, Atlanta

Preston Stanley Arkwright, *LL.D.*: President, Georgia Power Company; Emory Trustee

1942   Charles Howard Candler '98, '02M, *LL.D.*: Philanthropist; Chairman, Emory Board of Trustees

Edgar Hutchinson Johnson '91, *LL.D.*: Dean, Emory School of Business Administration

1943   Silas Johnson '11, *D.D.*: President, Wesleyan College

Spessard Lindsey Holland, Sr. '12, *LL.D.*: Governor, Florida

Thomas Kearney Glenn, *LL.D.*: Capitalist; Emory Trustee

[255]

James Edgar Paullin, *LL.D.*: Professor of Clinical Medicine, Emory School of Medicine

1944   Eugene Epperson Barnett '07, *LL.D.*: Secretary, International Y.M.C.A.

William Blount Burke '83, *D.D.*: Methodist Missionary, China

Ernest Cadman Colwell '23, '27T, *Litt.D.*: President, University of Chicago

Walter Franklin George, *LL.D.*: U.S. Senator from Georgia

Cordell Hull, *LL.D.*: U.S. Secretary of State

1945   Herbert Orlando Smith '28G, *L.H.D.*: Principal Boys' High School, Atlanta

James Walton Henley '23, '26T, *D.D.*: Methodist Minister, Nashville

1946   James Robert McCord, *D.Sc.*: Professor of Obstetrics and Gynecology, Emory School of Medicine

1947   Jere Asmond Wells, *LL.D.*: Superintendent, Fulton County (Georgia) Schools

1949   Arthur Hollis Edens '28, '38G, *LL.D.*: President, Duke University

Oren Austin Oliver '09D, *LL.D.*: Orthodontist, Nashville

Alben William Barkley '00, *LL.D.*: Vice-President of the United States

1951   James Clyde Adams '07, '26G, *D.D.*: Methodist Minister, Georgia

Franklin Nutting Parker, *L.H.D.*: Dean Emeritus, Candler School of Theology, Emory University

1952   Basil O'Connor, *LL.D.*: President, National Foundation for Infantile Paralysis

1954   Wallace McPherson Alston '27, '29G, *LL.D.*: President, Agnes Scott College

John Warren Branscomb '26, '28T, *D.D.*: Bishop, The Methodist Church

Robert DeBlois Calkins, *LL.D.*: President, Brookings Institution

George Esmond Clary '14, '17T, *D.D.*: Executive Secretary Southeastern Jurisdictional Council, The Methodist Church

David Alexander Lockmiller '27, '28G, *LL.D.*: President, University of Chattanooga

Paul Douglas West '24, '40G, *LL.D.*: Superintendent, Fulton County (Georgia) Schools

1954   *Degrees conferred at convocation celebrating Centennial of the School*
Oct.   *of Medicine*

Stanhope Bayne-Jones, *Sc.D.*: Director of Research, Medical Department, U. S. Army

Alfred Blalock, *Sc.D.*: Professor of Surgery, Johns Hopkins University; President, American College of Surgeons

Ferdinand Phinizy Calhoun '04M, *LL.D.*: Professor of Ophthalmology, Emory School of Medicine; Emory Trustee

John Farquhar Fulton, *Sc.D.*: Sterling Professor of Physiology, Yale University

Evarts Ambrose Graham, *Sc.D.*: Professor of Surgery, Washington University, St. Louis

Cyrus Cressy Sturgis, *Sc.D.*: Professor of Medicine, University of Michigan; President, American College of Physicians

1956   Ernest Mason Allen '26, '39G, *Sc.D.*: Chief, Division of Research Grants, National Institutes of Health

John Boswell Cobb '25T, *D.D.*: Methodist Missionary, Japan

Moses Hadas '22, *Litt.D.*: Jay Professor of Greek, Columbia University

Anthony Hearn '20, '20T, *D.D.*: Methodist Minister, Georgia

Nathaniel Guy Long, *D.D.*: Methodist Minister, Georgia

James Soule Pope '22, *Litt.D.*: Executive Editor, Louisville (Kentucky) *Courier-Journal and Times*

Sante Uberto Barbieri '33G, *L.H.D.*: Methodist Bishop, Central Conference of Latin America

Luther Alonzo Harrell '13, '19T, *D.D.*: Methodist Minister, Georgia; Emory Trustee

John Knox '24T, *S.T.D.*: Baldwin Professor of Sacred Literature, Union Theological Seminary, New York City

1957   Fletcher Marvin Green '21, *Litt.D.*: Kenan Professor of History, University of North Carolina

Russell Henry Oppenheimer, *Sc.D.*: Former Dean, Emory School of Medicine

David Morris Potter '32, *Litt.D.*: Coe Professor of History, Yale University

James Harris Purks, Jr. '23, *LL.D.*: Director, North Carolina Board of Higher Education

Louis Marvin Lester '08, '12G, *Ed.D.*: Director, Division of Instruction, Georgia State Department of Education

1957   *Degrees conferred at convocation celebrating the consecration of*
Sept.   *Bishops Hall of Theological Studies*

Marvin Augustus Franklin '15, *D.D.*: Bishop, The Methodist Church; Emory Trustee

Paul Neff Garber, *D.D.*: Bishop, The Methodist Church

Nolan Bailey Harmon '19T, *D.D.*: Bishop, The Methodist Church; Emory Trustee

Costen Jordan Harrell, *D.D.*: Bishop, The Methodist Church; Emory Trustee

Bachman Gladstone Hodge '21T, *D.D.*: Bishop, The Methodist Church

William Walter Peele, *D.D.*: Bishop, The Methodist Church

Clare Purcell '08, *D.D.*: Bishop, The Methodist Church

Roy Hunter Short, *D.D.*: Bishop, The Methodist Church

1958   Elbert Parr Tuttle, *LL.D.*: Judge, U. S. Fifth District Court of Appeals

1959   Henry Lumpkin Bowden '32, '34L, *LL.D.*: Lawyer; Chairman, Emory Board of Trustees

William Fletcher Quillian, Jr. '35, *Litt.D.*: President, Randolph-Macon Woman's College

1960   Charles Livingstone Allen '37T, *D.D.*: Methodist Minister, Atlanta

[257]

Henry Allen Moe, *Litt.D.*: Secretary-General, John Simon Guggenheim Memorial Foundation

Louis McDonald Orr '22, '24M, *Sc.D.*: President, American Medical Association

Thomas Fort Sellers '32M, *Sc.D.*: Director Emeritus, Georgia Department of Public Health

1961 *Degree conferred at special convocation*

Apr. Dean Rusk, *LL.D.*: U. S. Secretary of State

1961 Thomas Luther Gresham '28, '29G, *Sc.D.*: Chemist; Vice-President, A. E. Staley Manufacturing Company

George Warren Mundy '27, *LL.D.*: Lieutenant General, U. S. Army; Commandant, Industrial College of the Armed Services

Henry King Stanford '36, '40G, *LL.D.*: President, Birmingham-Southern College

James Frederick Wilson '35, '38T, *D.D.*: Methodist Minister, Georgia

1962 Eugene Robert Black, *LL.D.*: President, International Bank for Reconstruction and Development

Rolla Eugene Dyer, *Sc.D.*: Director of Research, Emory School of Medicine

John Adams Sibley, *LL.D.*: Chairman, Executive Committee, Trust Company of Georgia

1962 *Degree conferred at Opening Convocation*

Sir Ronald Syme, *Litt.D.*: Professor of Ancient History, Oxford University

1963 Lucius DuBignon Clay, *LL.D.*: General, U. S. Army (ret.); Chairman of Board, Continental Can Company

Comer Vann Woodward '30, *Litt.D.*: Sterling Professor of History, Yale University

Martin Dunaway Young '31, '32G, *Sc.D.*: Parasitologist, National Institutes of Health

Ralph Emerson McGill, *Litt.D.*: Publisher, *Atlanta Constitution*

1963 *Degree conferred at inauguration of President Atwood*

Nov. Deane Waldo Malott, *LL.D.*: President Emeritus, Cornell University

1964 *Degrees conferred at celebration of 50th Anniversary, Candler School*
Jan. *of Theology*

David William Brooks, *LL.D.*: General Manager, Cotton Producers Association; Chairman, Emory Committee of One Hundred

John Owen Gross, *D.D.*: General Secretary, Department of Educational Institutions, Board of Education, The Methodist Church

D. Trigg James, Sr. '25T, *D.D.*: Executive Secretary, Southeastern Jurisdictional Council, The Methodist Church

James W. Sells, *D.D.*: Executive Secretary, Southeastern Jurisdictional Council, The Methodist Church

John Owen Smith, *D.D.*: Bishop, The Methodist Church

1964 Enoch Smythe Gambrell, *LL.D.*: Attorney; Past President, American Bar Association

William Alexander Noble '16M, *Litt.D.*: Head, Salvation Army Medical Service, India

James Solomon Peters '08, *LL.D.*: Chairman, Georgia State Board of Education

1965   *Degrees conferred at Fiftieth Anniversary Convocation*

Jan.   Harllee W. Branch, Jr. '31L, *LL.D.*: President, The Southern Company; Emory Trustee

Richard H. Rich, *LL.D.*: President, M. Rich & Brothers Company

Carl Vinson, *LL.D.*: Member U. S. House of Representatives from Georgia

Goodrich Cook White '08, *L.H.D.*: Chancellor, Emory University

1965   Erich Heller, *Litt.D.*: Professor of German, Northwestern University

Marion Hines, *Sc.D.*: Professor Emeritus of Experimental Anatomy, Emory School of Medicine

Harold S. Johnson '41, *Sc.D.*: Professor of Chemistry, University of California, Berkeley

Robert K. Morton, *L.H.D.*: Professor of Sociology, Columbia University

Wernher von Braun, *Sc.D.*: Director, George C. Marshall Space Flight Center, Huntsville, Alabama

Douglas Maitland Knight, *LL.D.*: President, Duke University

1965   *Degree conferred at Opening Convocation*

Sept.   Vivian Hunter Galbraith, *Litt.D.*: Former Regius Professor of Modern History, Oxford University

[259]

Alumni Loyalty Fund

	Amount Given	Number of Donors	Per cent Participation
1949-50	$ 14,879.59		
1950-51	20,282.30		
1951-52	23,277.09		
1952-53	34,412.98		
1953-54	83,724.03	2,425	14.8
1954-55	66,567.19	2,694	15.8
1955-56	108,065.13	2,972	16.2
1956-57	155,480.29	4,177	20.3
1957-58	166,431.63	4,443	21.4
1958-59	208,719.71	4,687	22.1
1959-60	235,536.68	5,049	24.0
1960-61	244,775.04	5,436	25.5
1961-62	302,119.67	6,685	30.9
1962-63	353,192.43	8,021	36.8
1963-64	402,086.70	7,711	34.2
1964-65	506,670.20	8,725	37.3

Bibliography

A History of Emory University 1836-1936. By Henry Morton Bullock. Nashville, Parthenon Press, 1936.

Alumni History and Directory of Emory University. Edited by James A. Dombrowsky. Atlanta, Published by The Alumni Council Emory University, 1926.

History of the Emory Unit, Base Hospital 43, U.S. Army, American Expeditionary Forces. [Edited by Joel Chandler Harris, Jr.] Atlanta, Johnson Dallis Co., 1919.

Giant Against the Sky. The Life of Bishop Warren Akin Candler. By Alfred M. Pierce. Nashville, Abingdon-Cokesbury Press, 1948.

Asa Griggs Candler. By Charles Howard Candler. Emory University, 1950.

Adventure in Giving. The Story of the General Education Board. By Raymond B. Fosdick, with Henry F. Pringle and Katherine Douglas Pringle. New York, Harper & Row, 1962.

Until Now. A Brief History of Emory University Hospital and School of Nursing. By Maybelle Jones Dewey. Emory University, Georgia, Banner Press, 1947.

"The Atlanta-Southern Dental College: An Historical Sketch." By W. Edgar Coleman. In *The Asodecoan 1934*. Published by the Senior Class of the Atlanta-Southern Dental College.

"The Atlanta-Southern Dental College as a Factor in the Dental History of Georgia and the South." By Anderson M. Scruggs. In *Asodecoan 1938*.

Push the Button. The Chronicle of a Professor's Wife. By Maybelle Jones Dewey. Atlanta, Tupper and Love, 1951.

Report of the Educational Commission of The Methodist Episcopal Church, South, to the General Conference, Atlanta, Georgia, May 2, 1918.

Report of the Board of Trustees of Emory University of the General Conference of The Methodist Episcopal Church, South. 1922, 1926, 1930, 1934, 1938.

The Emory Alumnus, Vols. 1-40, 1924-64; *The Emory Magazine*, Vol. 41, 1965.

Report of the Board of Trustees of Emory University to the Southeastern Jurisdictional Conference of The Methodist Church. 1940, 1944, 1948, 1952, 1956, 1960, 1964.

Statement on Emory University College of Liberal Arts . . . . Presented to the Senate of Phi Beta Kappa, December, 1927.

Notes on the Proposed University Center in Atlanta. Published by the Committee on Educational Progress of the Emory University Alumni Association. 1938.

A Report from the President to the Alumni of Emory University, December first, 1939.

A Report to the Alumni and Friends of Emory University, by Dr. Harvey W. Cox; *Taking Stock and Looking Ahead*, by Dr. Goodrich C. White. September 1941.

Report of the President to the Board of Trustees. December 1, 1944.

Report to the President on the Development of the Graduate School. By Dr. Dumas Malone. October 1, 1945.

The College of Arts and Sciences, Purposes and Program. June 15, 1945.

The Emory Library: Where It Stands. November 1, 1948.

Fifteen Years of Progress and a New Program of Development. By President Goodrich C. White. December 1, 1951.

Report from the President of Emory University. 1958, 1959, 1962, 1964, 1965.

A Report of Progress at Emory University. 1962.

Emory University: A Self-Study. 1962.

Facts: Emory University. 1965.

INDEX

Abernathy, Chess   229
Academy, Emory University   22, 35, 181
Adams, George Bunch   151
Advanced Management Program   127
Adminstration Building   69, 87
Agnes Scott College   45, 47, 72
Agnor, William H.   166
Aidmore Hospital   90, 161
Air Force R. O. T. C.   75
Airov, Joseph   128
Akin Fund   188
Alabama Hall   21
Allan, Bryan L.   52
Allen, J. Fred   181
Allen, Young J.   4
Alma Mater, Emory   200
Alpha Epsilon Upsilon   39
Alumni Memorial Building   67, 75, 230
Anatomy Building   21
Andrew, Bishop J. O.   4, 142
Ansley, Bradford D.   84
Antoinette Gardens   33
Arant, Herschel W.   164
Archie, William C.   84
Arms, Thomas S.   218
Association of American Universities   25, 237
Atlanta Area Teacher Education Service   132
Atlanta Constitution   160
Atlanta Journal   41
Atlanta Journal and Constitution Magazine   106
Atlanta Medical College   4, 19, 148
Atlanta-Southern Dental College   54, 172
Atwood, Sanford S.   83

Bachmann, Jean George   151
Bain, James A.   84, 157
Baker, W. B.   88, 103, 141
Barker, Tommie Dora   30, 36, 170, 171
Barkley, Alben William   78, 183

Barnett, Albert Edward   146
Bartlett, Marcus   49, 127, 208
Basic Health Sciences, Division of   64, 68, 71
Beardslee, William A.   84, 133
Beasley, A. Wilburn   145
Beck Foundation   44, 131, 186, 189
Ben-Dor, Immanuel   96, 140
Bennett, Robert L.   154
Bessent, Ewell E.   70, 85
Biomedical Data Processing Center   96
Bishops Hall   88, 145
Blincoe, Homer   151
Block, Edward Bates   151
Board of Visitors   87
Boland, Frank K.   149, 150, 151
Bonnell Hall   85, 182
Boozer, Jack S.   212
Bourne, Geoffrey S.   162
Bowden, Henry L.   71, 83, 101, 102
Bowden, Mrs. Henry L.   180
Bowden, John M.   146
Bowen, Boone M.   140
Boyd, Clarence Eugene   116
Branch, Harllee W.   106
Bridges, S. Russell, Jr.   126
Brinkley, Sterling H.   29, 117
Brittain Award   105
Brittain, M. L.   44
Brock, I. W.   71
Brown, Frank Clyde   216
Bryan, Paul E.   164, 165, 168
Buhler, John E.   70, 174, 175
Bullock, Henry M.   46, 229
Bush, Arthur Dermont   151
Byrnes, Ralph K.   54, 174
Byron, Dora   78

Calhoun, F. Phinizy   150, 151, 157, 192
Calhoun Chair of Opthalmology   156
Calhoun Medical Library   69, 150, 191
Campbell, James LeRoy   151
Campus   205
campus, Druid Hills   14, 20, 89

[263]

Candler, Asa G. 7, 13, 14, 15, 29, 30, 41, 185
Candler, Charles Howard 42, 69, 76, 83, 191
Candler, Mrs. Charles H. 34, 88, 225
Candler, John S. 52, 164, 227
Candler Lectureship 79, 225
Candler Memorial Room 188
Candler Professorships 88, 102
Candler, Walter Turner 79, 88
Candler, Warren A. 6, 14, 24, 26, 46, 52, 72, 138, 139, 142, 181, 191, 217
Cannon, William R. 71, 136, 144, 145
Career Scholars Program 91, 120
Carnegie, Andrew 170
Carnegie Corporation 35, 127, 133, 170, 171
Carnegie Foundation 218
Carpenter, Francis W. 205
Centennial of College 45
Chamber Music Series 67, 225
Charvat, Frank J. 128
Chemistry Building 21, 33
Chewning, David 189
Church School Building 53
Clay Memorial Eye Clinic 156
Clegg, L. L. 61, 70, 71
Clifton Court Apartments 89
Clinic, Emory University 79, 87, 158
coeducation 72
Columbia Theological Seminary 45, 48, 144
Colwell, Ernest C. 70, 84, 133, 222
Committee of One Hundred 80, 144
Commonwealth Fund 77, 179
Communicable Disease Center 90, 160
Connally, Thomas W. 227
Cottle, Charles Sidney 128
Cox, Albert F. 118
Cox Hall 89
Cox, Harvey Warren 25, 50, 52, 219
Craft, George S. 70, 124
Crawford Long Hospital 53, 79, 89, 152, 161

Culp, Maurice S. 166
Cuttino, George P. 133

Davis, E. C. 53, 149
Davis, Walter R. 231
debating 43, 78, 105, 206
Dewey, Malcolm H. 27, 36, 116, 117, 201
Dewey, Maybelle Jones 179
Dickey Hall 88, 182
Dickey, James E. 8, 19
Dietz, Arthur T. 128
dining hall-auditorium 33, 90
Dobbs Hall 21, 89
Dobbs, Samuel C. 43, 48
Dombrowsky, James 201, 227, 228
Dooley 62, 205
Dowman, Charles E. 7
Dowman Hall 182
Dozier, Alberta 178
Duffee, Warren S. 205
Duncan, Bingham 57
Duncan, Elizabeth 228, 229
Duncan Lectureship 142
Duncan, Marjorie 231
Durham, Plato 14, 18, 27, 138, 140, 210
Dyer, Rolla E. 155

Eady, Virgil Y. C. 51, 182
Edens, A. Hollis 50, 56, 70, 184
Educational Commission M. E. Church S. 12, 138
Egleston Hospital 90, 161
Elkin, Daniel C. 151
Elkin, W. S. 20, 52, 148, 150
Embree, Edwin R. 43, 47
Emmerich, Charles O. 70, 86
Emory Alumnus 228
Emory, Bishop John 3
Emory Court Apartments 66
Emory Lake 31
Emory Park Apartments 68
Emory Players 42, 207
Emory Units 58, 149, 152
Emory University Quarterly 57
Emory Victory, M. S. 61
Emory Wheel 26, 27, 104, 106, 204
Engineering, Department of 64, 115

English, Thomas H.   43, 57, 186, 207
Eskew, Rhea 205
Evans, Letitia Pate   67, 151
Extension Department   29

Faculty Row   23
Farris, Jacob D.   220
Fattig, Perry W.   36
Ferguson, Ira A.   58, 152
Few, Ignatius   3
Field House   64, 66, 221
Fischer, Luther C.   53, 79, 152
Fishburne Building   29
Fitts, Ralph L.   218
Floyd, Arva C.   140
Ford Foundation   77, 90, 127, 157
Ford Foundation for the Advancement of Teaching   91
Fort, Ada   71, 179
Fort, Randolph   102, 229, 231
Foster, Sheppard W.   172
Franklin Foundation   146
Fraternity Row   28, 34, 52, 67
Freeman, G. Ross   143

Gambrell, Elizabeth   153
Gandy, Ray P.   231
Garber, Paul N.   146
Gateway, Haygood-Hopkins   52
General Education Board   26, 47, 48, 49, 76, 91, 132, 186
Geology Building   68
Geology Camp   68, 95
Georgia Heart Association   156
Georgia Mental Health Institute   161
Georgia School of Technology   6, 45, 48
Georgia State Woman's College   77, 184
"G. I. Bill of Rights"   61, 65
Gilbert Hall   66, 143
Glee Club   27, 42, 80, 200
Glenn Memorial   34, 90
Glenn, Thomas K.   34, 156
Glenn, Wadley K.   152
Goff, John H.   85, 125, 126
Goldsmith, William Stokes   151
Goldstein, Jacob H.   102
Goodchild, Chauncey G.   102
Gooding, Lydia M.   36, 171

Goodyear, Nolan A.   43, 116, 206
Gosnell, Cullen B.   37, 117, 189
Graduate Housing Center   89
Grady Hospital   41, 54, 159, 161
Gray Clinic   41, 89
Greek New Testament Project   80, 145
Griffin, Albert   124
Griffin, John A.   43, 78, 102, 225
Guy, J. Sam   39, 40, 116

Hamff, Christian   116, 200
Hansell, Granger   190
Harmon, Nolan B.   146
Harrington, H. R.   208
Harris Hall   34, 69
Harris, Hugh H.   138
Harris, Joel Chandler   58, 189
Hartford Foundation   157, 161
Hartley, Virgil A.   231
Hartshorne, Charles   102
Hartsock, Ernest   204
Harwell, Richard B.   136
Hayes, Charles W.   51
Haygood, Atticus G.   5
Health Services Board   70
Hentz, Hal F.   34, 49
Hepburn, William M.   71, 86, 166, 167
High Museum of Art   45, 48
Hilkey, Charles J.   30, 71, 165
Hill, DeLos L.   173
Hilley, Maude   87
Hinman, Thomas K.   172
Hinton, James   19, 30, 116, 185, 186, 189
History Building   68
Honor Council   120
Honors Day   105
Hopkins Hall   88
Hopkins, Isaac S.   6
Hornbostel, Henry   20
Howard, Clara E.   36, 170
Howard, Harry C.   138
Howlett, Ernest S.   202
Hudgens, Robert S.   50
Humphrey, Burwell W.   71, 155
Hund, James M.   126

Institute of Citizenship   37
integration   99
Institute of the Liberal Arts   63, 133

International Association of
  Universities   238

Jack, Theodore H.   23, 37, 38, 42,
  116, 130
Jackson, Charles A.   144
Jackson, Evalene   71, 171
Jarrell Lectureship   142
Jemison, Margaret   71, 185, 186
Johnson, Ben F.   86, 101, 167
Johnson, Edgar H.   19, 23, 52, 116,
  123
Johnson, Emmett S.   143
Johnson, Harold L.   128
Johnston, Thomas P.   132
Jones, Boisfeuillet   70, 71, 86, 155
Jones, William H.   85, 92
Jordan, G. Ray   102, 211
Jordan, Mildred   171, 191
Joslin, G. Stanley   86, 102, 167
Journal of Public Law   95, 167
Journalism, Department of   56, 64,
  115

Kane, Edward A.   203
Kellogg Foundation   126, 179
Kendrick, W. S.   148

Lagomarsino, Chess   202
Laird, Samuel L.   213
Lamar, L. Q. C.   164
Law Building   21
Law Day   167
Lawson, A. Venable   171
Lemonds, William   203
Lester, Charles T.   85, 134
Lester, James G.   36, 68, 102, 116,
  117, 217, 220
Library, Asa Griggs Candler   30,
  69, 87, 185, 187
Library for Advanced Studies   87,
  188
Lineback, Paul Eugene   151
Little Commencement   28, 43
Little Symphony   27, 201
Livingstone, Sir Richard   78
Loemker, Leroy E.   69, 102, 117,
  132, 136
Longstreet, A. B.   4
Longstreet Hall   69
Lovett Memorial   189
"Lower Slobbovia"   65

Loyalty Fund   76, 229
Lullwater Biology Field Laboratory
  95
Lullwater House   88
Lyle, Guy R.   71, 136, 187

McAlister Chair of Preventive
  Medicine   162
McCain, J. R.   44, 48
McCandless Fund   188
McCord, Jeff   95, 218, 220
McDonald Endowment   188
McDonough, Thomas E.   220, 222
McGhee, Joseph L.   151
McGregor Americana   190
McKenzie, Kermit E.   136
McLean, Ross H.   37, 116, 224
McTier, John T.   86
McTyeire Hall   53
Major, J. Russell   136
Malone, Dumas   51, 131
Malone, Pat   231
Manual Labor School   3
Martin, Boyce F.   50, 124
Martin, Edwin T.   103, 136
Martin, S. Walter   82
Mason, Wiley Roy   220
Massey, Dyar   84
Mathews, Joseph J.   102
Means, Alexander   3, 4
Means Hall   69
Medical Association of Georgia
  55, 153
Medical Centennial   58, 79, 157
Megahee, Percy   190
Melton, Wightman F.   116
Messick, J. Fred   116
Mew, George H.   30, 65, 70, 85,
  221
Miller, H. Prentice   86, 231
Miller, Julia   54, 178
Miller, Norman C.   230
Ministers Week   141
Mitchell, Albert S.   182
Mitchell, Anita Benteen   179
Mizell, Robert C.   46, 47, 77, 88
  124, 181, 228
Moore, Arthur J.   146, 182
Moulton, George H.   86, 175
"Mudville"   65
Murrah, W. B.   138

Museum   36, 88, 140
Myers, Orie E.   70, 86

National Foundation for Infantile
    Paralysis   154
National Heart Institute   95
National Institutes of Health   134,
    180
Neely, George A.   207, 208
Nelms, William S.   116
Nicholson, William Perrin   148
Nixon, Raymond B.   56, 115, 150,
    205, 228
Nursing Semicentennial   180

Oak Ridge Laboratory   96
Odum, Howard W.   22, 123, 190
Odum, Pauline   23, 87
Oglethorpe University   54, 153
Old Church, Oxford   181
Oliver, Oren A.   174
Omicron Delta Kappa   46
One Per Cent Plan   80, 144
Ophthalmological Research Center
    96
Oppenheimer, Russell H.   30, 50,
    150, 153
Orr Chair of Urology   162
Osborne, Joseph D.   174
Outler, John M.   86
Oxford   3

Papageorge, Evangeline   84, 157
Park, Robert E.   190
Parker Chair of Systematic Theology
    143
Parker, Franklin N.   18, 24, 48,
    139, 140, 141
Paullin, James Edgar   151
Parvis, Merrill M.   80, 145
Paty, Raymond R.   42, 50
Peebles, John B.   115, 116, 220
Peed, Mansfield Theodore   116
Pelham, Glenn   207
Pershing, John J.   85
Person, Weldon Edwards   151
Pettus, Clyde   192
Pfeiffer, Carl C.   84, 157
Phi Beta Kappa   38, 46, 58, 79,
    120, 237
Phillips, Howard M.   69, 85, 132
Phoenix   27, 203

Physics Building   21, 118
Physiology Building   21
Pierce, George F.   4, 5
Pierce Science Hall   90, 182
Prayer Chapel, Oxford   5, 242
Protestant Radio and Television
    Center   144
Purks, J. Harris   50, 70, 131
pushball   61, 80, 218

Quayle, Osborne R.   56, 117, 220
Quillian, Henry M.   165, 168
Quillian Lectureship   142

Radiation Research Field   95
Rast, J. Marvin   200
Read Confederate Collection   190
Rece, Ellis Heber   50, 85, 103,
    104, 208
Religious Emphasis Week   211
Research Committee, Business
    Executives   94, 125
Research Committee, University   94
Reserve Officers Training Corps   36
Rhodes, Robert C.   116
Rhodes Scholars   120
Rich Foundation   64, 124
Rich Memorial Building   66, 124
Richardson, Arthur P.   71, 84, 155,
    157, 159
Ritter, Alan L.   125
Roach, George S.   182
Roberts, Stewart R.   151
Robinson, David W.   85
Robinson, James D., Jr.   70, 155
Rockefeller Foundation   102
Rogers, Ernest   27, 204
Rohrer, Robert   106
Rosenwald Fund   36, 170
Royer, Elizabeth   191
Rozier, John   86
Rumble, Douglas   116
Rusk, Nina   85
Russell, Edith   208

Sam Jones Lectureship   141
Saunders Hall   89
Scarborough, J. Elliott   53, 84, 151,
    158
Sellers, Thomas F.   162
Semicentennial, University   105
Seney, George I.   6

Seney Hall 6, 242
Sforza, Count Carlo 59
Shatford Chair of Homiletics 145
Shea, Edward J. 220
Shelton, William A. 36, 138
Short, Roy Hunter 146
Shufelt, Lynn F. 132
Shutze, Philip 68
Siefkin, Gordon 70, 85, 125, 126
Sigma Xi 56, 237
Sitton, Claude 205
Sledd, Andrew 138
Smart, Wyatt Aiken 136, 139, 212
Smathers, Ray K. 217
Smith, Mrs. Bayne 202
Smith, Garland G. 43, 208
Smith Hall 88
Smith, James M. 133
Smith, L. Neal 52
Smith, Luther M. 5
Smith, Norman C. 84
Smith, Osborn L. 5
Smyke, E. J. 222
sororities 104
Sources & Reprints 57
Southern Association 8, 25, 237
Southern Methodist University 12
Southern University Conference
    237
Sowell, Waldo 230
Staar, Richard F. 136
Stead, Eugene A. 51, 153
Steadman, J. M. 116
Stephens, John C. 85, 209
Stipe, J. Gordon 19, 23, 56, 70,
    77, 116, 227
Stipe Lectureship 79, 225
Stipe Scholars 104
Stokes, Mack B. 143
Stone Hall 89, 182
Strickland, Bonnie Ruth 86
Strickler, C. W. 149, 151
Strozier, William A. 103
Stubbs, William B. 35, 50, 183,
    197
Student Lecture Association 224

Tate, Sam 21
Teachers College 28, 31
Theology Building 21, 146
Theology Semicentennial 103, 146

Thomas Hall 88
Thomas, James R. 4
Thomas Jefferson Award 103
Thomson Hall 66
Thomson, William D. 14, 15, 22,
    71, 164, 166, 189, 229
Tilton, Edward L. 185
"Trailertown" 65
Trimble, H. B. 50, 142, 144
"Troika" 83
Trump, Guy W. 85, 126
Tufts, Arthur 20
tuition charges 32, 92, 155
Tull Foundation 133, 157
Turner, E. K. 116
Turner, Malcolm E. 162
Turner, "Uncle Allen" 3
Tye, M. Myrtle 191

Unification Conference 142
Union Catalogue of Books 48, 131,
    186
University Center 44, 47
University of Georgia 45, 49
University Senate 77
Uppergate House 53

V-12 59
Vanderbilt University 10, 18
Veterans Administration Hospital
    90, 160
Village 53

Wager, Ralph E. 29, 117
Waitzman, Morton B. 156
Walters Chair of Pediatrics 156
Ward, Judson C. 70, 84
War Memorial 75
Warren, James E. 204
Watkins, Floyd C. 136
Watkins, William T. 141
Watson, Charles N. 74
Weens, H. Stephen 103
Wesleyana 191
Wesleyan College 72
Wesley Hall 68, 144
Wesley Memorial Church 15, 18,
    138
Westmoreland, John G. 148
Whisonant, Eugene D. 77, 144
Whitaker, Robert F. 51, 71, 152,
    228, 229

[268]

White, Chappell   209
White, Goodrich C.   30, 39, 42, 50,
  51, 55, 82, 106, 116, 124, 129,
  131, 159, 215
White, Goodrich C., Jr.   67, 225
Whitehead Chair of Surgery   48,
  151
Whitehead Foundation   151
Whitehead Memorial Room   68
Whitehead Surgical Pavilion   67,
  151
Whitman, W. Tate   103, 128
Wiley, Bell I.   102, 136
Wilhelmi, Alfred E.   103
Williams, Samuel Cole   22, 165,
  190
Winship Clinic   53, 151
Winship Hall   21, 89
Woman's Club   24, 189
Women's Honor Organization   74
Wood, R. Hugh   69, 152, 153, 157,
  158

Woodrow Wilson Fellowships   120
Woodruff Endowment for Medical
  Education   156
Woodruff Foundation   69, 77, 93,
  156
Woodruff, George W.   69, 162
Woodruff Memorial   69, 155
Woodruff Memorial-Henry
  Woodruff Extension   89, 161
Woodruff, Robert W.   53, 69, 151,
  162
Woodward, Comer M.   30
Woodward, Hugh A.   35, 181
Works, George A.   44
Wrigley, Eva   185

Yerkes Primate Research Center
  95, 162
Young, James Harvey   136
Young, Walter J.   139

Zeller, E. Jerome   85